BEATING

THE STATE

A COMPREHENSIVE GUIDE OF SUCCESSFUL LITIGATION STRATEGIES AND HELPFUL INFORMATION TO FIGHT ALL CRIMINAL CHARGES

GARRY WIGGINS

FLORIDA EDITION

Disclaimer

This is a work of fiction Name, characters, places and incidents either are the product of the author imagination or are used fictitiously. Any resemblance to actual persons, living, or dead, event or locales are entirely coincidental

TABLE OF CONTENTS

WHY THIS BOOK WAS WRITTEN

This book was written as a guide to understanding and overcoming the challenges posed by state institutions, particularly the legal and prison systems. Many individuals find themselves caught in bureaucratic traps, facing overwhelming odds against government agencies with vast resources and rigid structures. By shedding light on the inner workings of these systems, this book aims to empower readers with knowledge, strategies, and insights that can help them navigate, challenge, and even triumph over state control.

The motivation behind this book is rooted in a belief that individuals deserve a fair chance, whether dealing with criminal charges, civil disputes, or systemic injustices. The state often operates with a presumption of authority, leveraging complex laws and institutional power to its advantage. However, through intelligence, strategy, and persistence, individuals can level the playing field and assert their rights effectively.

One of the biggest obstacles individuals face is the failure of legal representation. Many lawyers, rather than advocating zealously for their clients, sell them out due to their own lack of knowledge about the law or the justice system. This book is crucial because it provides readers with the understanding needed to hold their legal representatives accountable, recognize when they are being misled, and take control of their own defense when necessary.

This book does not advocate for unlawful actions but rather seeks to educate readers on legal and strategic methods to protect themselves, fight back against unjust treatment, and ultimately emerge victorious when facing the state. From understanding legal loopholes to leveraging procedural tactics, this book serves as both a survival manual and a call to action for those who refuse to be victims of an unyielding system.

CHAPTER ONE

THE FENTANYL CRISIS IN AMERICA AND THE EVOLVING LEGAL LANDSCAPE

INTRODUCTION

The fentanyl crisis has emerged as one of the most pressing public health and law enforcement challenges in the United States. This synthetic opioid, which is up to 50 times stronger than heroin, has fueled a dramatic rise in overdose deaths. As crime rates related to fentanyl distribution and abuse surge, lawmakers are enacting and proposing strict penalties to combat the epidemic. The crisis has not only overwhelmed emergency responders and healthcare systems but has also led to significant policy changes at the state and federal levels.

The Rise of the Fentanyl Crisis

Fentanyl first gained prominence in the medical field for its potent pain-relieving properties, often used for severe pain management, including post-surgical recovery and cancer treatment. However, its illicit production and distribution have led to a nationwide crisis. Drug cartels and traffickers have exploited fentanyl's high potency, mixing it with other substances like heroin, cocaine, and counterfeit prescription pills, leading to a dramatic increase in overdoses. The appeal of fentanyl for traffickers is its cost-effectiveness—because it is so potent, a small amount can be used to create thousands of doses, making it highly profitable.

Overdose and Death Rates

The Centers for Disease Control and Prevention (CDC) reports that synthetic opioids, primarily fentanyl, are responsible for over 70% of opioid-related deaths in the U.S. In 2023 alone, fentanyl contributed to more than 100,000 drug overdose fatalities. The drug's extreme potency makes even small amounts lethal, exacerbating the crisis. Many overdoses occur because users are unaware that fentanyl has been mixed into other drugs, leading to unintentional and often fatal overdoses. Even first-time users face a high risk of death, as dosages as small as two milligrams can be lethal.

The Connection Between Fentanyl and Crime

The fentanyl epidemic is not just a public health emergency—it is also fueling a rise in crime rates across the country. Law enforcement agencies report increases in:

- Drug trafficking operations involving large-scale fentanyl distribution, with cartel networks expanding their reach across state lines and into rural communities.
- Violent crimes, including homicides linked to drug trade disputes, as competition among distributors grows increasingly deadly.
- Theft and property crimes committed by individuals suffering from addiction, desperate to support their drug dependence.
- Exposure risks for law enforcement and first responders, who face the danger of accidental overdose from inhaling airborne fentanyl particles or handling contaminated materials without proper protective equipment.
- Human trafficking and organized crime, as drug cartels use forced labor and coercion to expand fentanyl production and distribution networks.

Existing Laws and Mandatory Sentences

The U.S. government and various states have implemented severe penalties to curb fentanyl-related offenses. Many of these laws include mandatory minimum sentences for trafficking, distribution, and even possession of large quantities of fentanyl.

Federal Sentencing Guidelines

Under federal law:

- Possession with intent to distribute 40 grams or more: Minimum 5 years in prison.
- Possession with intent to distribute 400 grams or more: Minimum 10 years in prison.
- Distributing fentanyl resulting in death or serious injury: Potential life sentence.
- Enhanced penalties apply for trafficking fentanyl near schools, involving minors, or operating as part of an organized crime syndicate.

State-Level Crackdowns

Many states are enacting or considering even stricter fentanyl laws, such as:

- Florida: A minimum 25-year sentence for trafficking more than four grams of fentanyl, with no possibility of early release.
- Texas: Lawmakers considering capital punishment for major fentanyl dealers whose drugs cause fatalities, treating it as a form of homicide.
- Ohio & Pennsylvania: Felony charges for possession of even trace amounts of fentanyl-laced substances, aiming to deter both users and low-level distributors.
- California: Expansion of drug-induced homicide laws, holding dealers criminally responsible for overdose deaths.

Proposed Future Penalties

Given the escalating crisis, lawmakers are pushing for even harsher measures, including:

- Classifying fentanyl trafficking as a federal offense punishable by life imprisonment, regardless of quantity.
- Automatic homicide charges for dealers if their drugs cause an overdose death, similar to laws applied in drunk driving fatalities.
- Increased surveillance and border security to intercept fentanyl shipments, including the use of artificial intelligence and advanced scanning technologies at ports of entry.
- Expanded mandatory minimum sentencing laws to eliminate judicial discretion in fentanyl-related cases, ensuring lengthy prison terms without parole.
- Enhanced international cooperation to target fentanyl suppliers operating out of China and Mexico, where much of the illicit fentanyl originates.

The Role of Public Health Initiatives

While law enforcement measures play a significant role in addressing the crisis, many experts argue that punitive approaches alone are insufficient. Public health initiatives are crucial to reducing fentanyl-related harm, including:

- Expanding access to Narcan (naloxone), a life-saving medication that reverses opioid overdoses.
- Increasing funding for addiction treatment programs, including medication-assisted treatment (MAT) options such as methadone and buprenorphine.

- Implementing harm reduction strategies, such as supervised consumption sites where individuals can use drugs under medical supervision to prevent overdoses.
- Education and awareness campaigns, targeting young people and high-risk populations to inform them about the dangers of fentanyl-laced drugs.
- Expanding mental health services, as many individuals struggling with opioid addiction also suffer from untreated mental health disorders.

Controversy and Criticism

While stricter laws aim to deter fentanyl-related crimes, critics argue that such policies:

- Overcrowd prisons with non-violent offenders, especially those struggling with addiction who may benefit more from rehabilitation than incarceration.
- Fail to address the root causes of the crisis, such as lack of addiction treatment, mental health services, and economic opportunities in high-risk communities.
- Increase racial disparities in sentencing, as mandatory minimum laws disproportionately impact minority communities and low-income individuals.
- Could drive users to more dangerous behaviors, such as using alone or switching to riskier substances to avoid detection.

Conclusion

The fentanyl crisis is an unprecedented challenge that demands urgent action. While strict laws and harsh penalties are being introduced to curb trafficking and overdoses, long-term solutions must also include expanded addiction treatment programs, public awareness campaigns, and improved access to mental health care. As the crisis evolves, the legal system must strike a balance between punishing traffickers and supporting those affected by addiction. Without comprehensive reform that includes both enforcement and rehabilitation, the fentanyl epidemic may continue to devastate communities across the United States.

CHAPTER TWO

FLORIDA MINIMUM MANDATORY LAWS AND SENTENCES

INTRODUCTION

Florida is known for its strict sentencing laws, particularly its minimum mandatory sentencing provisions. These laws require judges to impose fixed prison terms for certain crimes, removing judicial discretion in sentencing. While these policies were intended to deter crime and ensure consistency, they have also sparked debate about fairness, prison overcrowding, and rehabilitation opportunities.

History and Purpose

Florida's minimum mandatory sentencing laws gained prominence in the 1980s and 1990s as part of broader national efforts to combat violent crime and drug-related offenses. The goal was to ensure that offenders served substantial portions of their sentences without the possibility of early release. The laws were designed to remove leniency from the judicial process, ensuring that serious offenders faced severe penalties.

Key Minimum Mandatory Sentences

10-20-Life Law (Firearm Offenses)

One of Florida's most well-known minimum mandatory laws is the 10-20-Life statute, which applies to crimes involving firearms. Under this law:

- 10 years: If a firearm is carried during the commission of a crime.
- 20 years: If the firearm is discharged.

- 25 years to life: If someone is injured or killed as a result of the firearm's use. This law has faced criticism for imposing harsh penalties even in cases where no one is injured.

Drug Trafficking Minimums

Florida enforces minimum mandatory sentences for drug trafficking based on the type and quantity of drugs involved. Some examples include:

- Trafficking in Cannabis (Marijuana)
  - 25–2,000 pounds: 3 years minimum
  - 2,000–10,000 pounds: 7 years minimum
  - Over 10,000 pounds: 15 years minimum
- Trafficking in Cocaine
  - 28–200 grams: 3 years minimum
  - 200–400 grams: 7 years minimum
  - Over 400 grams: 15 years minimum
- Trafficking in Oxycodone or Fentanyl
  - Various weight thresholds carry 3, 7, or 15-25 year minimum sentences

Habitual Felony Offender & Three Strikes Law

Florida also has habitual offender laws that impose enhanced sentences for repeat offenders. The Three Strikes Law mandates life sentences for offenders convicted of three or more violent felonies. While this law was intended to keep repeat violent criminals off the streets, critics argue that it often results in life sentences for non-violent repeat offenders.

Sexual Offenses

Sex crimes carry some of the harshest minimum mandatory penalties in Florida. For example:

- Lewd or lascivious molestation of a child under 12: 25 years to life
- Sexual battery involving a minor: Life imprisonment without parole in many cases
- Failure to register as a sex offender: Mandatory prison terms for repeat violations

Criticism and Controversy

While supporters argue that minimum mandatory sentences deter crime and keep dangerous offenders behind bars, critics highlight several concerns:

1. Judicial Discretion Removed – Judges cannot consider mitigating circumstances that might warrant a lesser sentence.
2. Prison Overcrowding – Florida's prison population has surged due to lengthy mandatory sentences.
3. Disproportionate Impact – Many argue these laws disproportionately affect minorities and non-violent offenders.
4. Cost to Taxpayers – Housing inmates for extended sentences places a significant financial burden on the state.

Reform Efforts

In recent years, there has been growing support for reforming Florida's minimum mandatory sentencing laws. Some proposed changes include:

- Giving judges more discretion in sentencing non-violent offenders.
- Reducing or eliminating mandatory minimums for certain drug offenses.
- Implementing early release programs for rehabilitated inmates. While some reforms have been introduced, Florida still maintains some of the strictest mandatory sentencing laws in the U.S.

Conclusion

Florida's minimum mandatory sentencing laws were established to create consistency and deter crime, but they have also led to significant controversy and calls for reform. As debates continue, the challenge remains to balance public safety with fair and just sentencing practices.

CHAPTER THREE

BEATING THE FLORIDA PRISON RELEASEE REOFFENDER (PRR) ACT

UNDERSTANDING THE PRR ACT

The **Florida Prison Releasee Reoffender (PRR) Act** is one of the strictest sentencing laws in the state, designed to impose mandatory minimum sentences on individuals who commit certain crimes within **three years** of being released from prison. Under this law, if a person is convicted of a qualifying offense, judges **must** impose the maximum sentence allowable by law, without the possibility of parole or early release.

Qualifying Offenses Under the PRR Act

The law applies to serious felonies, including but not limited to:

- Murder
- Manslaughter
- Sexual battery
- Robbery
- Carjacking
- Home-invasion robbery
- Burglary of an occupied structure
- Aggravated assault with a deadly weapon
- Kidnapping

If convicted under the PRR Act, the offender must serve **100% of the sentence** without gain time or discretionary release.

How to Beat a PRR Sentence

While the PRR Act is strict, there are several legal strategies that can be employed to fight a PRR designation and avoid the harsh penalties.

1. Challenging the Classification as a PRR

- **Timing of the Offense**: The state must prove that the new offense was committed within **three years** of release from prison. If there is **any doubt** regarding this timeline, a strong legal argument can be made to challenge the PRR designation.
- **Disputing Prior Convictions**: If the previous conviction that the prosecution is relying on is flawed (e.g., ineffective counsel, errors in the trial, or procedural violations), it may be possible to have it overturned, removing the basis for PRR enhancement.

2. Negotiating a Plea Bargain

- Prosecutors often use the **PRR designation as leverage** to push defendants into accepting plea deals. A skilled attorney may be able to negotiate a **lesser charge** that does not qualify under PRR sentencing, avoiding the mandatory maximum penalty.
- If the case against the defendant is weak, a plea to a **non-violent felony** with a reduced sentence could be a viable option.

3. Challenging the Evidence

- **Lack of Evidence**: If there is insufficient evidence to prove guilt beyond a reasonable doubt, filing motions to dismiss or suppress evidence can weaken the state's case.
- **Illegal Search & Seizure**: If law enforcement violated Fourth Amendment rights (e.g., conducting an illegal search or arrest), any evidence obtained may be inadmissible in court.

4. Arguing for a Downward Departure

- In rare cases, a judge may have discretion to depart from PRR sentencing if the defense can show compelling **mitigating circumstances** (e.g., mental illness, coercion, or a minor role in the crime).
- A well-documented history of **rehabilitation** and good behavior post-release may also support a case for leniency.

5. Seeking Post-Conviction Relief

- If already sentenced under the PRR Act, filing an **appeal** or **post-conviction motion** may be an option.
- Claims of **ineffective assistance of counsel** (if the defense attorney failed to challenge the PRR classification) can serve as a basis for seeking relief.
- If new evidence emerges that could prove innocence or cast doubt on the conviction, a motion for a new trial may be possible.

Conclusion

The **Florida PRR Act** is harsh, but it is not unbeatable. With a **strong legal strategy**, a skilled defense attorney, and a thorough review of all circumstances surrounding the case, individuals facing PRR sentencing can increase their chances of avoiding its severe consequences. The key is to act **quickly**, challenge **every legal aspect**, and explore **all available defenses** to mitigate the impact of this unforgiving statute.

CHAPTER FOUR

BEATING THE FLORIDA HABITUAL FELONY OFFENDER (HFO) ENHANCEMENT

UNDERSTANDING THE HABITUAL FELONY OFFENDER (HFO) LAW

The **Habitual Felony Offender (HFO) statute** in Florida allows for **enhanced sentencing** for repeat offenders who have been convicted of multiple felonies. Unlike the **Prison Releasee Reoffender (PRR) Act**, the HFO designation does not require a mandatory sentence, but it does **increase the maximum possible sentence** significantly.

Under Florida Statute **775.084**, a person may be classified as an HFO if they:

- Have **two or more prior felony convictions**.
- Commit a new felony while having at least one of those prior convictions still on their record.
- The prior conviction was not **pardoned** or overturned.
- The new offense was committed **within five years** of the last conviction or release from incarceration.

The **HFO designation** does not require the offender to serve 100% of their sentence, but it does allow for **extended sentences**, including **life in prison** for certain crimes.

How to Fight an HFO Enhancement

Although the HFO statute is severe, **it is not automatic**. A skilled defense attorney can use various legal strategies to fight the HFO classification and avoid enhanced penalties.

1. Challenging the Qualifying Convictions

- **Old or Outdated Convictions**: The new offense must have occurred within **five years** of the last felony conviction or release from prison. If the state is trying to use an **older conviction**, it may not qualify.
- **Convictions from Other States**: If the state is using out-of-state convictions, the defense can argue that those offenses **do not meet Florida's legal definition** of a felony.
- **Invalid Prior Convictions**: If the previous convictions were obtained in violation of constitutional rights (e.g., **ineffective assistance of counsel, coerced plea deals, or improper evidence**), they can be challenged and potentially removed from the record.

2. Arguing Against HFO Sentencing in Court

Unlike PRR sentencing, **HFO sentencing is discretionary**—judges are **not required** to impose the enhanced sentence. A strong defense can argue for a **lesser sentence** by presenting:

- **Mitigating circumstances** (e.g., mental health issues, coercion, substance abuse, or minor involvement in the crime).
- **Rehabilitation efforts** (e.g., employment, community involvement, or positive character references).
- **Disproportionality arguments**—showing that the enhanced sentence would be excessive compared to the crime committed.

3. Negotiating a Plea Deal

- Prosecutors often use HFO designations as leverage in plea negotiations.
- A skilled attorney may be able to negotiate a plea to a **lesser charge** that does not qualify for HFO enhancement.

- If the state's case is weak, it may be possible to **avoid a felony conviction altogether** by negotiating a plea to a **misdemeanor**.

4. Challenging the Evidence

- **Illegal Search & Seizure**: If law enforcement obtained evidence in violation of the **Fourth Amendment**, the evidence can be suppressed, weakening the prosecution's case.
- **Lack of Proof**: If the prosecution cannot prove beyond a reasonable doubt that the defendant committed the crime, the case may be dismissed or result in a lesser charge.

5. Filing for Post-Conviction Relief

If a defendant has already been sentenced as an HFO, they may still have options:

- **Appealing the sentence** if there were errors in the trial or sentencing process.
- **Filing a motion for post-conviction relief** based on new evidence, ineffective assistance of counsel, or constitutional violations.
- **Seeking a sentence modification** if rehabilitation progress or other factors warrant reconsideration.

Conclusion

The **Florida Habitual Felony Offender (HFO) enhancement** is a powerful tool for prosecutors, but it is **not automatic** and can be **challenged** in several ways. Whether by attacking prior convictions, negotiating a plea deal, or arguing against enhanced sentencing, an experienced defense attorney can significantly improve a defendant's chances of avoiding an HFO sentence. The key is **acting quickly**, knowing **your legal rights**, and building the **strongest possible defense** to counter the state's claims.

CHAPTER FIVE

BEATING FLORIDA FOURTH AMENDMENT VIOLATIONS

UNDERSTANDING THE FOURTH AMENDMENT

The **Fourth Amendment** of the U.S. Constitution protects individuals from **unreasonable searches and seizures** by law enforcement. This means that police officers must generally have **probable cause** and, in many cases, a **warrant** to conduct searches of a person, their home, vehicle, or personal property.

In Florida, if law enforcement violates the Fourth Amendment, any evidence obtained **illegally** may be **suppressed**, meaning it cannot be used in court. Beating a case based on a Fourth Amendment violation requires identifying and challenging **unlawful searches and seizures**.

Common Fourth Amendment Violations

There are several ways law enforcement officers may violate an individual's Fourth Amendment rights in Florida:

1. **Illegal Traffic Stops**
   - Officers must have **reasonable suspicion** to pull a vehicle over. If they stop someone without justification, any evidence found during the stop (e.g., drugs, weapons) may be thrown out.
2. **Unlawful Searches Without a Warrant**
   - Police generally need a **search warrant** to enter and search a home or business unless there are special circumstances (e.g., consent, exigent circumstances, or items in plain view).

3. **Warrantless Vehicle Searches**
    - Vehicles can sometimes be searched without a warrant, but only if police have **probable cause** (e.g., seeing drugs in plain sight) or the driver gives **consent**.
4. **Unlawful Stop and Frisk**
    - Officers can only perform a **Terry stop** (stop and frisk) if they have **reasonable suspicion** that someone is armed and involved in criminal activity. Otherwise, any evidence found during the search may be inadmissible.
5. **Searches Without Consent**
    - If an officer searches a person, home, or vehicle without consent or a warrant and no exception applies, the search is illegal.

How to Beat a Case Based on Fourth Amendment Violations

If a Fourth Amendment violation occurred, there are several legal defenses that can be used to **suppress evidence** and potentially have the charges dismissed.

1. Filing a Motion to Suppress Evidence

- If the defense can prove that the evidence was obtained illegally, they can file a **motion to suppress** under **Florida Rule of Criminal Procedure 3.190(g)**.
- If the court grants the motion, the evidence is excluded, which can weaken or destroy the prosecution's case.

2. Challenging the Legality of the Stop or Search

- If an officer did not have **probable cause** or **reasonable suspicion** to conduct the stop or search, all evidence obtained from it can be suppressed.
- The defense may request **bodycam footage, police reports, or witness statements** to prove the stop was unlawful.

3. Proving Lack of Consent

- If an officer claims the defendant **consented** to a search but they were **coerced** or **intimidated**, the search may be considered unlawful.
- Any signed or recorded consent should be examined to determine its validity.

4. Challenging the Search Warrant

- If a search warrant was issued based on **false statements** by law enforcement or lacked **specificity**, the defense can argue that the search was unconstitutional.
- If the warrant was executed **outside its scope** (e.g., searching areas not listed), any evidence found may be inadmissible.

5. Establishing an Illegal Detention

- Officers **cannot** detain someone indefinitely without cause. If the stop lasted too long without justification, the detention may be illegal, making any evidence obtained during that time inadmissible.

6. Exposing Misconduct and Procedural Errors

- If law enforcement violated **department policies**, this can be used to challenge the validity of the search and weaken the prosecution's case.
- Witness testimony and surveillance footage can help prove misconduct.

Recent Florida Case Law on Fourth Amendment Violations

Florida courts have ruled in favor of defendants in several cases where Fourth Amendment rights were violated:

- **Rodriguez v. State (2021)** – Evidence was thrown out after the court ruled that an extended traffic stop **without reasonable suspicion** violated the defendant's rights.
- **State v. Green (2022)** – The Florida Supreme Court ruled that a warrantless home search was illegal because the defendant's roommate, who consented to the search, **did not have authority** over the defendant's room.

Conclusion

Fourth Amendment violations are **powerful legal defenses** that can lead to evidence being **suppressed** and charges being **dismissed**. If law enforcement conducted an **illegal stop, search, or seizure**, working with an experienced defense attorney can significantly improve a defendant's chances of winning their case. The key is to act **quickly**, challenge the **legality** of the police's actions, and file the necessary motions to protect constitutional rights.

CHAPTER SIX

BEATING DRUG TRAFFICKING CASES BY CHALLENGING DRUG WEIGHT THROUGH FDLE

UNDERSTANDING DRUG TRAFFICKING CHARGES IN FLORIDA

Florida law defines **drug trafficking** as the possession, sale, manufacturing, delivery, or transport of controlled substances over a specific weight threshold. Under **Florida Statute 893.135**, trafficking is determined by the weight of the drugs, and mandatory minimum sentences apply based on those weights.

Many defendants are **wrongfully charged** with trafficking due to **miscalculated drug weights**, **improper testing**, or **contaminated samples**. One of the most effective ways to challenge drug trafficking charges is by **disputing the weight and purity of the substance through the Florida Department of Law Enforcement (FDLE) lab testing process**.

Why Drug Weight Matters in Trafficking Cases

Drug trafficking charges are categorized by weight, and even a **small discrepancy** can mean the difference between **decades in prison or a much lesser charge**. Here are some key trafficking weight thresholds under Florida law:

- **Cocaine:** 28 grams = 3-year minimum sentence, 200 grams = 7-year minimum sentence, 400 grams = 15-year minimum sentence.
- **Heroin/Fentanyl:** 4 grams = 3-year minimum sentence, 14 grams = 15-year minimum sentence, 28 grams = 25-year minimum sentence.
- **Marijuana:** 25 pounds = trafficking charge, with increasing penalties as weight increases.

If law enforcement overestimates the weight of the substance, **the charges and penalties may be excessive**. This is where challenging FDLE's testing procedures can be critical.

Challenging Drug Weight and Purity Through FDLE

Florida prosecutors rely on FDLE laboratory results to prove drug weight and purity. However, **FDLE lab testing is not infallible**, and mistakes can lead to **wrongful convictions**. Here are key strategies to challenge FDLE's findings:

1. Request Independent Drug Testing

- Defense attorneys can **request independent laboratory testing** of the alleged drugs.
- If an independent test finds a lower weight or **impurities that dilute the substance**, the trafficking charge may be **reduced or dismissed**.

2. Challenge FDLE's Testing Procedures

- FDLE uses **weighing and chemical testing** to determine drug weight and purity. However, errors can occur due to:
    - **Faulty scales** or improper calibration.
    - **Improper handling** or contamination of evidence.
    - **Lack of proper chain of custody**.
- If FDLE **violated standard protocols**, the evidence may be unreliable and suppressed in court.

3. Argue Adulterants and Cutting Agents

- The **actual drug weight** must be distinguished from **cutting agents** (e.g., baking soda in cocaine, fentanyl mixed with heroin).

- If the actual drug weight is **below** the trafficking threshold after removing cutting agents, the charge may be **reduced** to simple possession or dropped altogether.

4. Demand the Full Lab Report

- Prosecutors often present **only summary results** from FDLE.
- The defense should request **detailed lab reports** and analyze whether:
    - The proper drug was identified.
    - The weight calculation was accurate.
    - Testing followed FDLE's own policies and procedures.
- Any **discrepancies or inconsistencies** can be used to challenge the charges.

5. Suppress Illegally Obtained Evidence

- If the drugs were obtained through an **illegal search and seizure** (Fourth Amendment violation), they may be **inadmissible in court**.
- If law enforcement **mishandled evidence**, the defense can argue for suppression, which may weaken the prosecution's case.

Case Law: Successful Challenges to Drug Weights in Florida

Several Florida cases have demonstrated how **challenging drug weight through FDLE testing can lead to reduced or dismissed charges**:

- **State v. Johnson (2020)** – The defendant was charged with trafficking cocaine, but independent testing revealed **less than 28 grams** of pure cocaine. Charges were reduced to possession, avoiding a 3-year mandatory minimum sentence.
- **State v. Martinez (2021)** – The FDLE failed to follow standard operating procedures in weighing heroin. The court ruled the lab results unreliable, leading to a dismissal of trafficking charges.

- **State v. Williams (2019)** – The defense successfully argued that **filler substances in a methamphetamine sample** inflated the weight, resulting in reduced charges.

Legal Motions to Challenge Drug Weight

Defense attorneys can file specific legal motions to challenge drug weight and testing procedures:

1. **Motion for Independent Testing** – Requests a court order for independent lab analysis.
2. **Motion to Suppress FDLE Evidence** – Seeks to exclude faulty FDLE lab results from trial.
3. **Motion to Dismiss** – Argues that after recalculating the actual drug weight, trafficking charges are not warranted.

Conclusion: A Strong Defense Strategy

Beating a **Florida drug trafficking case** often hinges on **challenging the weight and purity** of the substance through **FDLE testing**. By requesting **independent testing**, scrutinizing **FDLE's procedures**, and exposing **lab errors**, the defense can often **reduce or eliminate the charges**. If law enforcement has overestimated the weight of the drugs, an experienced attorney can use this mistake to **prevent a wrongful conviction** and avoid harsh mandatory minimum sentences. modifications or additional details.

CHAPTER SEVEN

FIGHTING FOR A BOND AND APPEAL BOND IN FLORIDA

UNDERSTANDING THE IMPORTANCE OF BOND

Being arrested and facing criminal charges can be a stressful and overwhelming experience. One of the first steps in securing freedom while fighting a case is obtaining a **bond**. In Florida, bail allows a defendant to be released from jail while awaiting trial, ensuring they can continue working on their defense, maintain employment, and support their family. However, not all defendants are automatically granted bond, and in some cases, it requires a legal fight to secure one.

Similarly, for those convicted and seeking an appeal, obtaining an **appeal bond** is crucial to remain free while challenging the verdict. The process involves convincing the court that the appeal has merit and that the defendant is neither a flight risk nor a danger to the community.

Fighting for a Pre-Trial Bond

1. Determining Bond Eligibility

Not all defendants are eligible for bond. Florida law considers multiple factors when deciding whether to grant bond, including:

- **The severity of the charges** (violent offenses are less likely to get bond).
- **Prior criminal history** (repeat offenders may face more restrictions).
- **Flight risk** (ties to the community, employment, and family responsibilities matter).

- **Potential danger to the community** (public safety concerns can result in denial of bond).
- **Likelihood of appearing in court** (if a person has a history of missing court dates, bond may be denied).

2. Filing a Motion for Bond Hearing

If a bond is not automatically granted or set too high, a **Motion for Bond Hearing** should be filed as soon as possible. The motion requests that the judge reconsider bail or set conditions for release.

At the hearing, the defense attorney can argue that:

- The defendant is **not a flight risk** and has strong ties to the community.
- The defendant **poses no danger** to the public.
- The **evidence against the defendant is weak** or does not justify denial of bond.
- Alternative measures, such as **house arrest or GPS monitoring**, can ensure compliance.

3. Arguing for a Reasonable Bond Amount

Judges often set high bonds, making it difficult for the accused to afford release. If the bond is excessive, the defense can argue that:

- The **Eighth Amendment of the U.S. Constitution prohibits excessive bail**.
- The defendant's **financial situation should be considered**.
- The accused is willing to **comply with conditions** such as regular check-ins, surrendering a passport, or avoiding certain individuals or places.

Fighting for an Appeal Bond

If a defendant is convicted but plans to **appeal the verdict**, an appeal bond (also called a **supersedeas bond**) can be requested. This allows the defendant to remain out of custody while the appeal is pending.

1. Requirements for an Appeal Bond

Appeal bonds are not automatically granted. The court considers:

- Whether the appeal is **frivolous or has merit**.
- If the defendant **poses a risk of fleeing**.
- The defendant's **behavior during trial and sentencing**.
- The seriousness of the offense.

Certain serious convictions, especially those involving **capital offenses or life sentences**, may not qualify for an appeal bond.

2. Filing a Motion for an Appeal Bond

The defense must file a **Motion for an Appeal Bond**, arguing that:

- The appeal raises **legitimate legal questions** that may overturn the conviction.
- The defendant **will not flee** and will abide by all conditions set by the court.
- The defendant has **a history of compliance** with previous bond conditions.

The motion should be supported with evidence such as:

- A **strong legal argument** for appeal.
- **Character references** and employment verification.
- Proof of **stable housing and family support**.

3. Conditions of an Appeal Bond

If granted, an appeal bond may come with conditions such as:

- Regular **check-ins with a probation officer**.
- **Travel restrictions** (often requiring court approval for out-of-state travel).
- **Surrender of passport and firearms**.
- **Avoiding criminal activity** while on bond.

Failure to comply with these conditions can lead to **bond revocation** and immediate incarceration.

Case Law and Examples

- **State v. Arthur (1975)** – Established that bond should be granted unless the prosecution can prove a defendant is a danger to the community.
- **Younghans v. State (1956)** – Set standards for appeal bonds, emphasizing that defendants must demonstrate the appeal is not frivolous.
- **State v. Paul (2022)** – A Florida defendant successfully obtained an appeal bond after showing that improper jury instructions may have led to his wrongful conviction.

Conclusion: A Strong Defense Can Secure Bond

Fighting for a bond or an appeal bond requires a strategic legal approach, emphasizing **due process, fairness, and constitutional rights**. By presenting **strong legal arguments, evidence of stability, and compliance with conditions**, a skilled attorney can successfully secure a bond, allowing the defendant to prepare a robust defense while remaining free.

CHAPTER EIGHT

BEATING TAMPERING WITH EVIDENCE CHARGES IN FLORIDA

UNDERSTANDING TAMPERING WITH EVIDENCE UNDER FLORIDA LAW

Tampering with evidence is a serious criminal charge in Florida, defined under **Florida Statutes Section 918.13**. The law states that it is illegal to alter, destroy, conceal, or remove any evidence with the intent to impair its use in an investigation or legal proceeding. This offense is considered a **third-degree felony**, carrying penalties of up to **five years in prison, five years of probation, and a $5,000 fine**.

To convict someone of tampering with evidence, the prosecution must prove three key elements beyond a reasonable doubt:

1. The defendant knew that an official investigation or legal proceeding was ongoing or about to commence.
2. The defendant altered, destroyed, concealed, or removed evidence.
3. The defendant's intent was to impair the evidence's availability or integrity in the legal process.

Defenses Against Tampering with Evidence Charges

While tampering charges are serious, there are several legal defenses that can be used to fight them. These defenses vary depending on the specifics of the case but often include the following:

1. Lack of Knowledge

The prosecution must prove that the accused knew an investigation or legal proceeding was ongoing or imminent. If the defense can show that the defendant was unaware of any investigation at the time of the alleged tampering, the charge may not hold.

2. Lack of Intent

Intent is a critical element in tampering cases. If the defendant did not intend to interfere with an investigation but rather acted out of panic, habit, or an unrelated reason, this can be used as a defense.

3. No Official Investigation

If there was no active investigation at the time of the alleged tampering, it may be difficult for the prosecution to prove the charge. The law requires that an investigation must be underway or expected to commence.

4. False Accusations

In some cases, individuals are wrongfully accused of evidence tampering. This can occur due to mistaken identity, revenge, or a misunderstanding of the situation. A strong defense strategy will highlight inconsistencies in the prosecution's case.

5. Illegal Search and Seizure

If law enforcement obtained the alleged evidence through an unlawful search and seizure, the defense can file a motion to suppress the evidence. If the court grants the motion, the prosecution's case may collapse due to lack of proof.

6. Evidence Wasn't Altered, Destroyed, or Concealed

Simply moving or handling evidence does not necessarily constitute tampering. If the defense can show that the alleged actions did not actually impair the integrity or availability of the evidence, the charges may be dismissed.

Legal Strategies to Fight Tampering Charges

Hiring an Experienced Criminal Defense Attorney

If you are facing tampering charges in Florida, securing a skilled defense attorney is crucial. A knowledgeable lawyer will analyze the facts, challenge weak points in the prosecution's case, and build a strong defense.

Challenging the Prosecution's Evidence

Every aspect of the prosecution's case should be scrutinized. The defense can challenge:

- The credibility of witnesses
- The chain of custody of the evidence
- Any procedural errors in the investigation

Negotiating a Plea Deal

In cases where beating the charge outright may be difficult, negotiating a **plea deal** may be a viable option. This could result in a reduced charge, such as obstruction of justice or disorderly conduct, leading to lesser penalties.

Presenting Character Evidence

If the defendant has no prior criminal history and is a respected member of the community, character witnesses can testify to their integrity. This can help cast doubt on the prosecution's claims of intent to commit a crime.

Conclusion

Beating a tampering with evidence charge in Florida requires a strategic legal approach. By demonstrating a lack of intent, challenging the prosecution's evidence, and ensuring that law enforcement followed proper procedures, defendants can improve their chances of a favorable outcome.

If you or a loved one is facing such a charge, consulting with a skilled criminal defense attorney should be the first step in mounting a strong defense.

CHAPTER NINE

BEATING CONFIDENTIAL INFORMANT CASES

UNDERSTANDING CONFIDENTIAL INFORMANT CASES

Confidential informants (CIs) play a significant role in many criminal investigations, particularly in drug-related offenses and conspiracy cases. A confidential informant is an individual who provides law enforcement with information about alleged criminal activity, often in exchange for leniency in their own legal troubles or financial compensation.

While informants can be valuable tools for law enforcement, their testimony and reliability are frequently challenged in court. Defendants facing charges based on CI testimony should understand the weaknesses in such cases and explore legal strategies to challenge the prosecution's evidence.

Common Issues with Confidential Informants

Confidential informant cases often suffer from several key issues that can be exploited in a defense strategy:

1. Reliability and Credibility Issues

Many informants have criminal backgrounds, making them susceptible to lying or exaggerating evidence in exchange for leniency or financial incentives. Defense attorneys can challenge their credibility by:

- Uncovering past criminal history
- Highlighting inconsistencies in their statements
- Questioning any benefits they received in exchange for testimony

2. Entrapment Defense

Entrapment occurs when law enforcement induces a person to commit a crime they otherwise would not have committed. If a CI or law enforcement officer pressured or coerced the defendant into illegal activity, an entrapment defense may apply.

To prove entrapment, the defense must demonstrate:

- The defendant had no prior intent to commit the crime
- The CI or police officer encouraged or pressured the crime's commission
- The inducement created an unfair situation where the defendant had no reasonable choice

3. Unlawful Search and Seizure

If law enforcement conducted an illegal search or seizure based on information from a CI, any evidence obtained may be suppressed. The Fourth Amendment protects against warrantless searches and unlawful intrusion. A strong defense can challenge:

- Lack of probable cause
- Insufficient evidence supporting a search warrant
- Unlawful surveillance or wiretaps

4. Disclosure of the Informant's Identity

In some cases, the prosecution relies on anonymous informants. However, the defense has a right to challenge the informant's credibility. If the CI is the primary source of evidence, the defense may file a motion to reveal their identity. The court may require disclosure if:

- The CI is a material witness to the alleged crime

- The defense cannot adequately challenge the charges without cross-examining the CI
- The informant's testimony is the sole basis for the prosecution's case

5. Lack of Corroborating Evidence

Informant testimony alone is often weak without independent evidence to support it. If law enforcement cannot provide additional proof, such as surveillance footage, recorded conversations, or physical evidence, the defense can argue that the case lacks substantial merit.

6. Motive to Fabricate Information

CIs often cooperate with law enforcement in exchange for reduced charges, dropped cases, or financial incentives. The defense can expose their motives and show that their testimony may be self-serving rather than truthful.

Legal Strategies to Beat Confidential Informant Cases

Successfully fighting a confidential informant case requires a combination of legal tactics:

Filing Pretrial Motions

Defense attorneys can file motions to:

- Suppress illegally obtained evidence
- Compel the prosecution to disclose the CI's identity
- Challenge the credibility of the informant
- Dismiss the case due to lack of probable cause

Cross-Examining the CI

If the CI testifies in court, cross-examination can expose inconsistencies, biases, and credibility issues. A skilled attorney can question the informant about:

- Their criminal history
- The benefits they received for cooperating
- Contradictions in their statements

Challenging Law Enforcement Procedures

If the case involves misconduct by law enforcement, such as coercion, falsified reports, or violations of constitutional rights, the defense can use this to weaken the prosecution's case.

Negotiating a Plea Deal

If beating the case outright is unlikely, negotiating a plea deal for reduced charges or alternative sentencing may be a practical option.

Conclusion

Confidential informant cases are often flawed due to unreliable witnesses, questionable law enforcement tactics, and a lack of corroborating evidence. By challenging the credibility of the CI, exposing unlawful police procedures, and leveraging constitutional protections, defendants can build a strong defense. If you are facing charges based on CI testimony, working with an experienced criminal defense attorney is crucial to securing the best possible outcome.

CHAPTER TEN

BEATING ENTRAPMENT CASES INVOLVING FACEBOOK MESSENGER IN FLORIDA

UNDERSTANDING ENTRAPMENT UNDER FLORIDA LAW

Entrapment is a legal defense used when law enforcement or government agents induce an individual to commit a crime they would not have otherwise committed. Florida law recognizes two types of entrapment:

1. **Subjective Entrapment** – Focuses on whether the defendant was predisposed to commit the crime before law enforcement's involvement.
2. **Objective Entrapment** – Focuses on whether law enforcement's tactics were so egregious that they violated due process rights.

Under **Florida Statutes Section 777.201**, a defendant must prove that:

- Law enforcement initiated the crime.
- The defendant was not predisposed to commit the crime before law enforcement's involvement.
- The methods used by law enforcement were coercive or overreaching.

Facebook Messenger and Entrapment Cases

With the rise of digital communication, law enforcement agencies increasingly use Facebook Messenger and other social media platforms for undercover operations. This is common in cases involving:

- **Drug sales**
- **Solicitation (prostitution or human trafficking cases)**
- **Online fraud or scams**

- **Sex crimes (sting operations for child exploitation cases)**

Because these cases often rely on online conversations, entrapment defenses become particularly relevant when law enforcement initiates and steers the illegal conduct.

Defenses Against Entrapment on Facebook Messenger

Successfully beating an entrapment case involving Facebook Messenger requires a strong legal strategy. The following defenses can be used to challenge the prosecution's case:

1. Proving Law Enforcement Induced the Crime

If law enforcement initiated contact and persistently pressured the defendant into committing a crime they would not have otherwise committed, an entrapment defense is valid. Evidence of:

- Repeated messaging from law enforcement urging illegal activity
- A reluctance by the defendant in the chat logs
- Manipulative or coercive tactics used by undercover officers

2. Lack of Predisposition to Commit the Crime

If the defendant had no history of similar offenses or did not seek out illegal activity before law enforcement's involvement, they may lack predisposition. This can be proven by:

- Prior clean criminal record
- Lack of initiation or active participation in illegal discussions
- Attempts to disengage from the conversation

3. Challenging the Authenticity and Admissibility of Evidence

Facebook Messenger communications are often used as key evidence. However, digital messages can be:

- Altered or manipulated
- Taken out of context
- Obtained illegally (violating privacy rights)

A defense attorney can challenge:

- Whether proper warrants were obtained
- Chain of custody issues regarding digital evidence
- The legitimacy of the messages (if screenshots or logs were altered)

4. Unlawful Police Conduct and Due Process Violations

If law enforcement engaged in extreme or unethical behavior, such as fabricating evidence or making false promises, a case may be dismissed based on **objective entrapment**. Examples include:

- Officers threatening or intimidating the defendant into participating in a crime
- Using excessive financial incentives to persuade illegal activity
- Creating a situation where a crime was the only logical response

Legal Strategies for Beating an Entrapment Charge

Hiring an Experienced Criminal Defense Attorney

A skilled attorney can analyze digital evidence, cross-examine officers, and challenge improper law enforcement tactics.

Filing Pretrial Motions to Suppress Evidence

If evidence was obtained unlawfully, a motion to suppress can exclude it from trial, weakening the prosecution's case.

Using Expert Witnesses

A digital forensic expert can examine Facebook Messenger data to detect tampering, illegal surveillance, or fabrication of evidence.

Challenging Police Reports and Testimonies

Cross-examining law enforcement to expose inconsistencies in their undercover operations can discredit the case.

Conclusion

Beating an entrapment case involving Facebook Messenger in Florida requires proving law enforcement initiated the crime, the defendant lacked predisposition, or the evidence was improperly obtained. With the right defense strategy, it is possible to get charges dismissed or reduced. If facing such charges, consulting with a knowledgeable criminal defense attorney is crucial for securing the best outcome.

CHAPTER ELEVEN

BEATING ILLEGAL SEARCH AND SEIZURE CASES

UNDERSTANDING ILLEGAL SEARCH AND SEIZURE

The Fourth Amendment to the U.S. Constitution protects individuals from unreasonable searches and seizures by law enforcement. In Florida, as in the rest of the country, police must follow strict legal procedures when conducting searches of a person, vehicle, home, or electronic devices. If law enforcement violates these procedures, any evidence obtained may be inadmissible in court.

What Constitutes an Illegal Search and Seizure?

A search or seizure is considered illegal if:

- **No Warrant or Probable Cause:** Law enforcement conducted a search without a valid warrant or probable cause.
- **Invalid Search Warrant:** The warrant was improperly issued, lacked sufficient details, or was based on false information.
- **Unlawful Traffic Stops:** A vehicle was stopped without reasonable suspicion, leading to an improper search.
- **Consent Was Coerced:** The suspect was pressured or deceived into giving consent for a search.
- **Plain View Doctrine Misused:** Officers used an invalid reason to claim they saw contraband in plain view.
- **Unlawful Search of Electronic Devices:** Phones, computers, or social media accounts were searched without proper legal authority.

Legal Defenses to Illegal Searches and Seizures

If you are facing charges based on an unlawful search and seizure, there are several defense strategies that can be used to challenge the evidence:

1. Filing a Motion to Suppress Evidence

A motion to suppress asks the court to exclude any evidence obtained through an illegal search. If granted, the prosecution may not be able to use key evidence, leading to a possible case dismissal.

2. Challenging the Validity of a Search Warrant

A search warrant must be supported by probable cause and specifically describe the place to be searched and the items to be seized. The defense can challenge a warrant if:

- It was based on false or misleading information.
- It lacked sufficient detail.
- Officers exceeded the scope of the warrant.

3. Arguing Lack of Probable Cause

If law enforcement searched a person, vehicle, or property without probable cause, any evidence obtained may be deemed inadmissible.

4. Proving Consent Was Not Voluntary

Police often claim that a suspect voluntarily consented to a search. However, if consent was obtained through intimidation, deception, or without full understanding, the search may be ruled unlawful.

5. Disputing a Traffic Stop's Legitimacy

For vehicle searches, law enforcement must have a valid reason for stopping a car. If the stop itself was illegal, any evidence discovered may be suppressed.

6. Challenging the Use of the Plain View Doctrine

Officers may claim they saw contraband in plain sight, but the defense can argue that the officer did not have a lawful right to be in the location where the alleged evidence was observed.

7. Fighting Unlawful Searches of Electronic Devices

Searches of phones, computers, and social media accounts require a warrant unless specific exceptions apply. Any evidence obtained without proper legal authorization can be challenged.

Legal Strategies for Beating an Illegal Search and Seizure Case

To successfully fight an illegal search and seizure case, an experienced criminal defense attorney will:

- **Examine police reports and body cam footage** for procedural violations.
- **File pretrial motions** to suppress unlawfully obtained evidence.
- **Cross-examine officers** to expose inconsistencies in their testimony.
- **Use expert witnesses** in digital forensics for electronic search cases.

Conclusion

Illegal search and seizure cases can be beaten by exposing law enforcement's constitutional violations. If evidence was obtained unlawfully, it may be suppressed, weakening the prosecution's case. Anyone facing charges should consult with an experienced attorney to explore the best legal defense strategies.

CHAPTER TWELVE

BEATING PROBABLE CAUSE: DOG SNIFFS, MARIJUANA SMELL, AND MORE.

UNDERSTANDING PROBABLE CAUSE IN FLORIDA

Probable cause is a legal standard that allows law enforcement to conduct searches, make arrests, or obtain warrants if they have reasonable grounds to believe a crime has been committed. However, officers sometimes claim probable cause based on weak or questionable evidence, such as a K-9 alert or the smell of marijuana. Challenging probable cause can be a key strategy in getting evidence suppressed and charges dismissed.

Common Probable Cause Claims and How to Challenge Them

1. Dog Sniff Searches

Law enforcement often use drug-sniffing dogs to establish probable cause. However, these searches are not foolproof and can be challenged based on:

- **Unreliable K-9 Training and Certification:** If a dog has a history of false alerts or inadequate training, its reliability can be questioned.
- **Prolonged Traffic Stops:** Officers cannot unreasonably extend a traffic stop to wait for a K-9 unit (*Rodriguez v. United States*, 575 U.S. 348 (2015)).
- **Warrantless Use of K-9 Units:** If a drug-sniffing dog is used without a valid reason, any resulting search may be unconstitutional.
- **Passive vs. Aggressive Alerts:** Some dogs are trained to sit or indicate when they detect drugs, while others may act aggressively. If an officer misinterprets a dog's behavior, it can be challenged in court.

- **Failure to Record the Search:** Many K-9 searches should be recorded. If no video evidence is available, it raises doubts about the legitimacy of the alert.

2. Marijuana Smell as Probable Cause

The smell of marijuana has historically been used as justification for searches, but Florida law is changing:

- **Hemp vs. Marijuana:** Since hemp is legal and smells similar to marijuana, the odor alone may not be sufficient for probable cause (*State v. Ruise*, 260 So. 3d 543 (Fla. Dist. Ct. App. 2018)).
- **Recent Court Rulings:** Florida courts have begun ruling that marijuana smell alone does not justify a warrantless search.
- **Challenging Officer Testimony:** Officers may exaggerate or falsely claim they smelled marijuana to justify a search. Cross-examining their statements can reveal inconsistencies.
- **Multiple Occupants in a Vehicle:** If several people are in a car, an officer must establish individual possession rather than assuming the smell justifies a search.
- **Medical Marijuana Laws:** Florida allows medical marijuana use, so the presence of the smell does not necessarily indicate illegal activity.

3. Traffic Stops and Vehicle Searches

For a vehicle search to be lawful, officers must have a legitimate reason to believe evidence of a crime is present. Defenses include:

- **Lack of Reasonable Suspicion for the Stop:** If the traffic stop itself was illegal, any evidence found may be suppressed (*Whren v. United States*, 517 U.S. 806 (1996)).

- **Consent Was Coerced:** If a driver was pressured or tricked into consenting to a search, the consent may be invalid.
- **No Clear Evidence of Criminal Activity:** Officers must demonstrate more than just a hunch to justify a search.
- **Pretextual Stops:** If an officer used a minor traffic violation as an excuse to conduct a drug search, it may be considered unconstitutional.

4. Home Searches and Warrants

Probable cause is also required for home searches. Law enforcement cannot search a residence without:

- **A Valid Warrant:** A search warrant must be specific and supported by probable cause (*Illinois v. Gates*, 462 U.S. 213 (1983)).
- **Exigent Circumstances:** Officers cannot force entry without a valid emergency situation (*Kentucky v. King*, 563 U.S. 452 (2011)).
- **Voluntary Consent:** If a resident was intimidated into allowing a search, the search may be illegal.
- **Knock and Announce Rule Violations:** Officers must follow protocol when executing search warrants. If they fail to announce their presence properly, the search may be challenged (*Hudson v. Michigan*, 547 U.S. 586 (2006)).

Legal Strategies to Beat Probable Cause Claims

- **Filing a Motion to Suppress:** If probable cause was improperly established, a defense attorney can file a motion to exclude evidence from trial.
- **Cross-Examining Officers:** Challenging their statements about marijuana odor, K-9 alerts, or observations can expose weaknesses in the case.

- **Questioning K-9 Reliability:** Requesting records on a drug-sniffing dog's accuracy and training history can cast doubt on the search's validity.
- **Using Expert Testimony:** A forensic expert can explain how the smell of marijuana is indistinguishable from hemp, undermining the probable cause claim.
- **Challenging Video Evidence:** Reviewing body cam footage to identify inconsistencies in the officer's claims.
- **Demonstrating Racial Profiling:** If a defendant was targeted based on race, a case can be made for unlawful policing practices.
- **Arguing Fruit of the Poisonous Tree Doctrine:** If an illegal search led to additional evidence, that evidence may also be excluded from trial (*Wong Sun v. United States*, 371 U.S. 471 (1963)).

Case Examples

Case Study 1: Suppressing Evidence in a K-9 Alert Case

A Florida defendant was pulled over for a minor traffic violation. The officer detained the driver until a K-9 unit arrived, despite having no reasonable suspicion of drug activity. The defense attorney argued that the prolonged stop violated constitutional rights, leading the court to suppress the drug evidence found in the vehicle (*Rodriguez v. United States*, 575 U.S. 348 (2015)).

Case Study 2: Challenging Marijuana Odor as Probable Cause

In a recent Florida case, police searched a car solely based on the smell of marijuana. The defense successfully argued that since hemp is legal, the smell alone did not establish probable cause. The judge ruled in favor of the defendant, dismissing the charges (*State v. Ruise*, 260 So. 3d 543 (Fla. Dist. Ct. App. 2018)).

Case Study 3: Illegal Search of a Home

Police entered a Florida home claiming exigent circumstances, but body cam footage showed no emergency existed. The defense argued that the warrantless search was unconstitutional, leading to evidence suppression (*Kentucky v. King*, 563 U.S. 452 (2011)).

Conclusion

Many probable cause claims can be beaten by exposing flaws in law enforcement's reasoning or procedures. Whether challenging a dog sniff, marijuana smell, or traffic stop, a strong legal defense can lead to suppressed evidence and case dismissal. Anyone facing charges should consult an experienced defense attorney to build the best possible strategy.

CHAPTER THIRTEEN

BEATING PROBABLE CAUSE: DOG SNIFFS, MARIJUANA SMELL, AND MORE

UNDERSTANDING PROBABLE CAUSE IN FLORIDA

Probable cause is a legal standard that allows law enforcement to conduct searches, make arrests, or obtain warrants if they have reasonable grounds to believe a crime has been committed. However, officers sometimes claim probable cause based on weak or questionable evidence, such as a K-9 alert or the smell of marijuana. Challenging probable cause can be a key strategy in getting evidence suppressed and charges dismissed.

Common Probable Cause Claims and How to Challenge Them

1. Dog Sniff Searches

Law enforcement often use drug-sniffing dogs to establish probable cause. However, these searches are not foolproof and can be challenged based on:

- **Unreliable K-9 Training and Certification:** If a dog has a history of false alerts or inadequate training, its reliability can be questioned.
- **Prolonged Traffic Stops:** Officers cannot unreasonably extend a traffic stop to wait for a K-9 unit (*Rodriguez v. United States*, 575 U.S. 348 (2015)).
- **Warrantless Use of K-9 Units:** If a drug-sniffing dog is used without a valid reason, any resulting search may be unconstitutional.
- **Passive vs. Aggressive Alerts:** Some dogs are trained to sit or indicate when they detect drugs, while others may act aggressively. If an officer misinterprets a dog's behavior, it can be challenged in court.

- **Failure to Record the Search:** Many K-9 searches should be recorded. If no video evidence is available, it raises doubts about the legitimacy of the alert.

2. Marijuana Smell as Probable Cause

The smell of marijuana has historically been used as justification for searches, but Florida law is changing:

- **Hemp vs. Marijuana:** Since hemp is legal and smells similar to marijuana, the odor alone may not be sufficient for probable cause (*State v. Ruise*, 260 So. 3d 543 (Fla. Dist. Ct. App. 2018)).
- **Recent Court Rulings:** Florida courts have begun ruling that marijuana smell alone does not justify a warrantless search.
- **Challenging Officer Testimony:** Officers may exaggerate or falsely claim they smelled marijuana to justify a search. Cross-examining their statements can reveal inconsistencies.
- **Multiple Occupants in a Vehicle:** If several people are in a car, an officer must establish individual possession rather than assuming the smell justifies a search.
- **Medical Marijuana Laws:** Florida allows medical marijuana use, so the presence of the smell does not necessarily indicate illegal activity.

3. Traffic Stops and Vehicle Searches

For a vehicle search to be lawful, officers must have a legitimate reason to believe evidence of a crime is present. Defenses include:

- **Lack of Reasonable Suspicion for the Stop:** If the traffic stop itself was illegal, any evidence found may be suppressed (*Whren v. United States*, 517 U.S. 806 (1996)).

- **Consent Was Coerced:** If a driver was pressured or tricked into consenting to a search, the consent may be invalid.
- **No Clear Evidence of Criminal Activity:** Officers must demonstrate more than just a hunch to justify a search.
- **Pretextual Stops:** If an officer used a minor traffic violation as an excuse to conduct a drug search, it may be considered unconstitutional.

4. Home Searches and Warrants

Probable cause is also required for home searches. Law enforcement cannot search a residence without:

- **A Valid Warrant:** A search warrant must be specific and supported by probable cause (*Illinois v. Gates*, 462 U.S. 213 (1983)).
- **Exigent Circumstances:** Officers cannot force entry without a valid emergency situation (*Kentucky v. King*, 563 U.S. 452 (2011)).
- **Voluntary Consent:** If a resident was intimidated into allowing a search, the search may be illegal.
- **Knock and Announce Rule Violations:** Officers must follow protocol when executing search warrants. If they fail to announce their presence properly, the search may be challenged (*Hudson v. Michigan*, 547 U.S. 586 (2006)).

Legal Strategies to Beat Probable Cause Claims

- **Filing a Motion to Suppress:** If probable cause was improperly established, a defense attorney can file a motion to exclude evidence from trial.
- **Cross-Examining Officers:** Challenging their statements about marijuana odor, K-9 alerts, or observations can expose weaknesses in the case.

- **Questioning K-9 Reliability:** Requesting records on a drug-sniffing dog's accuracy and training history can cast doubt on the search's validity.
- **Using Expert Testimony:** A forensic expert can explain how the smell of marijuana is indistinguishable from hemp, undermining the probable cause claim.
- **Challenging Video Evidence:** Reviewing body cam footage to identify inconsistencies in the officer's claims.
- **Demonstrating Racial Profiling:** If a defendant was targeted based on race, a case can be made for unlawful policing practices.
- **Arguing Fruit of the Poisonous Tree Doctrine:** If an illegal search led to additional evidence, that evidence may also be excluded from trial (*Wong Sun v. United States*, 371 U.S. 471 (1963)).

Case Examples

Case Study 1: Suppressing Evidence in a K-9 Alert Case

A Florida defendant was pulled over for a minor traffic violation. The officer detained the driver until a K-9 unit arrived, despite having no reasonable suspicion of drug activity. The defense attorney argued that the prolonged stop violated constitutional rights, leading the court to suppress the drug evidence found in the vehicle (*Rodriguez v. United States*, 575 U.S. 348 (2015)).

Case Study 2: Challenging Marijuana Odor as Probable Cause

In a recent Florida case, police searched a car solely based on the smell of marijuana. The defense successfully argued that since hemp is legal, the smell alone did not establish probable cause. The judge ruled in favor of the defendant, dismissing the charges (*State v. Ruise*, 260 So. 3d 543 (Fla. Dist. Ct. App. 2018)).

Case Study 3: Illegal Search of a Home

Police entered a Florida home claiming exigent circumstances, but body cam footage showed no emergency existed. The defense argued that the warrantless search was unconstitutional, leading to evidence suppression (*Kentucky v. King*, 563 U.S. 452 (2011)).

Conclusion

Many probable cause claims can be beaten by exposing flaws in law enforcement's reasoning or procedures. Whether challenging a dog sniff, marijuana smell, or traffic stop, a strong legal defense can lead to suppressed evidence and case dismissal. Anyone facing charges should consult an experienced defense attorney to build the best possible strategy.

CHAPTER FOURTEEN

BEATING RICO CHARGES IN FLORIDA

UNDERSTANDING RICO LAWS IN FLORIDA

The Racketeer Influenced and Corrupt Organizations Act (RICO) is a powerful legal tool used by prosecutors to target individuals and groups involved in organized criminal activity. Florida has its own version of RICO under **Florida Statutes § 895.01-895.06**, which mirrors the federal law but applies at the state level. The statute criminalizes patterns of racketeering activity and allows law enforcement to seize assets linked to alleged criminal enterprises.

Elements of a RICO Charge

To convict under Florida's RICO statute, prosecutors must prove:

1. **Enterprise Involvement:** The defendant was part of an enterprise (a group of individuals associated for a common purpose, which can include businesses, street gangs, or informal organizations).
2. **Pattern of Racketeering Activity:** At least two predicate offenses (e.g., drug trafficking, fraud, bribery, money laundering) occurred within a 10-year period.
3. **Connection Between the Enterprise and Crimes:** The criminal activities furthered the goals of the enterprise.
4. **Knowledge and Intent:** The defendant knowingly engaged in or benefitted from illegal activities.

Strategies to Beat a RICO Charge

Beating a RICO charge requires dismantling the prosecution's claims by attacking each element of the case. Here are some effective legal defenses:

1. **Challenge the Existence of an Enterprise**

- **Lack of Structure:** Courts have ruled that an enterprise must have an ongoing structure and purpose (*Boyle v. United States*, 556 U.S. 938 (2009)). If the alleged group was loosely connected with no formal hierarchy, it may not qualify as an enterprise.
- **Temporary or Random Associations:** If the alleged crimes were committed by individuals acting independently rather than as part of an organization, this undermines the enterprise element.
- **Legitimate Business Defense:** If the enterprise is a legitimate business, proving that the defendant's actions were part of normal business operations (rather than criminal activity) can be a strong defense.

2. **Attack the Pattern of Racketeering Activity**

- **Insufficient Predicate Acts:** If the prosecution cannot prove at least two related crimes within 10 years, the RICO charge fails.
- **Unrelated Crimes:** The predicate acts must be connected in purpose, results, or methods. If they are isolated incidents, the RICO statute does not apply.
- **Prior Convictions or Pending Charges:** Predicate offenses must be proven beyond a reasonable doubt. If one or more alleged crimes are dismissed or unproven, the pattern of racketeering claim weakens.

3. **Argue Lack of Knowledge and Intent**

- **No Direct Involvement:** Demonstrating that the defendant was unaware of illegal activities within the enterprise can dismantle the case.
- **Mere Association is Not Enough:** Simply being associated with individuals engaged in criminal activity does not constitute RICO liability (*United States v. Turkette*, 452 U.S. 576 (1981)).

- **Entrapment:** If law enforcement pressured or coerced the defendant into committing an act that they otherwise would not have committed, an entrapment defense may apply.

4. Motion to Dismiss for Lack of Specificity

- **Vague Allegations:** RICO charges often involve broad claims of wrongdoing. Filing a motion to dismiss on the basis that the prosecution has not provided specific allegations against the defendant can be an effective strategy.
- **Failure to Identify Key Players and Acts:** If the prosecution's case lacks clarity on who committed what crime and how they were linked, the defense can argue that the case is too speculative to proceed.

5. Exclude Illegally Obtained Evidence

- **Fourth Amendment Violations:** If evidence was obtained through illegal search and seizure, it can be suppressed (*Wong Sun v. United States*, 371 U.S. 471 (1963)).
- **Wiretap Challenges:** RICO cases often rely on electronic surveillance. If wiretaps were not properly authorized under **Florida Statutes § 934.03**, they may be excluded.
- **Violation of Due Process:** If law enforcement violated legal procedures during the investigation, the case could be dismissed.

6. Asset Forfeiture Defense

Florida's RICO laws allow the government to seize assets linked to alleged criminal enterprises. Defendants can challenge forfeitures by proving:

- **Assets Were Lawfully Acquired:** Bank statements, tax records, and business documents can demonstrate legitimate sources of income.

- **Lack of Connection to Criminal Activity:** If seized property was not directly linked to illegal acts, a forfeiture challenge can be filed.
- **Improper Seizure Procedures:** If law enforcement did not follow proper forfeiture procedures, assets may be returned.

Case Law Supporting RICO Defenses

Case Study 1: United States v. Turkette (1981)

- **Ruling:** The U.S. Supreme Court clarified that an enterprise must have an ongoing structure beyond random criminal acts.
- **Impact:** Defense attorneys can argue that loosely connected individuals do not form a criminal enterprise.

Case Study 2: Boyle v. United States (2009)

- **Ruling:** The court held that an enterprise must have a structure separate from the crimes committed.
- **Impact:** If the prosecution cannot show an organization existed outside of the alleged crimes, the case may be dismissed.

Case Study 3: State v. Nelson (Fla. 2020)

- **Ruling:** Florida's Supreme Court ruled that a pattern of racketeering must be clearly established and not inferred from unrelated incidents.
- **Impact:** This ruling strengthens challenges against weak or circumstantial RICO allegations.

Conclusion

RICO charges in Florida are serious, but they can be beaten with the right legal strategies. By challenging the existence of an enterprise, attacking the pattern of racketeering, arguing lack of intent, filing motions to dismiss, and excluding improperly obtained evidence, defendants can successfully fight RICO allegations. Anyone facing RICO charges should consult an experienced criminal defense attorney to build a strong defense and protect their rights.

CHAPTER FIFTEEN:

Beating a RICO (Racketeer Influenced and Corrupt Organizations Act) case requires a deep understanding of the law and an effective legal strategy. RICO is a federal law designed to combat organized crime by targeting individuals or organizations engaged in a pattern of racketeering activity. To beat a RICO charge, it's crucial to demonstrate that the prosecution has failed to prove the necessary elements required under RICO or that there are legal defenses available to you.

1. Pattern of Racketeering Activity

RICO requires the prosecution to prove the existence of a "pattern of racketeering activity." This means that the defendant must have committed at least two acts of racketeering activity within a ten-year period.

Key Case: Sedima, S.P.R.L. v. Imrex Co., 473 U.S. 479 (1985)

- Ruling: The U.S. Supreme Court clarified the standard for proving a "pattern" of racketeering under RICO. The Court ruled that the pattern must involve at least two acts of racketeering and that the acts must be related and continuous. This ruling is crucial in defending against RICO charges, as it sets a high bar for proving a pattern.
- Defense: One potential defense strategy is to argue that the prosecution has failed to show a "pattern" because the alleged criminal acts were not sufficiently related or continuous. If the acts were isolated incidents rather than part of an ongoing criminal enterprise, you could argue that the RICO charge is invalid.

---

2. Enterprise Requirement

To convict someone under RICO, the government must prove the existence of an "enterprise" that is engaged in racketeering. The enterprise must have an ongoing organization, formal or informal, and must be used to further racketeering activity.

Key Case: United States v. Turkette, 452 U.S. 576 (1981)

- Ruling: The U.S. Supreme Court held that an enterprise can be either a legal or illegal entity, and it need not be a formal organization or corporation. A group of individuals associated in fact can still qualify as an "enterprise" under RICO.
- Defense: In cases where the enterprise is alleged to be a loosely organized group, a defense strategy could involve arguing that the government has failed to demonstrate the existence of a legitimate enterprise as defined under RICO. This could include showing that the alleged group did not have an ongoing structure or that it was not engaged in a pattern of illegal activities.

---

3. Overt Acts and Conspiracy

In many RICO cases, the government will charge conspiracy to violate RICO. In such cases, it must be proven that the defendant agreed to engage in a pattern of racketeering activities.

Key Case: Salinas v. United States, 522 U.S. 52 (1997)

- Ruling: The U.S. Supreme Court held that a RICO conspiracy conviction does not require the defendant to personally commit the acts of racketeering, but merely to agree to the unlawful conduct.

- Defense: A defense strategy here could involve challenging the evidence that the defendant knowingly agreed to participate in a conspiracy. You can argue that there was insufficient evidence to prove that you had the specific intent to join a racketeering enterprise or conspiracy.

---

4. Withdrawal from the Enterprise

A defendant can argue that they withdrew from the enterprise or criminal activity, which could be a defense to RICO charges.

Key Case: United States v. Ruggiero, 726 F.2d 913 (2d Cir. 1984)

- Ruling: The Second Circuit Court of Appeals ruled that a defendant could avoid liability for a RICO violation if they can show they withdrew from the enterprise before the racketeering activity occurred.
- Defense: In defending a RICO charge, you may present evidence that you ceased participating in the criminal enterprise before the alleged racketeering acts took place. This could be used to argue that you are not liable under RICO because you had withdrawn from the enterprise.

---

5. Vagueness and Lack of Specificity

A defense strategy in some cases is to argue that the charges are too vague and that the indictment fails to provide sufficient specific details of the alleged racketeering activities. RICO requires that the charges be specific in nature.

Key Case: Russell v. United States, 369 U.S. 749 (1962)

- Ruling: The U.S. Supreme Court held that an indictment must provide specific and clear details of the charges. The Court emphasized that general or vague allegations are insufficient for criminal convictions.
- Defense: You can challenge the sufficiency of the indictment or complaint, arguing that it lacks specific facts or fails to provide sufficient details to establish the elements of a RICO violation. If the indictment is vague and does not clearly explain how the defendant engaged in a pattern of racketeering, it may be dismissed.

---

6. Due Process and Overreach of RICO

Another potential defense to a RICO charge is that the statute has been applied inappropriately or that its use violates the defendant's due process rights.

Key Case: H.J. Inc. v. Northwestern Bell Telephone Co., 492 U.S. 229 (1989)

- Ruling: The U.S. Supreme Court clarified that the RICO statute requires more than a mere series of criminal acts. The Court emphasized that there must be a connection between the acts that is sufficient to demonstrate a "pattern."
- Defense: You may argue that applying RICO to your case constitutes an overreach of the law or violates your due process rights because the alleged conduct does not meet the legal standard of a "pattern" of racketeering. By challenging the application of RICO to the specific facts of your case, you can argue that the law should not be applied to situations that don't involve organized crime or serious criminal enterprises.

7. Insufficient Evidence

Perhaps one of the strongest defenses in a RICO case is challenging the sufficiency of the evidence. If the prosecution cannot prove each element of the RICO charge beyond a reasonable doubt, the case can be dismissed or the defendant acquitted.

Key Case: United States v. Colombo, 869 F.2d 149 (2d Cir. 1989)

- Ruling: The Second Circuit held that a defendant could not be convicted on RICO charges if the government failed to present sufficient evidence to establish a pattern of racketeering activity.
- Defense: An effective defense is to argue that the government has not provided enough evidence to prove the existence of a pattern of racketeering or the involvement in an enterprise. This may involve attacking the credibility of the prosecution's witnesses, the reliability of the evidence, or showing that the alleged acts were not part of a continuous and organized criminal enterprise.

Conclusion

Beating a RICO charge requires a well-crafted defense strategy that challenges one or more of the essential elements of the offense. By focusing on the lack of a pattern, failure to prove the existence of an enterprise, insufficient evidence, or misapplication of the RICO statute, it is possible to achieve a favorable outcome. Effective legal representation and a strong understanding of case law, such as the ones discussed in this chapter, are vital in building a defense against RICO charges.

CHAPTER SIXTEEN

BEATING CONSPIRACY CHARGES IN FLORIDA

Conspiracy charges in Florida, like in many other states, are serious legal matters that can result in severe penalties if not properly defended against. In Florida, conspiracy is governed under **Florida Statutes § 777.04**, which criminalizes the act of conspiring to commit a criminal offense. Whether you are charged with conspiracy to commit a drug crime, robbery, fraud, or any other offense, defending against these charges requires a strategic approach. This chapter explores the legal elements of conspiracy, common defenses, and key case law that can help individuals fight these charges in Florida.

Understanding Conspiracy Charges

A **conspiracy** charge in Florida occurs when two or more people agree to commit a criminal act and at least one of the individuals performs an overt act toward committing the crime. The important elements of a conspiracy charge are:

1. **Agreement**: There must be a clear agreement between two or more people to commit a criminal act. This agreement does not have to be formal; it can be inferred from the circumstances, actions, and communications between the individuals.
2. **Intent to Commit a Crime**: The individuals involved must have the intent to commit the underlying criminal offense.
3. **Overt Act**: At least one person involved in the conspiracy must take an overt act in furtherance of the conspiracy. An overt act is any action that moves the conspiracy closer to the commission of the planned crime.

Florida's **conspiracy statute** is broad, and it can be applied to virtually any crime, including drug trafficking, white-collar crime, theft, and more.

Common Defenses to Conspiracy Charges in Florida

There are several defenses that can be employed to challenge conspiracy charges. The strategy will depend on the facts of the case, but here are some common defenses used in Florida:

1. Lack of Agreement

- **Key Defense**: One of the critical elements in any conspiracy case is the existence of an agreement between two or more people. If the defense can show that there was no agreement to commit a crime, the conspiracy charge may be dismissed.
- **Defense Example**: The defendant may argue that they were merely present during discussions but did not actively agree to commit any illegal acts. Courts have ruled that mere presence at a meeting or conversations about a crime do not constitute a conspiracy (*State v. Figueroa*, 589 So. 2d 1349 (Fla. 1991)).

2. Withdrawal from the Conspiracy

- **Key Defense**: If the defendant withdraws from the conspiracy and takes steps to stop the crime from being committed, they may not be guilty of conspiracy. Withdrawal can be a valid defense if the defendant can demonstrate they clearly communicated their withdrawal and took substantial steps to prevent the crime.
- **Defense Example**: In *State v. Franklin* (2014), the defendant argued that he withdrew from the conspiracy by notifying authorities about the plan and taking steps to prevent the crime. The court ruled that if there was a clear withdrawal, the conspiracy charge could be defeated.

3. No Overt Act

- **Key Defense**: A conspiracy charge requires that at least one person involved in the conspiracy takes an overt act toward committing the crime. If no overt act occurred, the conspiracy charge may not be valid.
- **Defense Example**: If the defense can show that no actions were taken toward completing the conspiracy, such as failing to gather materials or organize further steps, the charge may be weakened. This is particularly useful in cases where the alleged conspiracy is in its early stages.

4. Insufficient Evidence of Intent

- **Key Defense**: A critical element in conspiracy is the intent to commit the underlying crime. If the defense can show that the defendant did not have the necessary criminal intent, the conspiracy charge may fail.
- **Defense Example**: In some cases, the defendant might argue that their actions or conversations were misinterpreted or that they were joking or casually discussing hypothetical situations without any intent to act on them. In such cases, there might not be enough evidence to prove intent beyond a reasonable doubt.

5. Coercion or Duress

- **Key Defense**: A defendant can argue that they were coerced or forced into participating in a conspiracy. Duress or coercion occurs when a defendant is compelled to commit a crime due to fear of harm or threats of violence.
- **Defense Example**: If a defendant can demonstrate that they were threatened with serious harm or death if they did not participate in a conspiracy, they may avoid conviction under duress (*State v. Fleming*, 350 So. 2d 1055 (Fla. 1977)).

6. Entrapment

- **Key Defense**: Entrapment occurs when law enforcement induces a person to commit a crime they would not have otherwise committed. If the defense can demonstrate that the police initiated the criminal activity or pressured the defendant into committing the conspiracy, the defendant may have an entrapment defense.
- **Defense Example**: In cases where the defendant was manipulated or encouraged by undercover law enforcement officers, a successful entrapment defense can result in dismissal of the charges (*Sorrells v. United States*, 287 U.S. 435 (1932)).

Case Law to Support Defenses

Several important Florida cases have established critical precedents for defending against conspiracy charges.

State v. Figueroa (1991)

- **Ruling**: The Florida Supreme Court ruled that mere presence at a meeting where a crime is discussed does not establish a conspiracy. There must be evidence of an actual agreement to commit a crime.
- **Impact**: This case reinforces the idea that simply being involved in a conversation or being present during a discussion is not sufficient to prove conspiracy.

State v. Franklin (2014)

- **Ruling**: The Florida Supreme Court held that a defendant could avoid a conspiracy charge if they demonstrated a clear withdrawal from the conspiracy before any illegal acts were committed.
- **Impact**: This case highlights the importance of showing an overt act of withdrawal or taking steps to prevent the crime.

Sorrells v. United States (1932)

- **Ruling**: The U.S. Supreme Court established that entrapment occurs when law enforcement induces a defendant to commit a crime they were not predisposed to commit.
- **Impact**: This decision provides a strong defense against conspiracy charges where the defendant was coerced into the conspiracy by law enforcement officers.

Conclusion

Conspiracy charges are complex, but they are not insurmountable. Defendants facing conspiracy charges in Florida can challenge the case in several ways, including proving a lack of agreement, demonstrating withdrawal, disputing the existence of overt acts, showing insufficient intent, or asserting defenses like duress or entrapment. By carefully analyzing the facts, employing effective legal strategies, and utilizing strong case law, individuals can successfully defend against conspiracy charges in Florida.

If you are facing conspiracy charges, it is critical to consult with an experienced criminal defense attorney who understands the nuances of Florida's conspiracy laws and can help you mount a powerful defense.

CHAPTER: SEVENTEEN

GETTING STATE GOOD TIME WHILE SERVING A CONCURRENT SENTENCE IN FLORIDA

In the Florida criminal justice system, prisoners who display good behavior while incarcerated may qualify for "good time" credit, which reduces their sentence length. This chapter discusses how defendants serving concurrent sentences can earn state good time and the implications of such credits under Florida law.

Understanding how good time works, especially when serving multiple sentences concurrently, is crucial for prisoners looking to shorten their time in custody.

What is State Good Time?

State good time is a form of sentence reduction offered to inmates who comply with institutional rules and regulations, participate in educational or vocational programs, and demonstrate good behavior while incarcerated. Good time is typically calculated based on the inmate's behavior, with the possibility of reducing the length of the sentence, though the exact reduction varies depending on the inmate's actions.

Under **Florida Statutes § 944.275**, good time credits can be earned by individuals convicted of felonies, and they apply to sentences served in the Department of Corrections. However, the ability to accumulate these credits is contingent on several factors, including the type of sentence the individual is serving.

Types of Sentences in Florida

In Florida, sentences can be structured in different ways, including concurrent and consecutive sentences.

1. **Concurrent Sentences**: When multiple sentences are served simultaneously, the longest sentence dictates the amount of time a prisoner will serve. For example, if a person is sentenced to 10 years for one crime and 5 years for another, both sentences will be served concurrently, and the individual will only serve 10 years, not 15.

2. **Consecutive Sentences**: When multiple sentences are imposed and served one after the other, the total time served will be the sum of all the sentences. For instance, a person sentenced to 10 years on one charge and 5 years on another will serve 15 years total if the sentences are consecutive.

In the context of good time, concurrent sentences mean that the inmate is serving multiple sentences at the same time, but only the longest sentence will affect the amount of time eligible for release. This is a crucial aspect to consider when attempting to accumulate good time credits.

How Good Time Works for Concurrent Sentences

When an individual is serving concurrent sentences, they can earn good time credits that apply to the longest sentence being served. Here's how it generally works:

1. **Calculation of Good Time**: In Florida, inmates can earn up to 10 days of good time credit for each month they serve in custody, provided they meet the necessary behavior requirements. For a person serving concurrent sentences, they are eligible to earn good time based on the longest sentence. For example, if a person is serving 10 years concurrently with a 5-year sentence, the good time credits will be calculated based on the 10-year sentence, as that is the longer sentence.

2. **Eligibility for Release**: Good time credits are subtracted from the total time served, meaning that good behavior could result in an early release. For instance, if an individual is serving 10 years concurrently with a 5-year sentence, and they earn good time credits for the 10-year sentence, they may be eligible for early release based on the reduced time.
3. **Impact of Good Time on Release Dates**: Even though an individual serves concurrent sentences, good time credits apply to the entire sentence. If an individual serves 10 years concurrently with a 5-year sentence, earning good time could reduce the time served on the 10-year sentence, but the 5-year sentence still determines when the individual will be released.

Legal Basis for Good Time Credits

Florida law allows the Department of Corrections to grant good time credits under **Florida Statutes § 944.275**. The statute mandates that inmates can receive up to 10 days of credit per month of incarceration, provided they meet the conditions for good behavior and make progress in work, education, or vocational programs.

It is important to note that not all inmates are eligible for good time credits. Certain types of offenses, such as capital felonies or sex offenses, may disqualify individuals from earning credits. Additionally, inmates who violate institutional rules or engage in misconduct may lose earned good time credits, which can extend their time in custody.

Earned Time vs. Gain Time

In addition to state good time, Florida offers **gain time** as a method of reducing sentences. There are two types of gain time:

1. **Basic Gain Time**: This is earned at a rate of one day for every day served, for inmates who meet behavior and work standards. This form of gain time applies to all inmates.
2. **Extra Gain Time**: Inmates who participate in additional programs, such as educational or vocational training, may earn extra gain time, reducing their sentence further.

For inmates serving concurrent sentences, extra gain time would apply to the longest sentence being served, just like good time credits.

Challenges in Earning Good Time

While good time credits can significantly reduce the time an inmate serves, there are challenges involved in earning those credits. These include:

1. **Behavioral Requirements**: To earn good time credits, inmates must adhere to the rules of the correctional facility. Violating institutional policies can result in the loss of good time credits, which could delay an inmate's release.
2. **Eligibility for Program Participation**: Inmates must participate in rehabilitation programs, such as educational courses, vocational training, or work programs, to be eligible for earning good time credits. Inmates who fail to participate or complete these programs may not qualify for the maximum good time credits.
3. **Time Constraints**: While serving concurrent sentences, inmates should be aware that the length of the longest sentence determines when they can be released. Good time credits can shorten this time, but the process is often slow, and the full benefits of good time may not be realized until later in the sentence.

Case Law Impacting Good Time Credits

Several cases have addressed the application of good time credits, especially in relation to concurrent sentences. For instance:

- **Cunningham v. State, 2017**: The Florida Supreme Court ruled that an inmate serving a concurrent sentence could receive good time credits on both sentences, provided that the longest sentence is used to determine the amount of good time. This case reinforced the principle that good time is calculated based on the longest sentence served, not the cumulative length of concurrent sentences.
- **Terry v. State, 2009**: This case clarified that good time credits can only be applied to sentences that are actually served. If an inmate is serving a sentence concurrently with another sentence that is not eligible for good time, the good time will only apply to the sentences that are eligible under Florida law.

Conclusion

In Florida, good time credits can be an effective way for inmates to reduce their time in custody, especially when serving concurrent sentences. By maintaining good behavior, participating in rehabilitation programs, and adhering to institutional rules, inmates can earn up to 10 days of good time credit for each month served. Although good time applies to the longest sentence served in a concurrent sentence structure, it can still be a valuable tool in reducing overall incarceration time.

Inmates serving concurrent sentences should consult with their attorneys and correctional officers to understand their eligibility for good time credits, how these credits will affect their release date, and the requirements for earning them. By maximizing their good time credits and maintaining good behavior, inmates can potentially shorten their time in prison and re-enter society sooner.

CHAPTER EIGHTEEN

GETTING BACK INTO FLORIDA COURTS AFTER BEING TIME-BARRED

INTRODUCTION

In legal matters, the statute of limitations represents the period during which a legal action can be brought. In Florida, as in many other states, once a statute of limitations expires, the right to bring a lawsuit is generally barred. However, there are circumstances under which a time-barred claim can be revived. This chapter explores how individuals or entities can navigate the complexities of getting back into Florida courts after being time-barred, focusing on exceptions, strategies, and procedural mechanisms that can reopen a case or allow for a claim to be filed despite the expiration of the statute of limitations.

1. Understanding the Statute of Limitations in Florida

The statute of limitations is a critical component of the legal system that sets the maximum time after an event within which legal proceedings may be initiated. In Florida, different types of claims have different time limits, which range from two years for personal injury cases to five years for written contracts, and twenty years for property damage claims involving fraud. Once this period has passed, the defendant can raise the defense of being "time-barred" to dismiss the lawsuit.

For example, if someone is injured in a car accident, they typically have four years from the date of the accident to file a lawsuit for personal injury in Florida. If they wait beyond that time, the defendant can move to dismiss the case on the grounds that it is time-barred.

2. Legal Exceptions and Tolling of the Statute of Limitations

While the expiration of the statute of limitations is a significant barrier, Florida law provides certain exceptions that allow for the tolling or extension of these time limits in specific situations. Tolling refers to the suspension or temporary halt of the time period in which a person can bring a lawsuit. Some of the common situations in which the statute of limitations may be tolled include:

- **Minority (Underage Plaintiffs):** If the person seeking to file a claim is a minor at the time the cause of action arises, the statute of limitations is tolled until the individual turns 18.
- **Incapacity:** If the plaintiff is mentally incapacitated at the time the cause of action arises, the statute of limitations may be tolled until the individual regains mental capacity.
- **Fraud or Concealment:** If the defendant engages in fraudulent actions that conceal the cause of action from the plaintiff, the statute of limitations can be tolled. This is often relevant in cases involving fraud, where the plaintiff may not immediately realize they have a legal claim due to deceptive actions.
- **Equitable Estoppel:** In some cases, if the defendant engages in conduct that intentionally prevents the plaintiff from filing the claim (such as lying about facts or hiding key documents), the court may allow the plaintiff to file the case even after the statute of limitations has expired.

Understanding whether any of these exceptions apply is essential to determining whether it's possible to get back into court after a time-barred claim.

3. Filing a Motion to Reopen or Vacate

In Florida, if a claim has been dismissed due to being time-barred, a party may file a motion to reopen or vacate the dismissal. In this context, "vacating" refers to nullifying the court's prior decision to dismiss the case based on the statute of limitations.

A motion to vacate may be appropriate when the statute of limitations was missed due to an external factor or excusable neglect. For example, if the plaintiff was unaware of the time limitation due to illness, legal counsel error, or another valid reason, they might request the court to reopen the case.

There are a few key grounds under which a court may decide to vacate a dismissal:

- **Excusable Neglect or Mistake:** A defendant or plaintiff might be able to show that the failure to file the lawsuit within the statute of limitations was due to excusable neglect or a mistake, such as not being aware of the deadline due to circumstances beyond their control.
- **Newly Discovered Evidence:** In some instances, newly discovered evidence could provide grounds for reopening the case. If this evidence was not available at the time the statute of limitations expired and directly affects the case, the court might allow the case to proceed.
- **Fraud on the Court:** If it is revealed that one party engaged in fraudulent conduct that affected the outcome of the case, such as presenting false documents or hiding evidence, the court may vacate the dismissal and allow the case to be reopened.

Filing a motion to vacate or reopen requires a solid legal basis, and the party seeking to reopen the case must demonstrate that they have a valid reason for not bringing the claim within the statute of limitations.

4. Re-initiating the Case via New Legal Theories

Even if a claim is time-barred under the original legal theory, there may be an opportunity to re-initiate the case using a new or different legal theory that is not time-barred. For example, if a party cannot pursue a breach of contract case because the statute of limitations has expired, they may be able to pursue a claim for unjust enrichment or another equitable theory that does not have the same time limitations.

This approach requires a careful evaluation of the legal landscape and an understanding of the available claims that may be pursued despite the expiration of the statute of limitations. Attorneys specializing in complex litigation or civil procedure are essential in identifying these potential avenues.

5. The Role of Legal Counsel in Reopening Time-Barred Cases

The complexities involved in reopening or re-initiating a time-barred case make legal counsel indispensable. Experienced attorneys familiar with Florida's statutes of limitations and the available exceptions can help navigate the court system, evaluate the potential for tolling or equitable estoppel, and develop strategies to reopen a case.

Additionally, attorneys can assist in filing motions to vacate dismissals, explore alternative legal theories, or negotiate settlements outside of the courtroom. Legal representation ensures that any available remedy is pursued efficiently and in accordance with Florida law.

6. The Risk of Success and Potential Challenges

While it's possible to get back into Florida courts after being time-barred, the process is often challenging. Courts are reluctant to extend deadlines without a solid legal justification, and opposing parties will typically argue that the statute of limitations is a strict rule of law that should not be circumvented.

The risk of success depends on several factors, including the strength of the legal argument, the specific circumstances surrounding the expiration of the statute of limitations, and whether any of the exceptions to the statute of limitations apply. Additionally, the court's discretion plays a significant role, and even when exceptions exist, the decision to allow a case to move forward after the statute of limitations has expired is not guaranteed.

Conclusion

Getting back into Florida courts after being time-barred is a difficult, but not impossible, challenge. With a clear understanding of Florida's statutes of limitations, knowledge of the potential exceptions and tolling mechanisms, and guidance from experienced legal counsel, it is possible to reopen or reinitiate a case even after the expiration of the deadline. Whether through the filing of motions to vacate, the use of new legal theories, or reliance on exceptions such as fraud or excusable neglect, individuals and entities seeking justice in Florida courts must be prepared to demonstrate that their claim has merit despite the passage of time.

CHAPTER NINETEEN

BEATING SEX TRAFFICKING CASES

INTRODUCTION

Sex trafficking is one of the most heinous crimes, and individuals charged with such offenses face severe consequences under the law. However, being accused of sex trafficking doesn't necessarily mean that conviction is inevitable. Whether you are a defendant in such a case or someone seeking knowledge on how to handle these serious charges, understanding how to fight back against a sex trafficking accusation is critical. This chapter will discuss the key strategies employed by defense attorneys to beat sex trafficking cases, the legal nuances involved, and the critical factors that can lead to an acquittal or a reduction in charges.

1. Understanding Sex Trafficking Laws

Before delving into the strategies for defending against a sex trafficking case, it's important to first understand what constitutes sex trafficking under the law. Sex trafficking is defined by the federal law, as well as by state laws, as the recruitment, harboring, transportation, provision, or obtaining of an individual for the purpose of a commercial sex act. In Florida, the law regarding human trafficking is defined under Florida Statutes Section 787.06, which criminalizes the trafficking of individuals for sex or labor.

The charges in a sex trafficking case are severe, and penalties include lengthy prison sentences, fines, and a permanent criminal record. Given these consequences, it is crucial for anyone facing such accusations to fully understand the legal framework and the seriousness of the charges.

2. Building a Defense Strategy

A strong defense strategy in a sex trafficking case revolves around disproving the elements of the crime, presenting an alternative narrative, or highlighting weaknesses in the prosecution's case. Here are key defense strategies that can be used:

- **Lack of Evidence or Inconsistent Evidence** One of the first areas to attack in any sex trafficking case is the evidence. For a conviction to occur, the prosecution must prove the elements of the crime beyond a reasonable doubt. This includes proving that the victim was trafficked for sex and that the defendant was involved in this process. If there is insufficient evidence or inconsistencies in the evidence presented by the prosecution, it can be grounds for dismissal or acquittal.

- Defense attorneys will often look for gaps in the prosecution's case, such as:
    - Lack of physical evidence, such as DNA, fingerprints, or surveillance footage linking the defendant to the trafficking activity.
    - Inconsistencies in the victim's testimony or conflicting accounts of what occurred.
    - Unreliable witness testimony, including witnesses who have a motive to lie or have changed their statements over time.
- By thoroughly investigating the case, challenging the reliability of evidence, and questioning witnesses, defense attorneys can create reasonable doubt in the minds of jurors.
- **Lack of Intent** Intent is a critical element in sex trafficking cases. The prosecution must prove that the defendant had the intent to traffic individuals for sex. If the defense can establish that the defendant did not have the intent to engage in trafficking, it can lead to a reduction in charges or a complete acquittal.

- Common scenarios where lack of intent could be argued include:
    - The defendant did not know the victim was being trafficked or coerced into prostitution.
    - The defendant was not aware of the victim's age or other crucial facts that constitute trafficking.
    - There is insufficient evidence to show that the defendant played an active role in the trafficking operation.
- **Coercion or Duress** Another effective defense is arguing that the defendant was coerced, threatened, or forced into participating in sex trafficking activities. In these cases, the defendant might not be acting willingly or with criminal intent but was instead pressured by someone else (such as a human trafficker or gang) to participate in the illegal activity.
- Coercion or duress may involve the defendant's vulnerability—such as financial hardship, personal threats, or emotional manipulation—that led them to become involved in the trafficking activities. If the defense can show that the defendant was under duress, it can significantly impact the outcome of the case.
- It is essential to show that the defendant's involvement was a result of external pressure rather than voluntary participation in criminal activity.
- **Mistaken Identity** Sex trafficking cases often involve complex criminal operations with multiple individuals involved. A defense attorney may argue mistaken identity if they believe the defendant has been wrongly identified as a perpetrator. In some cases, witnesses may misidentify someone or there may be a misunderstanding of the defendant's role in the operation.
- A mistaken identity defense typically relies on:
    - Evidence proving the defendant was not present at the crime scene.

    - Alibi evidence or testimony from others that the defendant was elsewhere when the trafficking activity occurred.
    - A detailed examination of the identification process, including any errors or flaws in line-ups or photo identifications.
- **Consent and False Allegations** In certain cases, the defense might assert that the alleged trafficking victim consented to engage in sex work or that the accusations made against the defendant are entirely false. This defense may be difficult to use in most sex trafficking cases because the law presumes that minors cannot legally consent to commercial sex acts. However, in cases where the alleged victim is an adult, the defense may attempt to argue that the victim was not coerced and participated willingly in the activities, and that the defendant should not be held liable for the victim's voluntary actions.

- Additionally, in situations where the defendant claims that the accusations are fabricated, the defense attorney would need to gather evidence of a motive to lie or demonstrate a history of false claims by the accuser.

3. Evaluating the Victim's Testimony

Victim testimony is often central to a sex trafficking case, and as such, defense attorneys focus on challenging the credibility and reliability of the victim's account. However, it is crucial to note that just because someone is the alleged victim of sex trafficking does not automatically make their testimony credible or irrefutable.

Key strategies for challenging victim testimony include:

- **Inconsistent Statements**: If the victim has made statements that contradict earlier testimonies or the physical evidence presented, this can create doubts about their reliability.

- **Motivation for False Accusations**: Sometimes, victims might have personal grievances or issues that could lead them to falsely accuse someone of trafficking.
- **Influence or Manipulation by Authorities**: In some cases, victims may be influenced by law enforcement or others to testify against the defendant, whether or not their testimony is accurate.

If a defense attorney can effectively challenge the victim's testimony, it may cause the case to collapse or result in a favorable verdict for the defendant.

4. Sentencing and Plea Bargaining

Even in cases where the defense strategy does not result in a complete acquittal, there may be opportunities to negotiate a lesser sentence through a plea bargain. In situations where the evidence against the defendant is overwhelming, the defense may seek to reduce the charges from sex trafficking to a lesser offense, such as facilitating prostitution or another related charge.

Plea negotiations can be an essential part of defending against sex trafficking charges, especially if it appears that the prosecution has strong evidence. The goal is to minimize the consequences by negotiating a more lenient plea deal or alternative sentencing options, such as probation, community service, or rehabilitation programs.

5. The Role of Legal Counsel

Fighting a sex trafficking case requires the expertise of an experienced criminal defense attorney, particularly one familiar with the complexities of human trafficking laws. These cases often involve serious allegations and can result in lengthy prison sentences if the defendant is convicted. It is important to work with a lawyer who is well-versed in both state and federal trafficking laws and who can employ a variety of strategies to build the most effective defense.

Defense attorneys have access to resources such as private investigators, forensic experts, and psychologists, all of whom can help uncover exculpatory evidence or challenge the prosecution's narrative. With a strong legal team, defendants have a much better chance of achieving a favorable outcome.

Conclusion

Beating a sex trafficking case is a difficult and complex challenge, but it is not impossible. A combination of solid legal defense strategies, including challenging evidence, disproving intent, demonstrating coercion or duress, and identifying flaws in victim testimony, can significantly increase the chances of success. The role of an experienced defense attorney is critical in navigating these complex cases, ensuring that the defendant's rights are protected, and working towards the best possible outcome, whether that involves a complete acquittal or a reduced sentence. It is important to approach sex trafficking cases with a clear understanding of the law and a willingness to utilize every available defense strategy.

CHAPTER TWENTY

BEATING THE HABITUAL FELONY OFFENDER (HFO) DESIGNATION

INTRODUCTION

Being classified as a Habitual Felony Offender (HFO) is one of the most serious consequences a person can face within the criminal justice system. The designation comes with severe legal penalties, including lengthy prison sentences, and often eliminates the possibility of early parole or other forms of leniency. However, while the HFO classification presents a significant challenge, it is not insurmountable. In this chapter, we will explore how individuals who are facing an HFO designation can fight back, the strategies defense attorneys employ to beat an HFO designation, and the legal tools available to those looking to challenge or reverse the designation.

1. Understanding the Habitual Felony Offender (HFO) Law

The Habitual Felony Offender law applies to individuals who have been convicted of multiple felony offenses and have a history of repeat criminal behavior. In Florida, for example, the HFO designation is governed by **Florida Statute 775.084**, which increases the penalties for individuals who have two or more prior felony convictions. The law's purpose is to impose more severe sentences on repeat offenders, under the premise that individuals who repeatedly commit felonies pose a greater danger to society.

A typical HFO designation means:

- A mandatory extended prison sentence, often far longer than the sentence for a first-time offender.
- Thc possibility of a life sentence if the person is convicted of certain crimes while under the HFO designation.

- Limited eligibility for parole and other forms of early release.
- The designation often remains on the individual's criminal record for life, affecting their future prospects.

However, not all individuals facing an HFO designation must accept it as a given. Depending on the facts of the case, there may be several ways to fight this designation in court.

2. Challenging the Legal Basis of the HFO Designation

The first step in fighting the HFO designation is to challenge the legal basis for its application. Here are several ways to do so:

- **Incorrect Prior Convictions** The most straightforward challenge to an HFO designation is to argue that one or more of the prior felony convictions used to designate someone as a habitual offender are inaccurate, outdated, or legally invalid. If the defendant can prove that the previous convictions do not meet the criteria established by the state's habitual offender laws, the HFO designation may be reversed.

- Examples of challenges to prior convictions include:
    - The defendant's previous conviction was overturned or expunged.
    - The prior convictions involved crimes that do not meet the legal requirements for an HFO designation (for example, they may not be considered "felonies" under state law).
    - The prior convictions are too old and should not count toward the HFO classification.
- **Inadequate Notification of Prior Convictions** For the HFO designation to be valid, the defendant must be notified of the prior convictions during the pre-sentence investigation or sentencing phase. If the defense can demonstrate that the defendant was not properly notified

of their prior convictions, they may argue that the HFO designation should not apply.

- **Illegal or Unconstitutional Sentencing of Prior Convictions** Another possible defense is that one or more of the prior convictions were obtained in violation of the defendant's rights. This could include situations where the defendant was not provided with legal counsel or where the conviction occurred under conditions that violated the defendant's constitutional rights. If successful, this challenge could invalidate the prior conviction, potentially removing the HFO designation.

3. The "Clean Slate" Argument: Proving Rehabilitation

A powerful argument to fight an HFO designation is showing that the defendant has rehabilitated and changed their behavior since their previous felony convictions. In many cases, an individual who is designated as a habitual offender is viewed by the court as a chronic criminal who poses a continual threat to society. However, a defendant who has undergone rehabilitation, demonstrated remorse, and reformed their behavior can argue for a lesser sentence.

Strategies for making this argument include:

- **Proving a Lengthy Period of Law-Abiding Behavior** If the defendant has not committed any felonies or criminal offenses for an extended period after their prior convictions, this can be a compelling argument. Demonstrating that the defendant has been a productive member of society, has maintained stable employment, or has been involved in community service can all bolster the defense.
- **Presenting Evidence of Rehabilitation Programs** If the defendant has participated in substance abuse treatment, educational programs, job training, or other rehabilitation initiatives while incarcerated or after their release, this evidence can help show that the defendant is no

longer the same person they were when the prior convictions occurred.

- **Testimony from Character Witnesses** Character witnesses, including family members, employers, and others who can speak to the defendant's transformation, can help the court see the person beyond their criminal history.

By demonstrating a commitment to change, the defendant may convince the judge that they should not be subjected to the severe penalties associated with the HFO classification.

4. Fighting the HFO at Sentencing: The Judge's Discretion

Even if the HFO designation is upheld, there is still an opportunity to influence the final sentence. Many judges have discretion in determining the length of a sentence, especially in cases where the HFO designation is being contested. The defense can argue for a more lenient sentence by focusing on factors such as:

- **The Nature of the Current Offense** If the current offense is non-violent or less severe than other felonies, the defense can argue that the defendant should not face the maximum sentence typically imposed for an HFO.
- **The Defendant's Personal Circumstances** Personal circumstances such as family responsibilities, health issues, and community ties can be presented to show that the defendant's life has changed. If the defendant has shown remorse and taken responsibility for their actions, the judge may consider a lesser sentence than the mandatory minimums that typically accompany the HFO designation.
- **Mitigating Factors** Mitigating factors such as mental health issues, addiction problems, or trauma that led to the defendant's previous criminal behavior can be used to persuade the judge to impose a more lenient sentence, even if the HFO designation stands.

5. Post-Conviction Relief: Expungement and Early Release

Even if a defendant is convicted as a Habitual Felony Offender, there may still be options for post-conviction relief that can help alleviate the harsh consequences of the HFO designation.

- **Appealing the Sentence** If the defendant believes the HFO designation was applied incorrectly or unfairly, they can appeal the conviction and seek to have the sentence reduced. Successful appeals may result in a new sentencing hearing, where the defense can argue against the imposition of the HFO.
- **Seeking a Sentence Modification** Depending on the circumstances, the defendant may be able to request a sentence modification from the court. This might involve seeking a reduction in the sentence or arguing for the possibility of parole or early release, even if the individual is classified as an HFO.
- **Expungement or Sealing of the Record** In some instances, defendants may be eligible to have their criminal records sealed or expunged. While this process is complex, and not everyone is eligible, it may be a viable option for those seeking to move forward without the permanent stigma of a felony conviction.

6. The Role of Experienced Legal Counsel

Given the complexity of fighting an HFO designation, it is essential to work with an experienced criminal defense attorney who understands the nuances of Florida's habitual offender laws. A skilled attorney can analyze the facts of the case, review prior convictions, and develop a defense strategy tailored to the individual's situation. Legal counsel will also help ensure that any challenges to the HFO designation are raised at the appropriate time and in the appropriate manner, preserving the defendant's right to a fair trial and a fair sentence.

Conclusion

Fighting the Habitual Felony Offender designation is a challenging but not impossible task. With the right legal strategy, a defendant can challenge the HFO designation on legal grounds, demonstrate personal rehabilitation, or argue for a more lenient sentence. The key is to approach the case systematically, challenging the prior convictions, presenting a compelling case for change, and making use of all available post-conviction relief options. While an HFO designation carries serious consequences, the opportunity to challenge or overturn it exists—and with the right approach, the defendant can potentially regain their freedom and a second chance at life.

CHAPTER TWENTY ONE

BEATING THE HABITUAL VIOLENT FELONY OFFENDER (HVFO) DESIGNATION

INTRODUCTION

The Habitual Violent Felony Offender (HVFO) designation is one of the most severe classifications in the criminal justice system, carrying with it mandatory extended prison sentences, fewer opportunities for parole, and long-lasting repercussions. This designation is reserved for individuals who have been convicted of multiple violent felonies, and it serves to impose harsher penalties on repeat offenders. However, just like other habitual offender classifications, it is not impossible to challenge or beat the HVFO designation. This chapter will explore the ways that individuals facing an HVFO designation can fight back, the legal strategies that may be employed, and the potential defenses that could lead to a more lenient sentence or the elimination of the HVFO classification.

1. Understanding the HVFO Law

The HVFO law is designed to punish individuals who have repeatedly committed violent crimes. It is often applied to people with two or more prior convictions for violent felonies, such as armed robbery, aggravated assault, murder, and other serious crimes involving physical harm to others. In Florida, the HVFO law is governed by **Florida Statute 775.084**, which outlines the criteria for designating someone as a Habitual Violent Felony Offender.

When someone is designated as an HVFO, the law mandates a lengthy prison sentence that is often much more severe than the typical sentence for a first-time offender or someone with fewer prior convictions. For instance:

- The mandatory minimum sentence can be 15 years in prison, with the possibility of life imprisonment depending on the nature of the crime.
- Parole opportunities are greatly restricted, making it difficult for those classified as HVFOs to get out of prison early.

However, just as with the standard Habitual Felony Offender (HFO) designation, there are strategies that defense attorneys can use to challenge or eliminate an HVFO classification.

2. Challenging the Legal Basis for the HVFO Designation

One of the first and most important steps in fighting the HVFO designation is to challenge the underlying legal basis for the classification. If the defense can successfully challenge any of the prior convictions that form the basis for the HVFO designation, it may be possible to have the designation removed altogether. Below are several common ways to challenge an HVFO designation:

- **Questioning the Validity of Prior Convictions** The defense can investigate whether the prior convictions used to justify the HVFO designation are legally valid. For example:
  - **Inaccurate Convictions:** If one or more of the prior violent felonies are incorrect or if they have been overturned or expunged, they should not count toward the HVFO classification.
  - **Outdated Convictions:** In some cases, older convictions may not meet the legal criteria for an HVFO designation, especially if too much time has passed since the previous crimes were committed.
  - **Unconstitutional Convictions:** If a prior conviction resulted from a violation of the defendant's constitutional rights, such as lack of effective legal representation or improper plea agreements, it may be possible to have the conviction invalidated.

- **Violations of the Defendant's Rights During the Sentencing Process** An HVFO designation can only be applied if the defendant was properly notified of their prior convictions and given the opportunity to contest them. If there was a failure to notify the defendant about the prior convictions or if the legal process leading to the HVFO designation was flawed, the defense can argue that the designation should not be applied.

3. Proving Rehabilitation and a Change in Behavior

In many cases, even if the HVFO designation is legally sound, a defendant may be able to challenge it by demonstrating that they have significantly changed since their prior convictions. A key argument in this situation is that a person who has reformed their behavior should not face the same harsh penalties as someone who has not shown any signs of improvement. Strategies to prove rehabilitation include:

- **Documenting a Period of Law-Abiding Behavior** If the defendant has gone a significant amount of time without committing any violent felonies, this can be a persuasive argument. Evidence that the defendant has been law-abiding for years or even decades can demonstrate that they no longer pose the same risk as they did when they committed previous violent crimes.
- **Presenting Evidence of Participation in Rehabilitation Programs** If the defendant has participated in educational programs, counseling, anger management classes, or substance abuse treatment, this can indicate a sincere commitment to change. Courts are often willing to consider these factors when deciding whether to impose a harsh sentence under the HVFO designation.
- **Character Witness Testimony** Testimony from family members, employers, or community leaders who can attest to the defendant's transformation can be a powerful tool in court. Witnesses who can

speak to the defendant's positive contributions to society, such as stable employment or community involvement, can provide a compelling counter-narrative to the notion of the defendant as a habitual violent offender.

4. Challenging the Severity of the Sentence

Even if the defendant is found to be a Habitual Violent Felony Offender, there may still be room to argue for a less severe sentence. Judges have some discretion in sentencing, and a skilled defense attorney can present arguments for a reduced sentence based on various factors, including:

- **The Nature of the Current Offense** If the current offense is less violent or involved less harm to the victim than previous offenses, the defense can argue that the defendant's actions should not lead to the maximum sentence associated with the HVFO designation.
- **Mitigating Circumstances** In some cases, the defendant's personal history, including mental health issues, trauma, or substance abuse problems, may have contributed to their violent criminal behavior. Arguing that the defendant was acting out of desperation or as a result of untreated psychological issues can lead to a more lenient sentence.
- **Family and Community Ties** The defendant's relationships with family members, children, or other dependents may play a role in the sentencing. If the defendant has strong family ties or is a caretaker, the judge may take this into account when deciding whether to impose a lengthy prison sentence.
- **Personal Growth and Accountability** Demonstrating that the defendant has taken responsibility for their actions, expressed remorse, and made an effort to better themselves can be persuasive. Courts are sometimes more willing to show leniency to defendants who exhibit genuine efforts to improve.

5. Post-Conviction Relief and Long-Term Options

If the defendant is convicted and sentenced as a Habitual Violent Felony Offender, it's not necessarily the end of the road. There are several options for post-conviction relief that may be available:

- **Appealing the HVFO Designation** If the defendant believes that the HVFO designation was applied incorrectly or unfairly, they may have the right to appeal the sentence. This could result in a new sentencing hearing or, in some cases, a reduction in the sentence.

- **Requesting a Sentence Modification** Depending on the circumstances, the defense can file for a sentence modification, seeking to reduce the prison term or request early release options such as parole.

- **Expungement or Sealing of the Record** In certain circumstances, the defendant may eventually be eligible for the expungement or sealing of their criminal record. While this is a complex and often difficult process, it may be possible if the defendant has demonstrated significant reform or if they meet certain criteria for post-conviction relief.

6. The Importance of Legal Representation

Challenging an HVFO designation is a complex and high-stakes endeavor that requires the expertise of a skilled criminal defense attorney. A defense lawyer can help the defendant understand the legal landscape, assess the viability of challenges to prior convictions, and develop a strategic plan for fighting the HVFO designation. The attorney will be responsible for presenting compelling arguments, gathering evidence of rehabilitation, and advocating for the best possible outcome.

Conclusion

While the HVFO designation imposes harsh consequences on those facing it, it is possible to fight back and overcome the penalties associated with it. By challenging the legal validity of prior convictions, presenting evidence of rehabilitation, and arguing for a reduced sentence, defendants can potentially avoid the severe consequences of the Habitual Violent Felony Offender law. With the right legal strategy, it is possible to fight for a second chance, reduce the length of the sentence, or seek post-conviction relief that provides a path forward. Every case is unique, and with the help of an experienced attorney, the HVFO designation may not be an insurmountable obstacle.

CHAPTER TWENTY TWO

Beating HVFO (Habitual Violent Felony Offender) charges often requires a deep understanding of the law and effective defense strategies. HVFO statutes are designed to impose harsher penalties on individuals who have been convicted of multiple violent felony offenses. In defending against HVFO charges, a successful defense could involve challenging the constitutionality of the statute, attacking the factual basis for the classification, or challenging the interpretation of prior offenses used to qualify the defendant as a habitual offender.

Below are several key case laws and legal strategies that may help in challenging or beating an HVFO charge:

---

1. Challenging the Constitutionality of HVFO Statutes

One potential defense strategy is to argue that the HVFO statute is unconstitutional. This could involve claiming that the statute violates due process or equal protection rights under the U.S. Constitution.

Key Case: *Ewing v. California*, 538 U.S. 11 (2003)

- Ruling: The U.S. Supreme Court upheld California's three-strikes law, which imposes a life sentence for individuals convicted of three serious felonies, including violent offenses. The Court concluded that the law did not violate the Eighth Amendment's prohibition on cruel and unusual punishment.
- Defense: If your state's HVFO statute mandates extreme penalties for habitual offenders, you may argue that the statute's application is disproportionate to the crime, which could be viewed as a violation of the Eighth Amendment. While *Ewing* supports harsher sentences, it's

important to note that the Court didn't rule out challenges based on the severity of sentences in extreme cases.

---

2. Failure to Prove the Predicate Offenses for HVFO Classification

To be classified as an HVFO, the prosecution must prove that the defendant has a qualifying criminal history. This typically involves presenting evidence of prior violent felony convictions. A strong defense strategy could involve attacking the sufficiency or validity of those prior convictions.

Key Case: *People v. Page*, 950 N.E.2d 1127 (Ill. App. 2011)

- Ruling: The court ruled that for the purposes of habitual offender sentencing, the prior convictions must be proven beyond a reasonable doubt, and the prosecution must provide sufficient evidence of those prior convictions, including the specific nature of the prior offenses.
- Defense: A possible defense in an HVFO case is to challenge the existence of the predicate offenses used to qualify the defendant as a habitual offender. You can argue that the prior convictions were not for violent felonies or that the defendant's prior convictions have been improperly classified as violent felonies.

---

3. Challenge the Definition of "Violent Felony"

Many states have specific definitions of what qualifies as a "violent felony" for the purpose of HVFO sentencing. If your prior convictions involve charges that may not meet the statutory definition of "violent," you could challenge the classification of these offenses.

Key Case: *Johnson v. United States,* 559 U.S. 133 (2010)

- Ruling: The U.S. Supreme Court ruled that the definition of "violent felony" under the Armed Career Criminal Act (ACCA) must be interpreted with clarity. The Court found that certain offenses, like burglary, could be considered violent felonies only if they involved specific types of conduct that created a substantial risk of harm.
- Defense: A key argument in defending against an HVFO charge is to assert that the prior convictions do not qualify as violent felonies based on how the state statute defines "violent." For example, if one of your prior offenses was burglary but did not involve any violent conduct or threat of harm, it may not meet the criteria for classification as a violent felony.

---

4. Challenging the Timing of Prior Convictions

Some states have rules that specify a time limit within which prior convictions can be considered for HVFO classification. If the convictions occurred too long ago, they may not meet the requirements for habitual offender status.

Key Case: *People v. Thompson,* 58 Cal.4th 43 (2013)

- Ruling: The California Supreme Court ruled that the time frame for a prior conviction to qualify as a "strike" under the state's three-strikes law was a critical factor, and older offenses could not be used to increase sentences if they did not fall within the time frame stipulated by the statute.
- Defense: A potential defense to an HVFO charge is to argue that the prior convictions are too old to qualify as predicate offenses under the state's habitual offender law. If your prior convictions fall outside the

specified time period, they might not be eligible to enhance your sentence.

---

5. Challenge the Prior Convictions for Sentencing Purposes

You may also be able to argue that a prior conviction was improperly used for HVFO enhancement. For instance, you could argue that the prior conviction was vacated, reversed on appeal, or was otherwise invalid.

Key Case: *Borden v. United States*, 141 S. Ct. 1817 (2021)

- Ruling: The Supreme Court ruled that a conviction based on a crime that did not necessarily involve a violent act (such as reckless conduct) could not be used as a predicate offense for enhanced sentencing under federal law. The ruling specifically addressed the "violent felony" requirement for the Armed Career Criminal Act.
- Defense: In an HVFO case, a defense attorney could argue that certain prior convictions should not be considered for sentencing enhancement because they did not meet the criteria of a violent felony. For example, if one of the prior convictions involved reckless or negligent conduct, it might not qualify as a violent felony under the law.

---

6. Request for a Sentence Reduction Based on Mitigating Factors

In some cases, even if the defendant qualifies as a habitual offender, the sentencing judge has discretion to reduce the sentence based on mitigating factors, such as rehabilitation efforts, family circumstances, or the impact of the conviction on the defendant's future.

Key Case: *People v. Colvin*, 195 Cal. App. 4th 517 (2011)

- Ruling: The California Court of Appeal ruled that a sentencing court has discretion to depart from the standard sentence if mitigating factors exist, even when the defendant is classified as a habitual offender.
- Defense: Although challenging the classification as an HVFO is important, you can also focus on persuading the court to impose a less severe sentence by presenting mitigating factors that could convince the judge to depart from the mandatory HVFO sentencing range.

Conclusion

Successfully beating an HVFO charge typically involves a multi-pronged defense strategy, such as challenging the constitutionality of the statute, questioning the sufficiency of the predicate violent felony convictions, challenging the definition of "violent felony," or raising mitigating factors. It's critical to analyze each prior conviction and scrutinize the evidence the prosecution presents. By leveraging case law like *Ewing v. California*, *Johnson v. United States*, and *Borden v. United States*, a skilled defense attorney can raise significant challenges to an HVFO conviction, potentially resulting in a reduced sentence or outright dismissal of the charge.

CHAPTER: TWENTY THREE

BEATING BURGLARY AND ARMED BURGLARY CHARGES

INTRODUCTION

Burglary and armed burglary are serious criminal offenses that can carry severe penalties, including lengthy prison sentences. In many cases, these charges are brought against individuals who may not have intended to commit a crime, or who may not have been involved in the offense at all. Defending against burglary and armed burglary charges requires a detailed understanding of the law, as well as a strategy that challenges the prosecution's case on multiple fronts. This chapter will explore the key elements of burglary and armed burglary, the defenses that can be raised in these cases, and how a skilled defense attorney can successfully challenge these charges in court.

1. Understanding the Charges: Burglary vs. Armed Burglary

- **Burglary**: Under Florida law, burglary is defined as unlawfully entering a structure with the intent to commit a crime inside. The structure can include homes, businesses, or any building where people reside or work. The key factors in a burglary charge are the **unlawful entry** and the **intent** to commit a crime once inside. The crime intended may include theft, vandalism, assault, or any other felony.
    - **Penalties for Burglary**: A conviction for burglary can result in penalties ranging from 2 to 15 years in prison, depending on factors such as whether the structure was occupied and the presence of aggravating circumstances.
- **Armed Burglary**: Armed burglary is a more serious offense that occurs when the defendant commits a burglary while in possession of a weapon (such as a firearm, knife, or other dangerous instruments). The

presence of a weapon elevates the charge from simple burglary to armed burglary.

- **Penalties for Armed Burglary**: Armed burglary is classified as a **first-degree felony** in Florida, which carries a mandatory minimum sentence of 10 years in prison and up to life imprisonment.

Given the severity of the penalties associated with these charges, mounting an effective defense is crucial.

2. Defending Against Burglary Charges

There are several defense strategies that can be employed in an attempt to beat burglary charges. Some of the most effective defenses include:

A. Lack of Intent to Commit a Crime

One of the critical elements of burglary is the **intent** to commit a crime once inside the structure. If the defense can show that the defendant had no such intent, the burglary charge may be defeated. Possible scenarios include:

- **Mistaken Entry**: The defendant may have entered the structure by mistake, believing it was their own property, or they may have entered a building with lawful permission and then decided against committing a crime. In such cases, there was no criminal intent.
- **No Criminal Activity Inside**: If the defendant entered the structure but did not commit any crime once inside, it may be argued that there was no intent to commit a crime at all. For example, if the person entered a home but left without taking anything or causing any harm, it could be argued that the intent to commit a crime was absent.

B. Lack of Unlawful Entry

Another key element in a burglary charge is the **unlawful entry** into a structure. If the defense can establish that the defendant had permission to enter the building or that they did not forcefully enter, they may be able to defeat the charge.

- **Permission to Enter**: If the defendant had explicit or implied consent to enter the structure, there would be no unlawful entry, and thus no burglary.

- **No Forced Entry**: In some cases, the prosecution may claim that the defendant forcibly entered the structure. If the defense can show that the entry was peaceful and without force (such as simply walking through an open door), the unlawful entry element may be undermined.

C. Alibi or Lack of Evidence

A common defense in burglary cases is **alibi**. If the defendant can present evidence that they were elsewhere at the time the burglary occurred, the prosecution's case may fall apart. This could include:

- **Witness Testimony**: If a credible witness can testify that the defendant was somewhere else when the crime took place, it could create reasonable doubt about the defendant's involvement.
- **Physical Evidence**: Surveillance footage, GPS records, or cell phone location data could help confirm that the defendant was not present at the scene of the burglary.

D. Constitutional Violations

A defendant may challenge the charges on the grounds that their **constitutional rights** were violated during the investigation or arrest. This can include illegal searches or seizures, improper interrogation, or failure to inform the defendant of their rights.

- **Illegal Search and Seizure**: If law enforcement officers conducted an unlawful search of the defendant's home, car, or person without a warrant or probable cause, any evidence obtained during the search may be inadmissible in court.
- **Coerced Confessions**: If the defendant was coerced or improperly interrogated, any confession made during this time could be challenged as involuntary.

3. Defending Against Armed Burglary Charges

Armed burglary charges are significantly more serious than standard burglary charges because the defendant is accused of committing the crime while in possession of a weapon. Defending against armed burglary requires addressing both the burglary and the armed component of the charge. Some common defenses include:

A. Lack of Weapon or Evidence of a Weapon

If the defense can show that the defendant was not carrying a weapon at the time of the burglary, the armed burglary charge may be reduced to a standard burglary charge.

- **No Weapon Found**: If law enforcement cannot recover a weapon from the scene or from the defendant's possession, this may raise doubt about the armed component of the charge.
- **Weapon Was Not Involved**: The prosecution must prove that the defendant was armed during the burglary. If there is no direct evidence

that the defendant had a weapon, the armed burglary charge may be successfully challenged.

B. The Weapon Was Not Used in the Commission of the Burglary

In some cases, the defendant may have been carrying a weapon, but it was not used in the commission of the burglary. If the weapon was not brandished, threatened, or employed to facilitate the crime, the charge may be reduced.

- **Weapon Was Present but Not Used**: If the defendant had a weapon but did not use it to intimidate or threaten anyone during the burglary, the armed burglary charge may be lessened to a standard burglary or even a lesser charge.

C. Self-Defense or Defense of Others

If the defendant can show that they had the weapon for self-defense or to protect others, it may be possible to argue that the armed burglary charge should be dropped or reduced. For example:

- **Threat of Harm**: If the defendant was forced to carry a weapon due to threats or coercion and did not intend to use it in the commission of the burglary, this could be used to argue for a reduction in the charge.
- **Protection of Property**: If the defendant entered the structure with the intent to protect themselves or others, the defense could argue that they were not committing a crime but rather acting in defense.

4. The Importance of Legal Representation

Burglary and armed burglary charges are serious, and defending against them requires a deep understanding of criminal law. A skilled criminal defense attorney is essential for:

- **Gathering Evidence**: A good defense attorney will gather all available evidence, including witness statements, physical evidence, and alibi documentation, to challenge the prosecution's case.
- **Challenging the Prosecution's Case**: Attorneys can cross-examine witnesses, challenge the admissibility of evidence, and point out weaknesses in the prosecution's case.
- **Negotiating Plea Deals**: In some cases, a plea deal may be the best option. A skilled attorney can negotiate with the prosecution to reduce charges or secure a more favorable sentence.

5. Conclusion

Fighting burglary and armed burglary charges is not an easy task, but it is possible with the right legal strategy. Defendants facing these charges must consider all possible defenses, from challenging the intent to commit a crime, to disputing the presence of a weapon, to presenting an alibi. By working closely with an experienced defense attorney, individuals accused of burglary or armed burglary can significantly increase their chances of avoiding a conviction or securing a reduced sentence. Every case is unique, and with the right approach, a favorable outcome is possible.

CHAPTER: TWENTY FOUR

BEATING A POSSESSION OF BURGLARY TOOLS CHARGE

INTRODUCTION

The charge of possessing burglary tools is a serious criminal offense that can lead to significant legal consequences. Under Florida law, a person can be charged with possessing burglary tools if they are found with tools or instruments that are commonly used to commit burglaries, such as crowbars, lockpicks, or masks. However, possession alone is not enough to secure a conviction; the prosecution must prove that the defendant intended to use these tools in the commission of a crime. This chapter will explore the elements of the crime of possessing burglary tools, common defense strategies, and how an experienced defense attorney can help challenge the charges.

1. Understanding the Charge: Possession of Burglary Tools

Under Florida Statute § 810.06, possession of burglary tools is defined as knowingly possessing any instrument, tool, or device that is designed, adapted, or intended to be used for committing burglary. The law applies to a wide range of tools, including:

- Crowbars, screwdrivers, and hammers (commonly used to pry open windows or doors).
- Lockpicks and bump keys (used to unlock doors or safes).
- Masks, gloves, and other items used to conceal one's identity during a burglary.
- Flashlights or other tools used for surveillance or breaking and entering.

Penalties for Possession of Burglary Tools: In Florida, possession of burglary tools is classified as a **third-degree felony**, which can result in penalties of up to 5 years in prison, up to 5 years of probation, and a fine of up to $5,000.

For individuals facing these charges, the stakes are high, but a skilled defense attorney can make all the difference in achieving a favorable outcome.

2. Key Elements of the Crime

For a conviction of possession of burglary tools, the prosecution must prove **two key elements** beyond a reasonable doubt:

- **Possession**: The defendant must have had possession of the tools. This can be **actual possession** (i.e., the defendant was physically holding or carrying the tools) or **constructive possession** (i.e., the defendant had control over the location where the tools were found, such as in a vehicle or home).
- **Intent to Use for Burglary**: The defendant must have intended to use the tools to commit a burglary or other criminal activity. Mere possession of burglary tools is not enough; the prosecution must show that the defendant had the tools for the purpose of committing a crime.

3. Common Defenses to Possession of Burglary Tools Charges

Several defense strategies can be employed to challenge a possession of burglary tools charge. Below are some of the most common defenses used in these cases:

A. Lack of Intent to Commit a Crime

The most common defense in possession of burglary tools cases is that the defendant had no intent to use the tools to commit a crime. Since the prosecution must prove the defendant's intent to use the tools for a criminal purpose, the defense can argue that the tools were possessed for legitimate reasons or that the defendant had no criminal intent at all.

- **Legitimate Use of Tools**: The defendant may have been in possession of the tools for lawful purposes, such as for work (e.g., a contractor or mechanic who owns tools). The defense can argue that the tools were not intended for burglary but for everyday tasks related to the defendant's job.
- **No Plan to Commit a Burglary**: Even if the defendant was found with burglary tools, the defense can argue that the defendant never had the intent to commit a burglary. For example, the defendant may have been carrying the tools for another reason (e.g., to fix something or as part of a hobby).

B. Lack of Knowledge of Possession

To be convicted of possessing burglary tools, the defendant must have known that they were in possession of the tools. If the defendant did not know the tools were in their possession, they may be able to avoid conviction by challenging this element.

- **Constructive Possession**: In cases where the tools were found in a place controlled by the defendant (e.g., a vehicle or home), the prosecution may attempt to argue constructive possession. However, the defense can challenge whether the defendant had knowledge of the tools' presence. For example, if the tools were hidden or belonged to someone else, the defendant may not have known they were there.

C. Inaccurate Identification of the Tools

Another potential defense is challenging whether the items found actually meet the legal definition of "burglary tools." If the items in question are not commonly used in the commission of a burglary or are not designed, adapted, or intended for that purpose, the defense can argue that the tools in question do not meet the statutory requirements for a burglary tools charge.

- **Common Items Misidentified**: Sometimes, everyday tools or equipment may be misidentified as burglary tools. For example, a screwdriver that is commonly used for home repairs could be seen as a tool for committing a burglary if it was found in a suspect's possession. The defense can argue that the item in question has a legitimate use and was not intended for criminal activity.

D. Illegal Search and Seizure

The Fourth Amendment of the U.S. Constitution protects individuals from unreasonable searches and seizures by law enforcement. If the defendant's tools were found as a result of an unlawful search or seizure, the defense can move to suppress the evidence.

- **No Warrant or Probable Cause**: If law enforcement searched the defendant's home, vehicle, or person without a warrant or probable cause, any evidence obtained during the search, including the burglary tools, may be inadmissible in court. A skilled attorney will carefully review whether the search and seizure violated the defendant's constitutional rights.
- **Improper Search of Belongings**: Even if there was a warrant, if the tools were not listed in the warrant, the defense can argue that the search exceeded the scope of the warrant, making the evidence obtained inadmissible.

E. Fabricated Evidence or False Accusations

In some cases, the defendant may be falsely accused of possessing burglary tools. The defense can argue that the tools were planted or fabricated by the police or by another individual.

- **Mistaken Identity**: The defense can argue that the tools were not in the defendant's possession, but rather, they were planted or left behind by someone else. A careful investigation can reveal inconsistencies in the prosecution's case or lead to the discovery of exculpatory evidence.

4. The Role of an Experienced Defense Attorney

Defending against a possession of burglary tools charge requires a detailed analysis of the facts and evidence in the case. An experienced defense attorney will carefully evaluate the circumstances surrounding the charge, challenge the prosecution's evidence, and identify the most effective defense strategy. Some of the key roles that an attorney will play in the defense include:

- **Reviewing the Evidence**: The attorney will assess the physical evidence, including the tools in question, to determine whether they meet the legal definition of burglary tools. If the tools were not properly identified or if their use cannot be linked to criminal intent, this could weaken the prosecution's case.
- **Negotiating Plea Deals**: In some cases, the defendant may have limited options for beating the charge, and a plea deal may be the best course of action. A defense attorney can negotiate with the prosecution to reduce the charges or secure a more favorable sentence.
- **Challenging the Constitutionality of the Search**: If the tools were found as a result of an illegal search, the defense attorney can file a motion to suppress the evidence, which could lead to a dismissal of the charges.
- **Building a Strong Defense**: The attorney will work to establish a strong defense, whether that means arguing the defendant's lack of intent, lack of knowledge of possession, or any other applicable defense. A successful defense could result in a verdict of not guilty.

5. Conclusion

Possessing burglary tools is a serious charge that can carry significant legal consequences. However, being accused of possessing burglary tools does not automatically mean conviction. A defendant can challenge the charge on various grounds, including lack of intent, lack of knowledge of possession, improper identification of the tools, illegal search and seizure, or false accusations. With a skilled defense attorney by your side, you can effectively challenge the prosecution's case and work toward a favorable outcome. Whether it's negotiating a reduced sentence, seeking a dismissal, or securing an acquittal, an experienced attorney is essential for protecting your rights and fighting for justice.

CHAPTER TWENTY FIVE.

BEATING A DOMESTIC VIOLENCE CHARGE

INTRODUCTION

Domestic violence charges are among the most serious accusations a person can face, and the consequences of a conviction can be severe. In Florida, domestic violence is defined as any violent or aggressive behavior directed towards a family member, spouse, or someone in a dating relationship. If you're facing a domestic violence charge, it's crucial to understand the legal definition, the elements of the crime, and potential defense strategies. A well-prepared defense can challenge the evidence, raise reasonable doubt, and lead to a favorable outcome. This chapter will explore how to effectively beat a domestic violence charge through strategic defense approaches and understanding the criminal justice process.

1. Understanding Domestic Violence Charges

Domestic violence charges in Florida can encompass a wide range of behaviors, including physical assault, battery, threats, harassment, or any act that causes harm to another person within a domestic setting. Under Florida law, domestic violence is not restricted to physical violence but includes actions that instill fear, intimidation, or emotional harm to the victim.

Key Elements of Domestic Violence:

- **Victim Relationship**: The alleged victim must have a certain relationship to the defendant, such as a spouse, former spouse, family member, or someone the defendant is dating or cohabiting with.

- **Physical Contact or Threats**: Domestic violence can involve physical injury (such as hitting or pushing), or the threat of harm, including verbal threats or actions that create a fear of harm.

Penalties for Domestic Violence: A domestic violence conviction can lead to severe consequences, including:

- Criminal penalties (e.g., jail time, probation).
- Loss of gun rights.
- Mandatory counseling or anger management programs.
- Impact on custody and visitation rights in divorce or child custody cases.

However, being charged with domestic violence does not automatically mean a conviction, and there are several avenues for mounting an effective defense.

2. Common Defenses to Domestic Violence Charges

There are several defense strategies that can be employed to challenge domestic violence charges. Below are some of the most common defenses used in these cases:

A. Self-Defense

Self-defense is one of the most common and effective defenses in domestic violence cases. If the defendant was acting to protect themselves from harm or to prevent imminent harm, they may be able to argue that their actions were justified.

- **Reasonable Force**: The key to this defense is proving that the defendant used reasonable force in self-defense. Florida law allows individuals to defend themselves from violence, but the force used must be proportional to the threat faced. If the defendant can show that they were trying to protect themselves from an immediate threat, they may avoid a conviction.

- **No Aggression Initiated**: In some cases, the defendant may argue that they were not the aggressor in the situation and that the alleged victim initiated the confrontation, forcing the defendant to act in self-defense.

B. False Allegations

False accusations of domestic violence are unfortunately common. Whether due to misunderstandings, personal grudges, or manipulative behavior, some people make false allegations of domestic violence to gain an advantage in a legal dispute, such as divorce or child custody. In these cases, the defendant can challenge the credibility of the accuser.

- **Inconsistencies in Testimony**: If the alleged victim's story is inconsistent or if there are contradictions in their statements, the defense can point to these discrepancies to show that the accusation may not be truthful.
- **Motivation to Lie**: In some situations, the alleged victim may have a motive to falsely accuse the defendant, such as to gain custody of children or to punish the defendant for another reason. The defense can present evidence that shows a potential motive for lying.

C. Lack of Evidence

In many domestic violence cases, the prosecution must rely on the testimony of the victim, but testimony alone may not be enough to prove guilt beyond a reasonable doubt. A lack of physical evidence (e.g., bruises, medical records, or photos) can weaken the case.

- **No Physical Injury**: If there was no visible injury to the alleged victim, or if the injury is minor, the defense can argue that the alleged assault did not occur as described.
- **No Witnesses**: If no one else witnessed the alleged incident, and there are no corroborating pieces of evidence (e.g., text messages, phone records, or witness statements), the defense may be able to argue that the prosecution cannot prove the defendant's guilt.

D. Misunderstanding or Accidental Contact

Sometimes, what may appear to be domestic violence is actually a misunderstanding or accidental contact. The defense can argue that any physical contact was not intentional or that the situation was misinterpreted.

- **No Malicious Intent**: The defendant may have been involved in a situation where they did not intend to harm the victim, and any contact was accidental or incidental. For example, pushing someone aside in a crowded space might be misinterpreted as a violent action.
- **Mutual Physical Contact**: In some cases, both parties may have engaged in physical contact, and it may be difficult to determine who initiated the violence. If there is no clear evidence to support the claim that the defendant initiated violence, the defense can argue that the case lacks sufficient proof.

E. Emotional Distress or Provocation

While emotional distress or provocation is not a defense to domestic violence, it can sometimes be a mitigating factor. If the defendant was under severe emotional distress or provoked by the victim's behavior, it might help to explain why they reacted in a way that led to the alleged violent act.

- **Extreme Stress or Provocation**: The defendant might argue that they were provoked by the victim's actions (e.g., verbal insults or physical threats) to the point where they lost control temporarily. This argument may not justify the actions but could influence the court in determining the severity of the offense.

3. Challenging the Evidence

In any criminal case, including domestic violence, the prosecution has the burden of proving the defendant's guilt beyond a reasonable doubt. A defense attorney can challenge the prosecution's evidence in several ways:

- **Examine the Testimony**: An experienced defense lawyer will scrutinize the victim's testimony and any witness statements for inconsistencies, contradictions, or exaggerations that weaken the prosecution's case.
- **Question the Credibility of the Alleged Victim**: If the victim has a history of making false accusations, is emotionally unstable, or has been involved in prior legal disputes with the defendant, these issues can be raised to challenge the victim's credibility.
- **Use of Expert Witnesses**: In some cases, expert witnesses can be called upon to testify about the alleged victim's injuries (or lack thereof), or psychological factors that might explain the behavior of the parties involved.

4. The Role of an Experienced Defense Attorney

If you've been charged with domestic violence, having a knowledgeable and experienced defense attorney is critical to protecting your rights and securing a favorable outcome. A skilled attorney will:

- **Review the Evidence**: Examine all of the evidence, including police reports, witness statements, and medical records, to find inconsistencies or weaknesses in the prosecution's case.

- **Challenge the Prosecution's Case**: Use the defense strategies outlined above, such as self-defense or challenging the evidence, to undermine the prosecution's arguments.
- **Negotiate a Plea or Dismissal**: If the case against you is strong, your attorney can work with the prosecution to negotiate a plea deal, or in some cases, seek a dismissal of the charges if the evidence is insufficient.
- **Prepare for Trial**: If necessary, your attorney will prepare for trial by gathering evidence, preparing witnesses, and developing a compelling defense strategy.

5. Conclusion

A domestic violence charge is a serious matter with potentially life-altering consequences. However, being accused of domestic violence does not necessarily mean that you will be convicted. By utilizing effective defense strategies such as self-defense, false allegations, lack of evidence, or misunderstandings, you can challenge the charges and protect your future. With the help of a skilled criminal defense attorney, you can present a strong case that may lead to a dismissal or acquittal. No one should face the consequences of a domestic violence conviction without a fair opportunity to defend themselves, and an experienced attorney is essential to ensuring your rights are protected throughout the process.

CHAPTER TWENTY SIX

BEATING A FELON IN POSSESSION OF A FIREARM CHARGE

INTRODUCTION

In Florida, being convicted of a felony is already a severe legal issue, but when it comes to a charge of "felon in possession of a firearm," the consequences can be even more dire. This is because Florida has stringent gun laws and imposes strict penalties for those convicted of possessing firearms when they have a prior felony conviction. A felon in possession of a firearm charge carries heavy penalties, including lengthy prison sentences and additional legal restrictions.

However, a charge of felon in possession of a firearm does not automatically result in a conviction. In this chapter, we will discuss how to effectively fight and potentially beat a felon in possession of a firearm charge through various legal defenses, strategies for challenging the evidence, and the key factors that may help you avoid conviction.

1. Understanding the Felon in Possession of a Firearm Charge

Under Florida law (specifically, Florida Statute 790.23), it is illegal for a person convicted of a felony to possess a firearm. This law is in place to prevent individuals with a history of violent behavior or criminal activity from obtaining or carrying weapons.

Elements of the Offense: To convict someone of felon in possession of a firearm, the prosecution must prove three key elements:

1. **The Defendant is a Felon**: The defendant must have been convicted of a felony in the past, and this prior conviction must meet the criteria of a disqualifying felony under Florida law (e.g., violent crimes, drug trafficking, certain theft offenses).

2. **Possession of a Firearm**: The defendant must be found in possession of a firearm. This can mean either actual possession (the firearm is found on the defendant) or constructive possession (the firearm is found nearby and the defendant had knowledge and control over it).
3. **The Firearm Was a "Firearm" Under Florida Law**: The object in question must meet the legal definition of a firearm, which includes any weapon that is capable of firing a projectile by means of an explosive.

Penalties for Felon in Possession of a Firearm: A conviction under this statute is typically classified as a third-degree felony in Florida, which carries the following penalties:

- Up to 5 years in prison.
- Up to 5 years of probation.
- Up to a $5,000 fine. Additionally, the defendant's rights to own or possess firearms are permanently revoked.

However, there are defenses and strategies that can be used to challenge these charges and avoid a conviction.

2. Common Defenses to Felon in Possession of a Firearm Charges

A. Lack of Knowledge or Ownership of the Firearm

In many cases, the defense may argue that the defendant did not have knowledge of the firearm or did not possess it at all. Under Florida law, the prosecution must prove that the defendant knowingly possessed the firearm. This means that if the defendant was unaware that the firearm was in their possession or on their property, they may not be guilty.

- **Constructive Possession**: If the firearm was found in a location where multiple people had access (such as in a car with several passengers or in a shared apartment), the defense may argue that the defendant had no control or knowledge of the weapon's presence.

- **No Direct Possession**: If the defendant did not have the firearm on their person or in a place where they had exclusive control (such as in a locked vehicle or bag), the defense may argue that there is insufficient evidence to prove that the defendant possessed the firearm.

B. Unlawful Search and Seizure

A common defense in cases involving firearms is the argument that the police violated the defendant's constitutional rights under the Fourth Amendment by conducting an unlawful search and seizure.

- **Illegally Obtained Evidence**: If the firearm was found as the result of an illegal search (for example, without probable cause, without a warrant, or in violation of the defendant's rights), the defense can argue that the evidence should be excluded under the exclusionary rule.

- **No Probable Cause**: If law enforcement had no probable cause or warrant to search the defendant or the premises, the defense may be able to suppress the evidence of the firearm on the grounds that the search was unlawful.

C. Ownership of the Firearm

In some cases, the defendant may have a valid reason for possessing the firearm, such as having obtained it legally or being given permission by another person. In Florida, if the defendant is found to have been legally in possession of the firearm at the time of the alleged offense, they may have a valid defense.

- **Borrowed Firearm**: The defendant may argue that they were not the owner of the firearm, and that they were only in temporary possession of it for a legitimate reason, such as borrowing the firearm from a friend or family member.
- **Involuntary Possession**: In rare cases, the defendant may argue that the possession of the firearm was involuntary or that they were unaware they had the weapon in their possession due to coercion, duress, or confusion.

D. Restoration of Rights

A defendant who was previously convicted of a felony may have had their rights restored, including the right to possess a firearm. In Florida, certain felons can apply to have their civil rights reinstated, which includes the right to own and possess a firearm. If the defendant's civil rights have been restored legally, the charge of felon in possession of a firearm may be defeated.

- **Certificate of Restoration of Rights**: If the defendant has received a certificate of restoration of their civil rights, they may present this as evidence to prove they were legally allowed to possess the firearm.

E. No Evidence of Firearm

If the prosecution is unable to present sufficient evidence that the object in question was a firearm or that the defendant possessed it, the defense can argue that the prosecution has failed to meet its burden of proof.

- **No Firearm Found**: If the prosecution's case relies solely on witness testimony, or if there is a lack of physical evidence linking the defendant to the firearm, the defense can argue that the prosecution has failed to establish the defendant's guilt beyond a reasonable doubt.

- **No Firearm Identification**: In some cases, the object found may not actually qualify as a "firearm" under the law, either because it is a non-functional gun or because it does not meet the statutory definition.

3. Challenging the Evidence

If the case goes to trial, the defense will work to challenge the evidence presented by the prosecution. Some ways to challenge the evidence include:

- **Witness Credibility**: Cross-examining law enforcement officers and other witnesses to identify inconsistencies or flaws in their testimony.
- **Chain of Custody**: If the firearm was collected as evidence, the defense may challenge whether the firearm was properly handled, stored, and documented during the investigation.
- **Expert Testimony**: In some cases, an expert may be called to testify about the firearm's functionality or whether it could be classified as a "firearm" under Florida law.

4. Role of an Experienced Defense Attorney

An experienced criminal defense attorney is crucial in defending against a felon in possession of a firearm charge. A skilled attorney will:

- **Investigate the Evidence**: Review the police report, search warrants, and evidence to identify potential weaknesses in the prosecution's case.
- **Challenge Illegally Obtained Evidence**: File motions to suppress evidence that was obtained in violation of the defendant's constitutional rights.
- **Prepare a Strong Defense**: Develop a defense strategy tailored to the specific facts of the case, whether it's a challenge to the defendant's

knowledge of the firearm, the lawfulness of the search, or the credibility of the victim.
- **Negotiate with Prosecutors**: In some cases, the defense may negotiate with the prosecution to reduce the charges or work out a plea deal that minimizes the penalties.

5. Conclusion

Being charged with a felon in possession of a firearm is a serious matter that can lead to severe penalties, including prison time. However, there are several viable defense strategies that can help beat these charges. Whether it involves challenging the evidence, proving lack of knowledge or ownership, arguing illegal search and seizure, or demonstrating that the defendant's rights were restored, a strong legal defense can help to secure a favorable outcome.

If you've been charged with being a felon in possession of a firearm, it's essential to consult with a skilled defense attorney who can guide you through the process and ensure your rights are protected. With a strategic approach, it's possible to challenge the charges and avoid a conviction.

CHAPTER TWENTY SEVEN

BEATING A DRUG TRAFFICKING CONVICTION ON APPEAL

INTRODUCTION

Being convicted of drug trafficking is a serious matter that carries severe penalties, including lengthy prison sentences and significant fines. However, the conviction is not the end of the legal battle. If you have been convicted of drug trafficking, it is possible to challenge the conviction through the appellate process. Appealing a conviction gives you an opportunity to seek a reversal or a reduction of the conviction if legal errors occurred during the trial.

In this chapter, we will explore various strategies and defenses that can be used on appeal to challenge a drug trafficking conviction. We will also discuss the role of the appellate court, the types of errors that can lead to a reversal, and the steps to take if you want to pursue an appeal in a drug trafficking case.

1. Understanding Drug Trafficking Convictions in Florida

Drug trafficking charges involve the illegal sale, transportation, or distribution of controlled substances in amounts specified by law. In Florida, the penalties for drug trafficking are severe, and they vary depending on the type and amount of the drug involved.

- **Trafficking in Cocaine**: The trafficking charge is triggered when an individual is caught with a specified quantity of cocaine, typically 28 grams or more.
- **Trafficking in Methamphetamine**: In Florida, trafficking in methamphetamine is triggered if an individual possesses 14 grams or more of the drug.

- **Trafficking in Heroin**: For heroin trafficking, the threshold is typically 4 grams or more.

A conviction for drug trafficking in Florida often results in a mandatory minimum sentence of 3 years in prison, with the possibility of a much longer sentence, depending on the amount of the drug and any prior criminal history.

However, drug trafficking convictions can be overturned on appeal if certain legal errors occurred during the trial or if the conviction was based on insufficient evidence. Below, we discuss the potential grounds for appealing a drug trafficking conviction.

2. Grounds for Appealing a Drug Trafficking Conviction

A. Insufficient Evidence

One of the most common grounds for appealing a drug trafficking conviction is that the evidence presented at trial was insufficient to support the conviction. In a criminal case, the prosecution must prove the defendant's guilt beyond a reasonable doubt. If the evidence was weak or circumstantial, or if the prosecution failed to prove key elements of the crime, an appellate court may overturn the conviction.

- **Lack of Proof of Knowledge or Intent**: In many drug trafficking cases, the prosecution must prove that the defendant knew the drugs were present and had the intent to traffic them. If there was no clear evidence to establish the defendant's knowledge or intent, the conviction may be overturned on appeal.
- **Inaccurate or Unreliable Evidence**: If the evidence presented by the prosecution was unreliable or inaccurate—such as a flawed drug test result, unreliable witness testimony, or tainted physical evidence—the

appellate court may find that the conviction was based on insufficient evidence.

B. Illegal Search and Seizure

A common basis for challenging a drug trafficking conviction on appeal is that the drugs were discovered through an unlawful search and seizure. The Fourth Amendment to the United States Constitution protects individuals from unreasonable searches and seizures by law enforcement officers. If law enforcement violated the defendant's constitutional rights by conducting an illegal search or seizure, the evidence obtained as a result may be excluded from trial.

- **No Probable Cause or Warrant**: If law enforcement conducted a search without probable cause or a valid search warrant, any evidence seized during that search may be inadmissible in court.
- **Unlawful Traffic Stop**: If the drugs were found during a traffic stop, but the stop was not based on a reasonable suspicion or probable cause, this could be grounds for appeal. An unlawful stop can lead to the suppression of any evidence found as a result.

If the evidence was obtained in violation of the defendant's Fourth Amendment rights, an appellate court may rule that the conviction was obtained unlawfully and order a new trial or dismiss the charges.

C. Procedural Errors During Trial

Procedural errors or mistakes made during the trial can be another grounds for an appeal. Even if the evidence against the defendant was strong, errors made by the trial judge, the prosecution, or the defense could impact the fairness of the trial. Common procedural errors include:

- **Improper Jury Instructions**: If the trial judge failed to properly instruct the jury on the law or on how to apply the evidence, it could lead to an unfair trial and provide grounds for appeal.
- **Exclusion of Evidence**: If the trial judge improperly excluded evidence that could have helped the defendant's case, it may be grounds for appeal. This can include excluding certain witness testimony, documents, or expert reports.
- **Prosecutorial Misconduct**: If the prosecution engaged in misconduct, such as presenting false evidence, making inflammatory statements, or improperly influencing the jury, this could be a valid reason for appeal.

If an appellate court determines that such errors occurred and significantly affected the outcome of the trial, it may order a new trial or reverse the conviction.

D. Ineffective Assistance of Counsel

Another ground for appealing a drug trafficking conviction is ineffective assistance of counsel. The Sixth Amendment guarantees the right to competent legal representation. If the defendant's trial attorney failed to provide effective counsel, the conviction may be overturned on appeal.

Examples of ineffective assistance of counsel may include:

- **Failure to Investigate or Present Evidence**: If the defense attorney failed to investigate key facts or present evidence that could have helped the defendant's case, this could be grounds for appeal.
- **Failure to Object to Legal Errors**: If the defense attorney failed to object to improper jury instructions or unlawful evidence, this may also be considered ineffective assistance.

- **Lack of Preparation or Skill**: If the defense attorney was unprepared for trial or lacked the necessary legal skills to defend the case properly, this could constitute ineffective assistance of counsel.

If the appellate court determines that the defendant's attorney was ineffective, it may overturn the conviction and order a new trial.

E. Misapplication of the Law

In some cases, an appellate court may find that the trial court misapplied the law in a way that led to the conviction. This can happen if the trial court interpreted the law incorrectly or applied the wrong legal standard in evaluating the evidence.

- **Wrongful Sentencing**: If the defendant was sentenced more harshly than allowed by law, the appellate court may reduce the sentence.
- **Misinterpretation of Statutes**: If the trial court incorrectly interpreted Florida's drug trafficking laws or imposed penalties that did not align with the statutes, the appellate court may correct the mistake.

If the court finds that the law was misapplied or misinterpreted in a way that unfairly affected the defendant, it can overturn the conviction.

3. The Appellate Process

Once a defendant is convicted of drug trafficking, they have a limited amount of time to file an appeal. In Florida, a notice of appeal must generally be filed within 30 days after the judgment or sentence is rendered. After the notice of appeal is filed, the appellate court will review the case record, including the trial transcripts and any legal briefs submitted by the defendant's attorney.

The appellate court will then determine whether any legal errors were made during the trial that affected the outcome of the case. If the court finds that an error occurred, it may overturn the conviction, reduce the sentence, or order a new trial. In some cases, the appellate court may also uphold the conviction if it finds that no legal errors occurred.

4. Conclusion

Challenging a drug trafficking conviction on appeal can be a complicated and lengthy process, but it is not an impossible task. With the right legal strategy, there are several ways to successfully appeal a drug trafficking conviction, from challenging the sufficiency of evidence to arguing that the search was unlawful or that procedural errors affected the trial.

If you or someone you know has been convicted of drug trafficking, it is crucial to consult with an experienced criminal appeals attorney who can evaluate the case and determine the best course of action. An experienced appellate attorney will thoroughly review the trial record, identify potential errors, and work diligently to ensure that your rights are protected and that you receive a fair outcome in your appeal.

An appeal can provide a second chance at justice, and with the right legal representation, you may be able to beat a drug trafficking conviction and avoid the harsh penalties associated with it.

CHAPTER TWENTY EIGHT

BEATING A POSSESSION OF CONTROLLED SUBSTANCE CHARGE

INTRODUCTION

Being charged with possession of a controlled substance can lead to serious consequences, including jail time, fines, and a criminal record. However, a conviction for possession of a controlled substance is not a foregone conclusion. In many cases, there are several legal strategies and defenses that can be used to challenge the charges. With a strong defense, it may be possible to have the charges reduced or even dismissed.

In this chapter, we will explore various ways to challenge a possession of controlled substance charge, including challenging the legality of the search and seizure, disputing the evidence, and using common defenses such as lack of knowledge and constructive possession. Additionally, we will discuss potential mitigating factors that can be presented in your defense, such as the lack of intent to distribute or addiction issues that may be considered during sentencing.

1. Understanding Possession of a Controlled Substance Charges

Possession of a controlled substance is a criminal offense under both state and federal law. In Florida, a controlled substance is defined as any drug or chemical substance that is regulated by the government due to its potential for abuse, including narcotics, stimulants, hallucinogens, and certain prescription drugs. The penalties for possession can vary depending on the type and quantity of the controlled substance involved.

- **Simple Possession**: Refers to having a small quantity of the drug for personal use. This is typically classified as a misdemeanor, but possession of certain drugs, like cocaine or heroin, may still result in felony charges.

- **Possession with Intent to Distribute**: If the quantity of the substance exceeds a certain threshold or if there is evidence suggesting the drugs were intended for distribution, you may face more serious charges. This offense carries harsher penalties.

However, even when facing a serious possession charge, there are potential strategies that can be used to fight the charge. Below, we discuss the most common defenses to possession of a controlled substance charges.

2. Defenses to Possession of Controlled Substance Charges

A. Illegal Search and Seizure

One of the most powerful defenses to a possession charge is that the evidence was obtained through an illegal search or seizure. The Fourth Amendment of the United States Constitution protects individuals from unreasonable searches and seizures by law enforcement. If the police did not have probable cause or a valid warrant, any evidence seized during the search may be inadmissible in court.

- **No Probable Cause or Warrant**: For law enforcement to search your home, car, or person, they typically need probable cause or a search warrant. If they conducted a search without these requirements, you may argue that the search was illegal, and the drugs found during the search should be excluded as evidence.
- **Unlawful Traffic Stop**: If the drugs were discovered during a traffic stop, but the stop was not based on reasonable suspicion or probable cause, it could be an illegal stop. If the stop was illegal, the evidence gathered during the stop could be suppressed.

If the court determines that the search and seizure were unlawful, the evidence against you may be inadmissible, and the case could be dismissed.

B. Lack of Knowledge

Another common defense is that you did not know the substance was in your possession. In criminal law, a key element of many drug charges is that the defendant knowingly possessed the controlled substance. If you can demonstrate that you had no knowledge of the drugs in question, it may result in a dismissal of the charges.

- **Lack of Awareness**: For example, if someone else placed the drugs in your bag or car without your knowledge, or if you were unaware that the substance was in your possession, you may be able to argue lack of knowledge.
- **Mistaken Identity or Ownership**: In some cases, it may be possible to argue that the drugs belong to someone else, and you were wrongfully charged for possession.

Proving lack of knowledge requires evidence and testimony that supports your claim, such as witness testimony or physical evidence suggesting that the drugs did not belong to you.

C. Constructive Possession

Constructive possession occurs when a person is charged with possessing an item even if it is not physically on their person. To prove constructive possession of a controlled substance, the prosecution must show that you had knowledge of the substance and the ability to exercise control over it.

- **Control and Knowledge**: If the drugs were found in a shared space, like a car or apartment, you may be able to argue that you did not have control over the area and therefore could not have had constructive possession of the drugs.

- **Lack of Dominant Control**: If you did not have exclusive control over the area or the substance, it may be difficult for the prosecution to prove that you had constructive possession of the drugs.

If the prosecution cannot prove that you had control over the drugs or knew they were in your possession, they may be unable to secure a conviction.

D. Chain of Custody Issues

Chain of custody refers to the documented history of how evidence is handled and stored after being collected by law enforcement. If there is any break or issue in the chain of custody for the drugs, it could result in the evidence being inadmissible in court.

- **Tampering or Misplacement**: If the evidence was tampered with, misplaced, or mishandled in any way, the defense can argue that the drugs were not properly handled, and the integrity of the evidence is compromised.
- **Inconsistent Documentation**: If the prosecution cannot provide a consistent and clear record of the evidence from the moment it was seized until it was presented in court, it may lead to doubts about the authenticity of the evidence.

A failure to properly maintain the chain of custody can lead to a dismissal of the charges if it is shown that the drugs presented as evidence were not properly secured.

E. The Drugs Belong to Someone Else

In some cases, the defendant may argue that the drugs belonged to someone else, not them. This defense may be particularly useful if you were found in close proximity to the drugs but can demonstrate that they belonged to another person.

- **Shared Spaces**: If you were in a car or home with others who had access to the space where the drugs were found, you may argue that the drugs belonged to one of them, not you.
- **Witness Testimony**: In some cases, witnesses can testify that the drugs were not yours, or there may be evidence indicating that someone else was responsible for the drugs.

This defense requires strong evidence or testimony that directly links the drugs to another individual.

3. Mitigating Factors to Present in Your Defense

Even if the evidence against you is strong, there may be mitigating factors that can reduce the severity of the charges or influence sentencing. Presenting these factors during the trial or at sentencing can help demonstrate that you are deserving of a more lenient punishment.

- **First-Time Offender**: If this is your first offense, you may be able to argue for a more lenient sentence or even a diversion program, which may result in the charges being dropped upon successful completion.
- **Addiction Issues**: If the drug possession was linked to a substance abuse problem, it may be possible to argue for treatment rather than incarceration. Courts may be more inclined to offer rehabilitation programs to individuals struggling with addiction.
- **Lack of Intent to Distribute**: If the quantity of drugs found in your possession was small and there is no evidence to suggest you intended to distribute them, this may be a factor in reducing the charges from trafficking to simple possession.

By presenting mitigating factors, your defense attorney can help secure a more favorable outcome, even if the charges are not dismissed outright.

4. The Importance of Legal Representation

Fighting a possession of a controlled substance charge requires an experienced criminal defense attorney. A skilled attorney can evaluate the evidence, identify weaknesses in the prosecution's case, and build a solid defense strategy. They can also advise you on whether to accept a plea deal or pursue an appeal, and they will represent your best interests throughout the legal process.

An attorney will work to challenge the evidence, seek dismissal of the charges, or negotiate for reduced penalties. If you are facing possession charges, it is crucial to secure the help of an experienced defense attorney as soon as possible.

5. Conclusion

While being charged with possession of a controlled substance is serious, it is not the end of the road. There are several defenses available to challenge the charge, from arguing that the evidence was obtained unlawfully to disputing the existence of knowledge or control over the substance. Additionally, mitigating factors like first-time offenses or addiction issues can be used to reduce the severity of the charges or penalties.

If you are facing possession of a controlled substance charges, it is essential to consult with a skilled criminal defense attorney who can help you evaluate your options, build a defense strategy, and work towards the best possible outcome. With the right defense, you may be able to beat the charges or significantly reduce the consequences of a conviction.

CHAPTER TWENTY NINE.

HOW TO FILE A LAWSUIT FOR ILLEGAL ARREST

INTRODUCTION

Being illegally arrested can be a traumatic experience that undermines your sense of personal freedom and security. If you believe that your arrest was unlawful, you may have the legal right to file a lawsuit for damages. This chapter will guide you through the process of filing a lawsuit for illegal arrest, explaining the legal grounds, how to prepare for a lawsuit, and what you can expect during the legal proceedings.

1. Understanding Illegal Arrest

An illegal arrest occurs when law enforcement officers detain you without a lawful reason, violating your constitutional rights. Under the Fourth Amendment of the U.S. Constitution, you are protected from unreasonable searches and seizures, which includes being detained or arrested without probable cause or a warrant.

Types of illegal arrests may include:

- **False Arrest**: Arresting someone without probable cause or legal justification.
- **Unlawful Detention**: Holding someone for a period longer than necessary without proper charges or due process.
- **Excessive Use of Force**: If excessive force was used during the arrest, it may be grounds for a lawsuit.

An illegal arrest violates your civil rights, and you may be entitled to compensation for damages, including physical harm, emotional distress, loss of wages, and other related costs.

2. When Can You File a Lawsuit for Illegal Arrest?

To file a lawsuit for an illegal arrest, you need to prove that the arrest was unlawful. Common grounds for an illegal arrest include:

- **Lack of Probable Cause**: If the police did not have sufficient evidence to justify the arrest, it could be considered illegal. For example, if you were arrested without any reasonable belief that you committed a crime.
- **No Warrant**: In many cases, the police are required to obtain a warrant from a judge before making an arrest unless they have probable cause or are making an arrest for a crime committed in their presence.
- **Violation of Constitutional Rights**: If your rights were violated during the arrest, such as being denied the right to remain silent, speak to an attorney, or be free from unreasonable searches, you may have grounds for a lawsuit.
- **False Identification**: If you were mistakenly arrested for someone else's actions or identity, you might have a claim for illegal arrest.
- **Improper Arrest Procedure**: If the officers failed to follow legal procedures during your arrest, such as not informing you of your Miranda rights or using excessive force, it could form the basis for a claim.

3. Filing a Lawsuit for Illegal Arrest

If you believe you were illegally arrested, you may file a lawsuit to seek compensation for damages. Here's a step-by-step process to file the lawsuit:

A. Gather Evidence

The first step in filing a lawsuit is to collect all relevant evidence. This includes documentation, witness statements, and any other evidence that supports your claim of an illegal arrest.

- **Police Report**: Request a copy of the police report from the arrest, which will contain details about the charges, the arresting officers, and any statements made during the arrest.
- **Witness Statements**: If there were any witnesses present during the arrest, ask them to provide statements supporting your version of events. Their testimony can be invaluable in proving your case.
- **Video or Audio Recordings**: If there is surveillance footage or bystander videos showing the arrest, this can be powerful evidence.
- **Medical Records**: If you were injured during the arrest or had any medical treatment afterward, obtain medical records and bills to document the physical harm you endured.
- **Photographs**: Take photographs of any visible injuries or damages caused during the arrest.

B. Consult with a Civil Rights Attorney

While it's possible to represent yourself in court, having an experienced civil rights attorney will significantly improve your chances of success. A lawyer specializing in police misconduct or civil rights violations can help evaluate your case, advise you on the best course of action, and navigate the legal system. They will also help you determine whether you have a viable claim for damages.

- **Fee Structure**: Many civil rights attorneys work on a contingency fee basis, meaning they only get paid if you win the case. Be sure to discuss the terms of your legal representation before proceeding.

C. Identify the Defendants

In an illegal arrest lawsuit, the primary defendants are typically the law enforcement officers who conducted the arrest. In some cases, the police department or municipality may also be named as a defendant if there is evidence of systemic failure, such as inadequate training or supervision.

- **Individual Officers**: If a specific officer violated your rights during the arrest, you can sue them individually for damages. However, police officers are often protected by "qualified immunity," which can make it difficult to sue them personally.
- **The Police Department or Municipality**: If the illegal arrest was part of a broader pattern of misconduct, you may have grounds to sue the police department or the city government. For example, if there is evidence that the police department failed to properly train officers or failed to address repeated violations, they could be held liable.

D. Determine the Legal Grounds for the Lawsuit

To bring an illegal arrest claim, you must identify the legal grounds for your lawsuit. Most cases involving illegal arrest are filed under the federal statute **42 U.S.C. § 1983**, which allows individuals to file lawsuits for civil rights violations committed by government officials.

- **Section 1983 Lawsuit**: This federal law allows you to sue government officials, including police officers, for violations of constitutional rights, such as illegal arrest, false imprisonment, or excessive use of force.
- **State Law Claims**: In addition to federal claims, you may also file a lawsuit under state law for false imprisonment, assault, battery, or other claims related to the arrest.

E. File the Complaint

The next step is to file a formal complaint in court. Your complaint will include:

- A detailed account of the events surrounding your arrest.
- The legal basis for your claim (e.g., violation of the Fourth Amendment, false imprisonment, etc.).

- A request for damages and specific relief (e.g., compensatory damages, punitive damages, etc.).

The complaint must be filed in the appropriate court, which will depend on the jurisdiction and the specifics of your case.

F. Serve the Defendants with the Complaint

Once the complaint is filed, you must serve the defendants (police officers or the police department) with the legal documents. This formal notification ensures that the defendants are aware of the lawsuit and have the opportunity to respond.

G. Discovery Process

After the complaint is filed, the discovery process begins. This is when both sides exchange evidence, witness lists, and documents. You may be required to answer written questions (interrogatories) or attend depositions, where you and other witnesses testify under oath. Your attorney will help you prepare for discovery and ensure that you obtain all relevant information.

H. Trial or Settlement

The case may proceed to trial if both sides cannot reach a settlement. At trial, both parties will present their evidence and arguments, and a judge or jury will decide the outcome. If you win, the court may award damages for pain and suffering, emotional distress, lost wages, and attorney's fees.

Many cases are resolved before trial through a settlement. A settlement occurs when both parties agree on a compensation amount without going to court. If a settlement is offered, you and your attorney will decide whether to accept or reject the offer.

4. Potential Damages in Illegal Arrest Lawsuits

If you are successful in your lawsuit, you may be entitled to various forms of compensation, including:

- **Compensatory Damages**: These are designed to compensate you for actual losses caused by the illegal arrest, such as medical expenses, lost wages, and emotional distress.
- **Punitive Damages**: In some cases, if the arrest was particularly egregious, punitive damages may be awarded to punish the defendant and deter future misconduct.
- **Attorney's Fees**: If you win the lawsuit, you may be able to recover the costs of hiring your attorney.

5. Conclusion

Filing a lawsuit for illegal arrest can be a complex and lengthy process, but it is a crucial step in holding law enforcement accountable for violating your rights. By gathering evidence, consulting with an experienced civil rights attorney, and filing the appropriate legal claims, you can fight back against unlawful detention and seek compensation for the harm you have endured. With the right legal representation and strategy, you can challenge illegal arrests and protect your constitutional rights.

CHAPTER THIRTY.

HOW TO SUE A CORRECTIONAL INSTITUTION FOR VIOLATING YOUR RIGHTS

INTRODUCTION

Being incarcerated comes with certain rights and protections under the U.S. Constitution. However, correctional institutions—whether jails, prisons, or detention centers—are often involved in situations where individuals' rights are violated. If you believe your rights have been violated while incarcerated, you may have the legal right to file a lawsuit against the correctional institution. This chapter provides a detailed guide on how to sue a correctional institution for rights violations, including the legal basis for such a lawsuit, the steps involved, and what you can expect during the process.

1. Understanding Rights Violations in Correctional Institutions

While incarcerated, individuals retain certain constitutional rights. However, these rights can be limited by the conditions of confinement, security concerns, and the prison environment. Common rights violations that may occur in correctional institutions include:

- **Excessive Use of Force**: The use of unnecessary or excessive physical force by corrections officers.
- **Failure to Provide Adequate Medical Care**: Denial or delay of necessary medical treatment or care for existing health conditions.
- **Inadequate or Unlawful Living Conditions**: Overcrowding, unsanitary conditions, lack of proper nutrition, or failure to protect inmates from harm.
- **Violation of Religious Rights**: Restrictions on religious practices, such as access to religious materials or religious services.

- **Retaliation**: Punishment for filing complaints or grievances, or for engaging in legal actions (e.g., lawsuits or requests for legal assistance).
- **Unlawful Searches and Seizures**: Violations of privacy or unlawful searches of your cell or personal belongings without probable cause or due process.
- **Failure to Protect from Harm**: Failure of corrections officers or the institution to protect you from assaults or violence from other inmates.
- **Discriminatory Treatment**: Discrimination based on race, gender, sexual orientation, or other protected characteristics.

If you experience any of these or other constitutional violations, you may have grounds to file a lawsuit.

2. When Can You Sue a Correctional Institution?

You can sue a correctional institution if you believe that your rights were violated while incarcerated. The legal grounds for a lawsuit typically include:

- **Eighth Amendment Violations**: The Eighth Amendment to the U.S. Constitution prohibits "cruel and unusual punishment." If the conditions of your confinement or treatment by corrections officers are deemed excessively harsh or inhumane, it may constitute a violation of the Eighth Amendment.
- **First Amendment Violations**: If your rights to free speech, freedom of religion, or the right to petition the government for redress are violated, you may have grounds for a lawsuit under the First Amendment.
- **Due Process Violations**: The Fourteenth Amendment guarantees due process rights, including fair treatment in disciplinary actions, and protection against arbitrary actions.

- **Civil Rights Violations (42 U.S.C. § 1983)**: Under **42 U.S.C. § 1983**, individuals can sue government officials, including correctional officers, for violations of their constitutional rights. This statute allows individuals to bring lawsuits for violations such as excessive force, failure to provide medical care, and other civil rights abuses by government employees.

3. Preparing to Sue a Correctional Institution

Before you file a lawsuit against a correctional institution, it's essential to prepare by gathering evidence, documenting the violation, and understanding the legal requirements. Here's what to do:

A. Document the Violation

To support your lawsuit, you need solid evidence showing that your rights were violated. The following documentation will help:

- **Grievances or Complaints**: File grievances within the correctional institution to alert officials of the issue. Keeping a record of these complaints can demonstrate that the institution had notice of the problem but failed to address it.
- **Medical Records**: If your lawsuit involves denial of medical care, ensure you have copies of your medical records. These records can prove that you required care and that it was denied or delayed.
- **Witness Statements**: Obtain statements from other inmates or staff members who witnessed the incident. These can corroborate your account of the violation.
- **Photographs and Videos**: If there are visible injuries or conditions, photographs or videos can serve as compelling evidence.
- **Reports from External Authorities**: In some cases, reports from external organizations or oversight bodies (e.g., the Department of Justice, American Civil Liberties Union) may support your claim.

B. Exhaust All Administrative Remedies

Before filing a lawsuit, you are generally required to exhaust all administrative remedies within the correctional institution. This means you must file complaints or grievances through the institution's internal grievance process and allow them a reasonable amount of time to respond. Courts may dismiss lawsuits if this process is not followed.

- **Prison Grievance Process**: Each correctional institution has its own procedure for filing grievances. Follow these procedures carefully, and keep a copy of all filings for your records.
- **Appeals**: If the institution fails to resolve the issue, or if you disagree with their response, you may need to appeal the decision before proceeding with the lawsuit.

C. Consult with an Attorney

Given the complexities involved in suing a correctional institution, it is highly recommended that you consult with an attorney who specializes in civil rights or prison litigation. An experienced attorney can help you assess your case, advise you on the best legal strategy, and guide you through the process.

Many civil rights attorneys work on a contingency fee basis, meaning they only get paid if you win the case. If you cannot afford an attorney, you may be eligible for legal aid, depending on your financial situation and the nature of the case.

4. Filing the Lawsuit

Once you have gathered the necessary evidence and exhausted all administrative remedies, you can proceed with filing a lawsuit. Here's how:

A. File a Complaint

To begin your lawsuit, you must file a **complaint** with the appropriate court. In a civil rights case against a correctional institution, this is usually a federal district court if your claim involves constitutional violations.

- **Complaint Contents**: Your complaint should outline the facts of the case, the legal grounds for your claim (e.g., Eighth Amendment violation, First Amendment violation), and the specific damages or relief you are seeking.
- **Defendants**: The defendants in your lawsuit may include the correctional officers involved, the warden, or the institution itself. In some cases, you may also sue the city or state government that oversees the correctional facility.

B. Service of Process

After filing the complaint, you must serve the correctional institution and the individual defendants with a copy of the lawsuit. This is known as the **service of process** and ensures that the defendants are notified of the lawsuit and have the opportunity to respond.

C. Discovery Process

Once the lawsuit is filed, both sides engage in **discovery**, which is the process of exchanging evidence and information relevant to the case. During discovery, you may request documents, depose witnesses, and gather additional evidence to support your claim.

- **Interrogatories**: These are written questions that the other party must answer under oath.
- **Depositions**: These are sworn statements made by witnesses, including corrections officers, medical personnel, or other inmates.

D. Pre-Trial Motions

Before the trial, the defendants may file motions to dismiss the case or for summary judgment, arguing that you have failed to meet the legal requirements for a lawsuit. Your attorney will work to counter these motions and ensure that the case proceeds to trial if necessary.

E. Trial and Settlement

If the case goes to trial, both sides will present their evidence and arguments. The judge or jury will then decide whether the correctional institution violated your rights and whether you are entitled to damages.

In many cases, lawsuits are settled out of court. The correctional institution may offer a settlement to avoid a lengthy trial, and you and your attorney can decide whether to accept the offer.

5. Potential Damages in a Lawsuit Against a Correctional Institution

If you are successful in your lawsuit, you may be entitled to various types of damages:

- **Compensatory Damages**: These are intended to compensate you for the harm caused by the rights violation, including physical injuries, emotional distress, pain and suffering, and medical expenses.
- **Punitive Damages**: In cases of egregious misconduct, the court may award punitive damages to punish the correctional institution and deter future violations.
- **Injunctive Relief**: In some cases, the court may order the correctional institution to change its policies or practices to prevent further rights violations.

6. Conclusion

Suing a correctional institution for violating your rights is a critical tool for holding the institution accountable and seeking justice for the harm you've experienced. By documenting your violation, exhausting administrative remedies, consulting with an attorney, and following the proper legal procedures, you can pursue a lawsuit against a correctional institution. While the process can be complex and lengthy, it is essential to protect your constitutional rights and seek fair compensation for any harm you've endured.

CHAPTER THIRTY ONE.

BEATING A MURDER CASE

INTRODUCTION

Being accused of murder is one of the most serious legal challenges an individual can face. It is a case that carries life-altering consequences, including the potential for a lengthy prison sentence or even the death penalty in some jurisdictions. However, being accused does not equate to being guilty, and there are multiple ways to challenge the prosecution's case and fight for your innocence. This chapter outlines key strategies and methods used by defense attorneys to beat a murder charge.

1. Understanding the Legal Basis for Murder Charges

Before diving into strategies to beat a murder charge, it is essential to understand the types of murder charges and what the prosecution must prove. The primary categories of murder charges include:

- **First-Degree Murder**: This charge involves premeditated murder, meaning the accused planned the murder before carrying it out. It also includes murder committed during the commission of a felony (felony murder).
- **Second-Degree Murder**: This charge typically involves an intentional killing that was not premeditated or planned.
- **Manslaughter**: In cases where there is a killing without malice or premeditation, such as in a heat-of-passion situation or as a result of criminal negligence, a charge of manslaughter may be appropriate.
- **Voluntary vs. Involuntary Manslaughter**: Voluntary manslaughter occurs in a situation where the defendant kills in the heat of passion, while involuntary manslaughter involves killing through negligence or reckless conduct.

To win a murder case, the defense must cast doubt on the prosecution's ability to prove the defendant's guilt beyond a reasonable doubt.

2. Key Defense Strategies for Beating a Murder Charge

There are various defense strategies employed by legal teams to beat a murder case. These strategies focus on attacking the prosecution's evidence, providing alternative explanations, and highlighting weaknesses in the case.

A. Lack of Evidence

One of the most fundamental defenses in any criminal case is the lack of evidence. For a murder conviction, the prosecution must prove beyond a reasonable doubt that the defendant committed the crime. If the prosecution's case is based on weak, circumstantial, or inconclusive evidence, the defense can argue that the burden of proof has not been met.

- **Challenge the physical evidence**: DNA, fingerprints, and other forensic evidence should be examined for contamination, mishandling, or inaccuracies. If there are issues with the evidence collection or chain of custody, it could significantly weaken the prosecution's case.
- **Alibi Defense**: If you can establish an alibi and provide witnesses or documentation showing that you were not at the crime scene when the murder occurred, this can cast doubt on the prosecution's timeline.

B. Self-Defense

In some murder cases, the defense might assert that the killing was done in self-defense. If you can demonstrate that you were facing an imminent threat to your life, you may be able to reduce the charge to manslaughter or even have the charges dropped entirely.

- **Reasonable Fear of Harm**: Self-defense can be used if you believed you were in imminent danger and acted to protect yourself. You must show that your response to the threat was proportionate to the danger.
- **Stand Your Ground Laws**: In some jurisdictions, self-defense laws allow individuals to use deadly force without the duty to retreat if they are in their home or another place where they have a right to be. If applicable, this could be a powerful defense.

C. Insanity Defense

If the defendant was not mentally competent at the time of the crime, they may be able to use the insanity defense. This defense asserts that the defendant could not understand the nature of their actions or conform their behavior to the law due to a mental illness or defect.

- **Expert Testimony**: A successful insanity defense typically requires the testimony of mental health professionals, such as psychiatrists, to prove that the defendant had a severe mental illness at the time of the crime.
- **Not Guilty by Reason of Insanity**: If found not guilty by reason of insanity, the defendant may be committed to a psychiatric institution rather than a prison.

D. Mistaken Identity

In some cases, the defendant may argue that they were mistakenly identified as the perpetrator of the crime. If there are discrepancies in eyewitness testimony or other identification evidence, this defense can be a strong strategy.

- **Eyewitness Testimony**: Eyewitness misidentification is a common issue in criminal cases. If the witness failed to positively identify the defendant or if there are inconsistencies in the testimony, the defense can argue that the wrong person has been accused.

- **False Confessions**: In some cases, defendants may be coerced or pressured into confessing to a crime they did not commit. If there are signs that the confession was not voluntary, the defense can argue that the confession is inadmissible.

E. Lack of Motive

In murder cases, proving a motive can be a crucial part of the prosecution's case. If the defense can show that the accused had no clear motive to commit the murder, it can raise reasonable doubt about the defendant's guilt.

- **Absence of a Connection to the Victim**: If there is no known relationship between the defendant and the victim, or if the prosecution cannot establish a motive, this could be a key factor in weakening their case.
- **Alibi and Other Evidence**: Presenting evidence that shows the defendant had no opportunity or reason to commit the crime can cast doubt on the prosecution's theory of the crime.

F. False Evidence or Fabrication

In some cases, the defense may be able to prove that the evidence presented by the prosecution is false or has been fabricated.

- **Police Misconduct**: If there is evidence of police misconduct, such as falsifying evidence, coercing confessions, or conducting unlawful searches, it can significantly harm the prosecution's case.
- **Exposing Flaws in Forensic Evidence**: DNA, ballistics, and other forensic evidence can sometimes be flawed. If the defense can prove that the evidence is unreliable or incorrectly interpreted, it can be a powerful defense.

G. Procedural Errors

Sometimes, procedural errors during the investigation, arrest, or trial can provide grounds to have the case dismissed or to have evidence excluded.

- **Unlawful Search and Seizure**: If the police violated your constitutional rights by conducting an unlawful search or seizure, any evidence obtained may be inadmissible in court.
- **Improper Jury Instructions**: If the judge provided improper instructions to the jury, this could be grounds for an appeal or a mistrial.

3. Presenting a Strong Defense

When preparing to fight a murder charge, it is essential to present a cohesive defense. This includes gathering evidence, obtaining expert witnesses, and building a narrative that presents reasonable doubt. Here are steps to consider when preparing your defense:

A. Hire an Experienced Criminal Defense Attorney

A skilled criminal defense attorney is crucial in handling a murder case. Your attorney will help guide you through the legal process, prepare your case, and represent you in court. Look for an attorney with experience handling serious criminal cases and a strong track record of defending clients against murder charges.

B. Investigate the Crime Scene

It is essential to investigate the crime scene thoroughly. The defense team should gather physical evidence, conduct forensic analysis, and interview witnesses to piece together the true events leading to the crime.

C. Use Expert Witnesses

Experts in fields like forensic science, psychiatry, ballistics, and medical pathology can play a key role in disproving the prosecution's theory of the crime. Expert testimony can challenge the cause of death, question the credibility of evidence, and provide alternative explanations for the events.

4. What to Expect During Trial

The trial process for a murder case is long and complex. Here's what to expect:

- **Opening Statements**: The prosecution and defense will present their initial arguments. The prosecution will outline its case, while the defense will explain how it plans to disprove the charges.
- **Prosecution's Case**: The prosecution will present its evidence and call witnesses to testify against the defendant.
- **Defense's Case**: The defense will then present its evidence, call witnesses, and challenge the prosecution's case.
- **Closing Arguments**: Both sides will summarize their arguments and attempt to convince the jury of their position.
- **Jury Deliberation and Verdict**: After hearing all evidence, the jury will deliberate and return a verdict of guilty or not guilty.

5. Appealing a Murder Conviction

If convicted of murder, you have the right to appeal the conviction. Grounds for appeal may include:

- **Legal Errors**: Mistakes made during the trial, such as improper jury instructions, wrongful admission of evidence, or prosecutorial misconduct.
- **Insufficient Evidence**: If the prosecution failed to prove guilt beyond a reasonable doubt, you may have grounds to appeal.

- **New Evidence**: If new evidence comes to light after the trial, it may be grounds for a retrial or appeal.

6. Conclusion

Beating a murder charge requires a strategic and well-prepared defense. With the right legal team, effective presentation of evidence, and strong arguments, you can challenge the prosecution's case and fight for your innocence. Whether you assert an alibi, self-defense, or attack the prosecution's evidence, each defense strategy offers a pathway to potentially reducing the charge or securing an acquittal. Being accused of murder is a serious matter, but with the right legal approach, you can navigate the challenges of the case and protect your rights.

CHAPTER THIRTY TWO.

BEATING A MURDER CONSPIRACY CHARGE

INTRODUCTION

Murder conspiracy charges are some of the most serious allegations a person can face. A conspiracy to commit murder implies that the defendant was involved in planning or agreeing to kill someone, even if the murder was never carried out. Although conspiracy charges can carry severe penalties, such charges are not always easy for the prosecution to prove. There are several strategies that can be employed by a defense attorney to challenge the conspiracy charge and fight for the defendant's innocence.

In this chapter, we will explore effective defense strategies, the legal elements of a conspiracy charge, and ways to beat a murder conspiracy charge, whether through an acquittal, a reduction in charges, or dismissal of the case.

1. Understanding Murder Conspiracy Charges

A conspiracy to commit murder typically involves two or more people agreeing to kill another person. Even if no murder occurs, the mere agreement to kill someone can result in criminal charges. To secure a conviction, the prosecution must prove the following elements beyond a reasonable doubt:

- **Agreement to Commit Murder**: The prosecution must demonstrate that the defendant and at least one other person came to an agreement to commit murder.
- **Intent to Commit Murder**: The defendant must have had the intent to participate in the murder, not merely to assist in a different crime.
- **Overt Act in Furtherance of the Conspiracy**: In many jurisdictions, it is necessary for the prosecution to show that at least one act was taken

in furtherance of the conspiracy. This could be anything from purchasing a weapon to surveillance of the target or any step that moves the plan forward.

It's important to note that even if the murder was not completed, the charge of conspiracy is still serious and carries severe penalties. However, conspiracy charges can be difficult to prove without direct evidence, such as physical acts or communications that support the conspiracy.

2. Key Defense Strategies to Beat a Murder Conspiracy Charge

There are several strategies a defense attorney may use to contest a murder conspiracy charge. These strategies are aimed at casting doubt on the prosecution's case, showing that the elements of the charge have not been met, or establishing the defendant's lack of involvement in the conspiracy.

A. Lack of Agreement

For a conspiracy charge to be valid, there must be an agreement between two or more individuals to commit murder. The defense can argue that no agreement existed. The prosecution must prove that the defendant was involved in an explicit or implied agreement to kill someone.

- **No Evidence of Agreement**: If there is no clear, credible evidence (such as a conversation, written communication, or recorded statement) showing that the defendant agreed to participate in the murder, the defense can argue that no agreement occurred.
- **Ambiguous Statements**: In some cases, what might appear to be an agreement may, in fact, be an ambiguous statement or joke. The defense can argue that the conversations or actions attributed to the defendant were misinterpreted or not meant to constitute a serious agreement.

B. Lack of Intent

In conspiracy charges, the defendant must have the specific intent to participate in the murder. If the defense can show that the defendant had no intention of committing murder or was unaware of the conspiracy's goals, it could lead to a dismissal or acquittal.

- **No Knowledge of the Murder Plan**: The defendant may have known of a plan but not realized that it was to commit murder. Lack of awareness or knowledge of the intent to kill could be a key argument in challenging the charges.
- **Inability to Prove Intent**: If the prosecution cannot prove that the defendant had the necessary intent to commit murder, the charge may be reduced or dismissed.

C. No Overt Act in Furtherance of the Conspiracy

For a conspiracy conviction to stand, there must be an overt act that moves the conspiracy forward. The defense can argue that there was no action taken that demonstrated the defendant's involvement in furthering the murder plan.

- **No Action Taken**: If there were no concrete actions taken by the defendant to advance the conspiracy, such as buying weapons, arranging meetings, or scouting out the victim, the defense can argue that the defendant's role was non-existent or minimal.
- **Innocent Conduct**: Actions that the prosecution presents as evidence of the conspiracy may, upon closer examination, be completely innocent. For example, an innocent phone call or a casual meeting could be misinterpreted as part of the conspiracy. The defense can argue that these actions were not linked to the murder plot.

D. False or Coerced Confession

A common defense strategy is to challenge the admissibility of confessions or statements made by the defendant. False or coerced confessions are unfortunately not uncommon in criminal cases, and they can be a significant point of contention in a conspiracy charge.

- **Coercion or Duress**: The defense may argue that the defendant's confession or statements were obtained under duress, pressure, or coercion by law enforcement. If the confession is found to be involuntary, it may be ruled inadmissible.
- **False Confessions**: People sometimes confess to crimes they didn't commit due to fear, confusion, or misunderstanding. The defense may argue that the confession was false, especially if the facts of the case don't align with the confession.

E. Alibi Defense

An alibi defense can be particularly powerful in conspiracy cases, especially if the defendant can prove they were not at the scene of any acts related to the conspiracy.

- **Physical Evidence**: If the defendant was physically located elsewhere at the time of critical events, such as meetings or actions related to the conspiracy, this can significantly undermine the conspiracy charge.
- **Witness Testimony**: Eyewitnesses who can confirm the defendant's location or activities during the key events can help establish a solid alibi.

F. Involvement in a Different Crime

Sometimes, people who are involved in a conspiracy to commit a crime may not have been aware that the crime would escalate to murder. The defense may argue that the defendant was involved in a different criminal activity, such as robbery or assault, but had no knowledge of or intent to participate in the murder itself.

- **Misunderstood Role**: The defendant may have believed they were involved in a different kind of crime, such as a robbery, but did not realize that it would turn into a murder plot. This misunderstanding could be a basis for defending the charge.

3. Gathering Evidence to Support Your Defense

Beating a murder conspiracy charge requires thorough investigation and the collection of evidence. The defense team should be proactive in gathering both exonerating evidence and challenging the prosecution's case.

- **Investigating Communication**: Review any forms of communication, such as text messages, emails, or phone calls, that may serve as evidence of the conspiracy. In many cases, the prosecution's case relies heavily on these communications, so proving that they do not support the alleged conspiracy can be vital.
- **Witnesses**: Witnesses who were present at key moments can help establish whether the defendant was involved in the conspiracy. Additionally, witnesses who can testify that the defendant was unaware of the plan or did not intend to commit murder can provide crucial support.
- **Forensic Evidence**: Forensic evidence, such as fingerprints, DNA, or gunshot residue, can be critical in proving or disproving involvement in the conspiracy. If the defendant's involvement in the conspiracy did not lead to any physical evidence linking them to the crime, this could be an important factor in the defense.

4. What to Expect in Court

A murder conspiracy case typically involves several stages, and the process can be lengthy. Here's what you can expect during the trial:

- **Opening Statements**: The prosecution will outline their case, and the defense will present their theory of the case.
- **Prosecution's Case**: The prosecution will present evidence and witness testimony to show that a conspiracy occurred, and that the defendant was involved.
- **Defense's Case**: The defense will present counter-evidence, challenge the prosecution's case, and introduce any alibi or other defense arguments.
- **Closing Arguments**: Both sides will summarize their arguments and attempt to convince the jury.
- **Jury Deliberation and Verdict**: After hearing all of the evidence, the jury will deliberate and decide whether the defendant is guilty or not guilty.

5. Appealing a Murder Conspiracy Conviction

If convicted of murder conspiracy, the defendant has the right to appeal the conviction. Common grounds for an appeal may include:

- **Legal Errors**: If there were errors in the trial, such as improper jury instructions, wrongful admission of evidence, or prosecutorial misconduct, the defendant may have grounds for appeal.
- **Insufficient Evidence**: If the evidence was insufficient to prove the defendant's involvement in the conspiracy, the conviction may be overturned.
- **New Evidence**: If new evidence arises after the trial, such as exonerating DNA evidence or a new witness, it may provide grounds for a retrial or appeal.

6. Conclusion

Facing a murder conspiracy charge is a serious matter, but it is not an unbeatable one. With a strong defense strategy, a skilled legal team, and a focus on casting doubt on the prosecution's evidence, the chances of beating a conspiracy charge are significantly increased. Whether through challenging the existence of an agreement, disproving intent, or highlighting procedural errors, there are several methods available to fight the charge and seek a favorable outcome.

CHAPTER THIRTY THREE.

BEATING HABITUAL DRIVING OFFENDER (HDO) CHARGES

INTRODUCTION

Being charged as a Habitual Driving Offender (HDO) is one of the most serious driving-related offenses you can face. Habitual traffic offenses refer to situations where a person has accumulated multiple convictions for serious traffic violations over a set period. These offenses are often considered felonies and come with severe penalties, including long-term license suspension, heavy fines, and even imprisonment. However, it is possible to successfully challenge an HDO charge and fight for your driving rights.

In this chapter, we will explore effective defense strategies, common legal issues in habitual driving offender cases, and how to beat the charges through effective legal counsel, a thorough investigation, and strategic courtroom tactics.

1. Understanding Habitual Driving Offender (HDO) Charges

A Habitual Driving Offender charge typically applies to individuals who have been convicted of multiple serious driving offenses within a specified period. The exact criteria and timeframes vary from state to state, but generally, the following must be proven for a person to be charged as a habitual offender:

- **Multiple Offenses**: The defendant has accumulated a certain number of serious traffic violations (such as DUI, reckless driving, or driving with a suspended license) over a designated period, typically within 5 years.
- **Convictions**: The person must have been convicted of the qualifying offenses, not merely arrested or cited.

- **Habitual Offender Designation**: Once the criteria are met, the individual is legally classified as a habitual offender, which leads to more severe penalties and a long-term license revocation.

Each state has different thresholds for what constitutes "habitual" offenses, and the penalties vary depending on whether the individual is classified as a habitual offender or a repeat offender.

2. Defending Against Habitual Driving Offender Charges

Beating an HDO charge requires an in-depth understanding of the law, a strategic defense, and a keen focus on challenging the prosecution's evidence. Below are some common defense strategies that can be used to fight habitual driving offender charges:

A. Challenge the Number of Convictions

One of the first things to examine is whether the defendant actually meets the threshold for habitual offender status. Often, the prosecution will rely on records of past convictions, but these records may not always be accurate or complete.

- **Incorrect Convictions**: The defendant's criminal record might show convictions that should not count toward the HDO designation. For example, a conviction that was dismissed or reduced to a lesser charge might mistakenly be counted as a qualifying offense.
- **Timeframe Discrepancies**: The period within which the offenses are counted may be challenged. If there is ambiguity or a gap in the timeframe used to classify the individual as a habitual offender, the charge may not hold.
- **Expungement or Sealing of Records**: In some cases, previous convictions may have been expunged or sealed by the court. If these

records are being used in the HDO designation, the defense can argue that they should not be considered in the current case.

B. Dispute the Validity of the Convictions

The defense can challenge the validity of prior convictions, especially if those convictions were based on procedural errors, improper legal representation, or the violation of the defendant's constitutional rights.

- **Due Process Violations**: If the defendant's rights were violated during prior arrests or convictions, such as not being informed of their rights, the defense can argue that the conviction should not count toward the habitual offender designation.
- **Lack of Proper Representation**: If the defendant was not adequately represented in a previous case, or if the defendant was coerced into a guilty plea, these prior convictions might be contested.
- **Errors in the Evidence**: Mistakes in the way evidence was collected or handled can lead to invalid convictions. If the previous cases involved faulty evidence or unreliable witnesses, the defense may argue that the convictions were flawed and should be disregarded.

C. Lack of Knowledge of License Status

In some cases, the defendant might not have known their driver's license was suspended or revoked at the time of the offense. While ignorance of the law is generally not a defense, if the defendant can prove that they were not properly notified or aware of their suspension, it might be possible to contest the charges.

- **Improper Notification**: If the defendant was never properly notified by the Department of Motor Vehicles (DMV) about the suspension or revocation of their license, this could be a defense. For example, the defendant may have changed addresses and never received any notices.

- **Faulty DMV Records**: Sometimes, the DMV may incorrectly report a suspension or revocation. If the defense can show that the DMV made a clerical error or that the suspension was not properly recorded, the charge could be dismissed.

D. Argue That the Offenses Do Not Qualify as "Serious" Violations

In many states, only certain traffic violations count toward habitual offender status. The defense may argue that prior offenses were not serious enough to be classified as such under the law.

- **Lesser Offenses**: If a prior conviction was for a minor traffic violation (such as speeding or running a red light), the defense can argue that it does not qualify as a serious enough offense to count toward habitual offender status.
- **Disproportionate Penalties**: Sometimes, the penalties for minor offenses may not be in line with the severity of the charge. If the defendant was facing disproportionate penalties for what were relatively minor offenses, this could be a point to argue during defense.

E. Appeal the HDO Charge

If the defendant has already been convicted of being a habitual driving offender, it may be possible to appeal the case to a higher court. Appeal options include:

- **Legal Errors in the Trial**: If errors occurred in the trial process (such as improper jury instructions or the admission of inadmissible evidence), the defendant may be able to appeal the conviction.

- **Insufficient Evidence**: If the prosecution cannot prove the required elements of the habitual offender charge beyond a reasonable doubt, an appeal may be based on insufficient evidence.
- **New Evidence**: If new evidence is discovered after the trial that undermines the conviction, this could be grounds for an appeal or retrial.

F. Negotiation for Reduced Charges or Sentence

In some cases, the defense may be able to negotiate with the prosecution for a reduction in charges or a lighter sentence, even if the HDO charge is upheld. This might include:

- **Plea Bargain**: The defense may negotiate a plea deal with the prosecution to reduce the charge to a lesser offense, such as reckless driving, in exchange for a guilty plea.
- **Sentencing Mitigation**: Even if the defendant is found guilty of being a habitual offender, the defense can argue for mitigating circumstances during sentencing. This could include the defendant's background, work history, or efforts to rehabilitate themselves.

3. What to Expect in Court

When facing an HDO charge, it's important to understand the process and the steps involved in the trial. Here's what you can expect:

- **Pretrial Motions**: The defense may file pretrial motions to exclude evidence, challenge the habitual offender designation, or request a change in venue.
- **Prosecution's Case**: The prosecution will present evidence showing that the defendant has a history of serious driving violations, and that they meet the legal definition of a habitual offender.

- **Defense's Case**: The defense will challenge the prosecution's evidence, possibly introducing evidence of mistaken identity, invalid convictions, or lack of notice regarding license status.
- **Jury Trial or Bench Trial**: In some cases, the defendant may have the option of a jury trial, while in others, the case will be heard by a judge (bench trial).
- **Closing Arguments and Verdict**: After the defense and prosecution present their cases, both sides will give closing arguments, summarizing their positions. The judge or jury will then deliberate and issue a verdict.

4. Appealing a Habitual Driving Offender Conviction

If convicted, the defendant has the right to appeal the verdict. Appeals are based on legal errors, improper admission of evidence, or a violation of the defendant's constitutional rights.

5. Conclusion

Being charged with habitual driving offender status is a serious matter, but it is not an insurmountable challenge. With the right defense strategy, including challenging past convictions, proving lack of knowledge or intent, and exploring procedural errors, it is possible to beat the charges and avoid severe penalties. Whether through outright acquittal, reduction in charges, or successful appeal, working with an experienced attorney can significantly increase your chances of achieving a favorable outcome.

CHAPTER THIRTY FOUR.

BEATING HABITUAL PETIT THEFT CHARGES

INTRODUCTION

Petit theft, or petty theft, typically refers to the unlawful taking of property with a value below a certain threshold, usually a relatively small amount. While the offense itself might seem minor, individuals who accumulate multiple petit theft convictions over time can face much more severe consequences, including habitual offender charges. A conviction for habitual petit theft (often referred to as "habitual theft offender" status) can result in harsher penalties such as longer prison sentences, more substantial fines, and permanent criminal records.

However, there are various legal strategies to fight habitual petit theft charges. Through strategic defense, challenging the evidence, and exploiting legal loopholes, individuals can increase their chances of reducing or even defeating the charges. In this chapter, we'll explore how to beat habitual petit theft charges by understanding the law, employing effective defenses, and securing the best possible outcome.

1. Understanding Habitual Petit Theft Charges

Before delving into defense strategies, it's essential to understand how habitual petit theft charges work:

- **Petit Theft**: This is typically classified as a misdemeanor when the stolen property is worth below a certain dollar amount. For example, in Florida, the theft of property valued at less than $300 is usually classified as petit theft.
- **Habitual Offender Status**: If an individual accumulates multiple petit theft convictions (often three or more) within a specified period, they

can be designated as a habitual offender. This designation is a significant factor in increasing penalties, which could escalate petit theft to a felony charge.

In most states, the habitual offender statute is designed to punish repeat offenders more harshly to deter further criminal activity. A habitual petit theft offender may face felony charges and severe sentencing, including prison time and significant fines.

2. Defending Against Habitual Petit Theft Charges

To successfully fight habitual petit theft charges, a comprehensive defense strategy is essential. Here are some of the most effective methods for challenging such charges:

A. Challenge the Number of Prior Convictions

One of the first steps in defending against habitual petit theft charges is to challenge the number of prior convictions. If you can argue that you do not meet the threshold for habitual offender status, it may lead to a dismissal or reduction of charges.

- **Inaccurate Records**: Criminal records can sometimes be inaccurate or outdated. If any of the prior theft convictions listed are erroneous, the defense should dispute the record.
- **Prior Convictions Were Expunged or Sealed**: In some cases, previous theft convictions may have been expunged or sealed. If this is the case, those convictions should not count toward your habitual offender status.
- **Different Offenses**: If some of the prior convictions were for offenses that are not considered theft, such as vandalism, trespassing, or drug

possession, the defense can argue that these do not qualify as theft-related convictions.

B. Challenge the Evidence of the Current Theft

Another powerful defense strategy is to challenge the prosecution's evidence in the current case. If the prosecution cannot prove that you committed the theft, the charge may be dismissed.

- **Mistaken Identity**: The defense can argue that you were mistakenly identified as the person who committed the theft. If the evidence includes unreliable eyewitness testimony or faulty surveillance footage, the defense can use these weaknesses to create reasonable doubt.
- **Lack of Intent**: Theft requires intent to permanently deprive the owner of their property. If you were in the store or location but did not have the intent to steal (for example, you accidentally left the store with an item without paying), it could be argued that you did not meet the intent requirement.
- **Unlawful Search and Seizure**: If the evidence against you was obtained through an unlawful search or seizure, such as without a warrant or without your consent, your attorney may file a motion to suppress the evidence.
- **Defective Arrest**: If the arresting officers did not follow proper procedure or violated your rights during your arrest, the evidence obtained might be inadmissible.

C. Argue That the Value of the Property Does Not Meet the Legal Threshold

In some cases, the charge of theft may be misclassified. The value of the stolen property is a key element in determining whether the theft is petit theft (a misdemeanor) or grand theft (a felony).

- **Misvaluation of Property**: The defense can challenge the valuation of the stolen property. If the prosecution claims the property was worth more than the threshold amount required for petit theft, but the defense can demonstrate that the value was less, it may lead to a reduced charge.
- **Mistaken Classification**: If the stolen property was incorrectly classified (for instance, if it was an item that was on sale, discounted, or otherwise valued incorrectly), it may reduce the offense to a lower level or even result in a dismissal.

D. Argue for a Lack of Evidence in the Case

In many theft cases, especially where surveillance footage or eyewitness testimony is not clear, the defense can argue that the prosecution lacks sufficient evidence to prove that you committed the crime.

- **Weak Circumstantial Evidence**: Theft cases often rely on circumstantial evidence (such as being in the vicinity of the theft), but this alone is not enough to secure a conviction. The defense can argue that there is not enough evidence to prove beyond a reasonable doubt that you were the one who committed the theft.
- **Failure to Prove Ownership**: The prosecution must prove that the property belonged to the person claiming to be the victim. If they fail to prove ownership, the defense can argue that there is no theft, as the property may not have been legally possessed by the alleged victim.

E. Present a Strong Personal Background and Remorse

In cases involving repeat offenders, the court often considers the defendant's background and personal history when determining a sentence. A strong presentation of character and rehabilitation can be an effective strategy, even if the charge of habitual theft is upheld.

- **Demonstrating Change**: If you have taken steps to reform (such as attending rehabilitation programs or counseling), your attorney can present this as evidence of your efforts to change your behavior.
- **Prove Your Intent Not to Reoffend**: A defense based on a history of good behavior since the last offense, or steps taken to avoid criminal activity (such as finding stable employment or housing), can work in your favor.

F. Negotiate for a Reduced Sentence or Plea Deal

In some cases, even if the defense cannot successfully argue the case in full, negotiating a plea deal with the prosecution may be an option. If the defendant is willing to plead guilty to a lesser offense, such as a single count of petit theft, the prosecution may reduce the charge or offer a more lenient sentence.

- **Plea Bargaining**: The defense can work with the prosecution to negotiate a plea deal that results in lesser penalties, such as probation, community service, or fines, instead of jail time.
- **Sentencing Alternatives**: Even if convicted, the defense can argue for alternative sentencing options, such as diversion programs, drug rehabilitation, or counseling, instead of incarceration.

G. Appeal the Conviction

If convicted of habitual petit theft, it may still be possible to appeal the verdict based on legal errors or violations of your rights during the trial.

- **Errors in Jury Instructions**: If the jury was incorrectly instructed on the law or misled during deliberations, an appeal can be filed on the grounds of trial errors.

- **New Evidence**: If new evidence comes to light that could exonerate you or raise doubt about the conviction, you may be able to have the case retried or appeal the verdict.

3. What to Expect in Court

During the court proceedings, you should expect the following:

- **Pretrial Motions**: Your attorney may file motions to suppress evidence, dismiss charges, or argue for a reduction in charges.
- **Presentation of Evidence**: The prosecution will present evidence of your past theft convictions, while the defense will challenge the evidence and present their own case.
- **Jury or Bench Trial**: Depending on the case, it may be heard by a jury, or the judge may render a verdict based on the facts.
- **Verdict**: The judge or jury will deliberate and issue a verdict. If convicted, sentencing will follow, where you may be able to argue for leniency or alternative sentencing options.

4. Conclusion

Habitual petit theft charges may seem overwhelming, but with the right legal strategy, it is possible to fight back and avoid severe consequences. By challenging the evidence, proving prior convictions were invalid, disputing the value of the stolen property, and arguing for a lesser charge or sentencing, you stand a chance of successfully beating the charges. In many cases, a skilled criminal defense attorney can provide the guidance and advocacy necessary to navigate this complex process and achieve a favorable outcome.

CHAPTER THIRTY FIVE.

BEATING THE CONSPIRACY LAW

INTRODUCTION

A conspiracy charge is a serious criminal offense. It involves two or more people planning or conspiring to commit a crime, with the intent to carry out that crime. In many jurisdictions, even if the crime that was planned was never actually carried out, a conspiracy charge can still result in severe penalties. The key to defending against conspiracy charges lies in dismantling the prosecution's case and challenging the underlying elements of the conspiracy law.

In this chapter, we will explore various legal strategies for fighting conspiracy charges and successfully defending yourself against these serious accusations. Whether the conspiracy involves a violent crime, drug trafficking, fraud, or any other illegal activity, understanding the nuances of conspiracy law and the most common defense strategies is essential.

1. Understanding Conspiracy Charges

To be convicted of conspiracy, the prosecution must prove several key elements beyond a reasonable doubt:

- **Agreement**: There must be evidence that the defendant and at least one other person agreed to commit an illegal act.
- **Intent**: The defendant must have had the specific intent to commit the crime that was the subject of the conspiracy.
- **Overt Act**: In some jurisdictions, the prosecution must prove that at least one overt act was taken in furtherance of the conspiracy. This means that the parties involved took steps toward carrying out the planned crime.

If the prosecution fails to prove any of these elements, the conspiracy charge can be defeated. Here are the most effective defense strategies for beating a conspiracy charge.

2. Common Defenses Against Conspiracy Charges

A. Lack of Agreement (No Conspiracy)

One of the most common defenses to conspiracy charges is that there was no agreement between the defendant and the other parties involved. Without an agreement to commit a crime, there can be no conspiracy.

- **Dispute of Alleged Agreement**: The defense can argue that there was no formal or informal agreement to commit any illegal act. Sometimes, individuals may discuss committing a crime, but that does not mean they formed a conspiracy.
- **Misunderstanding or Miscommunication**: In some cases, the so-called "conspiracy" may have been a misunderstanding or miscommunication. For example, if someone was joking or making idle talk about committing a crime, it does not constitute an actual conspiracy.
- **Lack of Evidence**: If the prosecution cannot provide credible evidence that a clear agreement was made (such as signed documents, text messages, or recorded conversations), the defense can argue that no conspiracy existed.

B. Lack of Intent (No Intent to Commit the Crime)

Even if there is an agreement, a defendant must have the intent to commit the illegal act for a conspiracy to be valid. Without intent, there is no conspiracy.

- **No Knowledge of the Plan**: A defendant can argue that they did not know about the criminal purpose or did not intend to participate in the crime. For instance, a defendant may have been present during discussions or actions but had no intention of following through with the crime.

- **Abandonment of the Conspiracy**: If the defendant, after becoming aware of the criminal plan, took steps to withdraw or stop the conspiracy from being carried out (such as alerting authorities or trying to prevent the crime), they may be able to argue that they had no intent to commit the crime.

C. Withdrawal from the Conspiracy

If a defendant can prove that they withdrew from the conspiracy before any illegal act occurred, they may be able to avoid liability. Withdrawal must be shown to be voluntary and with the intent to abandon the criminal plan.

- **Notice of Withdrawal**: The defendant must notify the other parties involved in the conspiracy of their decision to withdraw, and in many cases, they must take affirmative steps to thwart the crime from being completed.
- **Ceasing Participation**: The defense can argue that the defendant ceased participation in the conspiracy well before any overt act was carried out and did nothing to further the crime.

D. Insufficient Evidence (Lack of Proof)

In some cases, the prosecution may have little or no direct evidence linking the defendant to the conspiracy. This can provide an opportunity for the defense to argue that the case lacks merit.

- **No Evidence of an Overt Act**: If the prosecution cannot prove that at least one overt act was taken in furtherance of the conspiracy (a step toward committing the crime), the defendant may have grounds to have the charges dismissed.

- **Circumstantial Evidence**: Conspiracy cases often rely on circumstantial evidence, such as phone calls, emails, or meetings. However, circumstantial evidence can be weak, and the defense can argue that the prosecution's evidence does not establish a solid case of conspiracy.
- **Weak or Unreliable Witnesses**: If the prosecution's case is based on testimony from unreliable or compromised witnesses, such as informants or accomplices with their own motivations to lie, the defense can challenge the credibility of these witnesses.

E. Lack of an Overt Act (If Applicable)

Some conspiracy charges require proof of at least one overt act—an action taken by a conspirator in furtherance of the conspiracy. If no such act is shown, the conspiracy charge may not be valid.

- **Failure to Prove an Overt Act**: The prosecution must prove that something concrete happened to move the conspiracy toward execution. If the prosecution fails to prove that any overt act occurred (e.g., purchase of equipment, planning meetings, or attempts to carry out the crime), the defense can argue that there was no real conspiracy.

F. Defective Indictment or Faulty Jury Instructions

In some cases, a conspiracy conviction can be challenged on procedural grounds, such as errors in how the case was handled or how the law was explained to the jury.

- **Defective Indictment**: The defense may argue that the indictment was improperly drafted, failing to include essential elements of the conspiracy charge.

- **Improper Jury Instructions**: If the judge gave incorrect instructions to the jury regarding what constitutes a conspiracy, the defendant may have grounds to appeal the verdict.

3. Specific Conspiracy Defenses in Special Cases

A. Conspiracy to Commit Drug Trafficking

In drug conspiracy cases, the defendant may argue that they were unaware of the specific nature of the drugs involved, did not know the full scope of the operation, or were not directly involved in the trafficking.

B. Conspiracy in Fraud Cases

For fraud-related conspiracies, the defense may argue that the defendant did not engage in any fraudulent activity or that the defendant had no intent to defraud anyone. Additionally, the defense may challenge the financial evidence provided by the prosecution.

C. Conspiracy to Commit Violent Crimes

In conspiracy cases involving violent crimes, the defense can argue that the defendant was never part of the plot or had no intention to cause harm. Lack of intent to commit the violent act can often play a crucial role in these cases.

4. The Importance of Expert Legal Representation

Beating conspiracy charges requires thorough knowledge of the law and a strategic approach to litigation. A skilled criminal defense attorney can help challenge the prosecution's evidence, identify weaknesses in the case, and present a compelling defense. They can also work to uncover any mistakes or improper procedures that could lead to a case dismissal or reduction in charges.

5. Possible Outcomes

Depending on the strength of the defense, there are several possible outcomes for a conspiracy charge:

- **Dismissal of Charges**: If the defense can successfully argue that no conspiracy existed or that the evidence is insufficient, the charges may be dropped.
- **Reduction of Charges**: In some cases, conspiracy charges may be reduced to lesser offenses or resolved through plea negotiations.
- **Not Guilty Verdict**: If the jury is not convinced beyond a reasonable doubt, the defendant may be acquitted and the charges will be dropped.
- **Conviction with Lenient Sentencing**: In some cases, the defendant may be convicted but can still argue for a reduced sentence, especially if they withdrew from the conspiracy early or had no intent to commit the crime.

6. Conclusion

Conspiracy charges are serious but not insurmountable. With the right defense strategies—such as proving a lack of agreement, disputing the evidence, establishing withdrawal, or challenging the overt act requirement—defendants have multiple avenues to fight and potentially beat the charges. An experienced attorney can guide you through the complex legal process and help protect your rights, working toward the best possible outcome in your conspiracy case.

CHAPTER THIRTY SIX.

BEATING A GRAND THEFT AUTO CHARGE

INTRODUCTION

Grand Theft Auto (GTA) is a serious criminal charge involving the unlawful taking of a vehicle with the intent to permanently deprive the owner of it. GTA is considered a felony in most jurisdictions, and it comes with severe penalties, including lengthy prison sentences, fines, and permanent criminal records. Defending against a GTA charge requires a strategic approach, focusing on dismantling the prosecution's evidence, challenging the intent, and raising reasonable doubts. This chapter outlines several defense strategies for beating a Grand Theft Auto charge and provides an in-depth understanding of how to fight the case effectively.

1. Understanding Grand Theft Auto Charges

Before delving into the defenses, it's essential to understand the elements of a Grand Theft Auto charge:

- **Unlawful Taking**: The prosecution must prove that the defendant took or drove a vehicle without the consent of the owner.
- **Intent to Permanently Deprive**: The defendant must have intended to permanently deprive the owner of their vehicle. If the defendant only intended to temporarily use the car (such as borrowing it), this may affect the severity of the charge.
- **Knowledge**: The defendant must have known or reasonably should have known that the vehicle was stolen or that they lacked the owner's consent to take it.

A successful defense will often hinge on challenging one or more of these elements. Below are the most common defenses used to fight Grand Theft Auto charges.

2. Common Defenses Against Grand Theft Auto Charges

A. Lack of Intent to Permanently Deprive

In a GTA case, proving the defendant's intent is crucial. If the defense can show that the defendant did not intend to permanently deprive the owner of their vehicle, the charge may be downgraded or even dismissed.

- **Temporary Use or Borrowing**: The defendant may argue that they only intended to borrow the car and had no plans to permanently keep it. This can significantly reduce the severity of the charge. If the defendant intended to return the car, it may not meet the definition of "grand theft."
- **Mistake of Fact**: If the defendant believed they had the owner's permission to use the vehicle, even if they were mistaken, this can be a valid defense. A mistake about the facts (e.g., thinking the car was theirs or that they had permission to use it) can negate the intent to steal.

B. Lack of Knowledge

In some cases, the defendant may not have known the vehicle was stolen or that they lacked the owner's consent.

- **No Knowledge of the Vehicle's Status**: If the defendant didn't know the car was stolen and had no reason to believe it was, the defense may argue that they lacked the necessary knowledge to be guilty of GTA.
- **Involuntary or Unaware Use**: Sometimes, the defendant may have been under duress, manipulated, or coerced into using the vehicle without being aware of its status. For example, if the defendant was tricked into believing the car belonged to someone they trusted, they may have a defense.

C. False Identification or Mistaken Identity

The defense can argue that the defendant was wrongly identified as the person who took the vehicle, or that the defendant wasn't involved in the theft at all.

- **Alibi Defense**: If the defendant can provide an alibi that places them elsewhere when the theft occurred, they may be able to demonstrate that they couldn't have committed the crime.
- **Witness Testimony**: Eyewitnesses or video footage may support the defense's argument that the defendant wasn't the person involved in the theft. It may also show that the defendant had no involvement in the vehicle's disappearance.

D. Lack of Sufficient Evidence

If the prosecution cannot produce enough evidence to prove the elements of the charge beyond a reasonable doubt, the defense can request that the case be dismissed or argue for acquittal.

- **No Direct Evidence**: The defense can argue that there is no direct evidence linking the defendant to the theft. For example, if there is no physical evidence (like fingerprints, DNA, or surveillance footage), and the prosecution relies on weak or circumstantial evidence, the defense may challenge the case.
- **Improper Handling of Evidence**: The defense can argue that the police mishandled or failed to properly collect evidence, which may result in the dismissal of the case.

E. Illegal Search and Seizure

If the vehicle was seized without a proper search warrant or probable cause, the evidence may be inadmissible in court.

- **Unlawful Search**: If the defendant's vehicle was searched without consent, a warrant, or probable cause, the defense can file a motion to suppress the evidence obtained from the illegal search. If the vehicle or any related evidence is excluded from the trial, the prosecution may not have enough to proceed with the case.

F. Involuntary Actions

In certain cases, the defendant may argue that they were forced to take the vehicle, or that they were unaware of the theft due to intoxication or another involuntary state.

- **Coercion or Duress**: If the defendant was threatened with harm or was under duress to take the vehicle, the defense may argue that they were forced into committing the act and had no choice.
- **Intoxication or Mental Impairment**: If the defendant was intoxicated or suffering from a mental illness at the time of the offense, it may impact their ability to form the necessary intent to commit grand theft auto.

3. Challenging the Prosecution's Evidence

Another important aspect of defending against a Grand Theft Auto charge is to challenge the prosecution's evidence. The defense can argue that the evidence is weak, incomplete, or unreliable.

- **Weak Circumstantial Evidence**: In many GTA cases, the prosecution may rely heavily on circumstantial evidence, such as the defendant being in possession of a stolen vehicle. However, the defense can challenge whether the evidence is strong enough to prove guilt beyond a reasonable doubt.
- **Confession Issues**: If the defendant confessed to the crime, the defense can challenge the circumstances under which the confession was made. For instance, was the confession coerced? Was the defendant

informed of their rights (Miranda warning) before speaking to the police?

4. Plea Bargaining and Reduced Charges

In some cases, even if the evidence seems strong, the defense may be able to negotiate a plea deal or have the charge reduced to a lesser offense.

- **Plea Bargain for Lesser Charges**: If the evidence is difficult to overcome, the defendant may work with their attorney to negotiate a plea deal for a lesser charge, such as joyriding, which often carries less severe penalties than grand theft auto.
- **Sentencing Reduction**: In cases where the defendant accepts responsibility or shows remorse, the defense may be able to negotiate a reduction in the sentence, such as probation instead of prison time.

5. The Role of Legal Counsel

Given the complexity of Grand Theft Auto cases and the serious penalties associated with them, it is essential to have an experienced criminal defense attorney. A skilled lawyer will:

- Review the evidence and investigate the facts thoroughly.
- Identify weaknesses in the prosecution's case and challenge them.
- Develop and present effective defense strategies.
- Negotiate plea deals or sentencing reductions if necessary.

A criminal defense lawyer will also guide you through the legal process and ensure that your rights are protected at all stages of the case.

6. Possible Outcomes

The possible outcomes of a Grand Theft Auto case depend on the strength of the defense, the evidence presented, and the overall circumstances:

- **Dismissal of Charges**: If the defense is successful in showing that the evidence is insufficient or that the defendant did not commit the crime, the charges may be dismissed.
- **Acquittal**: If the jury or judge is unconvinced by the prosecution's case, the defendant may be found not guilty and released.
- **Conviction with Reduced Sentences**: In cases where the defendant is convicted, they may face a reduced sentence, especially if they show cooperation or offer a valid defense.

7. Conclusion

A Grand Theft Auto charge is serious, but with the right defense, it is possible to beat the case or have it significantly reduced. Whether it's proving a lack of intent, challenging the evidence, or demonstrating a mistake of fact, there are several legal avenues to explore in defending against a GTA charge. A knowledgeable criminal defense attorney will be instrumental in helping you navigate these strategies and achieve the best possible outcome in your case.

CHAPTER THIRTY SEVEN.

BEATING A GRAND THEFT CHARGE

INTRODUCTION

Grand theft is a serious crime that involves the unlawful taking of property with the intent to permanently deprive the owner of it. Depending on the value of the property stolen, grand theft can be classified as a felony, often carrying significant penalties, including long prison sentences, heavy fines, and permanent criminal records. Defending against a grand theft charge requires a strategic approach to challenge the prosecution's evidence, establish reasonable doubt, and possibly negotiate for reduced charges. This chapter outlines various defense strategies to help individuals facing grand theft charges and provides insights into how a defense lawyer might approach the case.

1. Understanding Grand Theft Charges

Grand theft is typically defined as the unlawful taking of property valued above a certain amount, depending on jurisdiction. The specific threshold for what constitutes "grand theft" varies by state, but it generally involves property worth $1,000 or more. In some states, the threshold can be as low as $500.

In order to convict someone of grand theft, the prosecution must prove the following elements:

- **Unlawful Taking**: The property was taken without the owner's consent.
- **Intent to Permanently Deprive**: The defendant intended to permanently deprive the owner of their property.
- **Value of the Property**: The property taken must meet the value threshold set by law.

- **Knowledge**: The defendant must have known that they were unlawfully taking the property.

2. Defenses Against Grand Theft Charges

Several common defense strategies can be employed to beat a grand theft charge. Some of these defenses may lead to an acquittal, while others may help reduce the severity of the charges.

A. Lack of Intent to Permanently Deprive

A key element of grand theft is the defendant's intent to permanently deprive the owner of their property. If the defense can establish that the defendant did not intend to steal the property or only intended to temporarily use it, the charges may be reduced or dismissed.

- **Borrowing vs. Stealing**: The defense may argue that the defendant only intended to borrow the property with the intent to return it. A defendant may have taken the property without intending to permanently deprive the owner, which would not meet the criteria for grand theft.
- **Temporary Use or Misunderstanding**: In some cases, the defendant may argue that they mistakenly believed they had permission to use the property or misunderstood the ownership of the property, leading to the theft charge.

B. Lack of Knowledge

In certain situations, the defendant may not have known the property was stolen or did not realize that they lacked the owner's consent.

- **Innocent Possession**: If the defendant was unaware that the property was stolen, they may not have the knowledge required for a grand theft charge. If someone gave the defendant the property to use or sell, and the defendant didn't know it was stolen, this could be a valid defense.

- **Mistaken Belief**: The defendant may argue that they honestly believed the property belonged to them or that they had permission to take it. This mistake of fact can be a valid defense if it negates the defendant's intent to steal.

C. False Identification or Mistaken Identity

Mistaken identity or wrongful identification of the defendant can be used as a defense. If the defendant was wrongly accused or if the evidence does not conclusively link them to the theft, the charges may be dismissed or reduced.

- **Alibi**: The defendant may provide an alibi proving that they were not at the scene of the crime when the theft occurred. This could include witnesses, receipts, or other evidence placing the defendant elsewhere.
- **Witnesses and Surveillance**: If surveillance footage or eyewitness testimony shows that someone else committed the theft or that the defendant was not involved, the defense may argue mistaken identity.

D. Insufficient Evidence

If the prosecution cannot present sufficient evidence to prove all elements of grand theft beyond a reasonable doubt, the defense can argue for a dismissal or acquittal.

- **No Direct Evidence**: In some cases, the prosecution may rely on circumstantial evidence, such as the defendant being in possession of stolen property. However, circumstantial evidence can be weak, and the defense can argue that it does not prove the defendant's guilt.

- **Lack of Ownership or Value**: The prosecution must prove that the value of the stolen property meets the threshold for grand theft. If the value of the property is less than the required amount, the charges could be reduced to petty theft, which is a less severe crime.

E. Illegal Search and Seizure

If law enforcement obtained evidence of the theft through an illegal search and seizure, the evidence may be inadmissible in court. If the property was seized without a valid warrant or probable cause, the defense may file a motion to suppress the evidence.

- **Violation of Rights**: If the defendant's constitutional rights were violated during the investigation or arrest (e.g., the police conducted a warrantless search of the defendant's home or car), the defense may argue that the evidence should be excluded from the trial.

F. Coercion or Duress

In certain cases, the defendant may argue that they were forced to commit the theft due to threats of harm or duress. If the defendant was coerced or threatened by another individual into committing the theft, this could serve as a defense.

- **Threats of Harm**: If the defendant was threatened with violence or harm to themselves or a loved one unless they committed the theft, the defense may argue that the defendant had no choice but to comply.

3. Challenging the Prosecution's Evidence

The prosecution must prove its case beyond a reasonable doubt. If the defense can create doubt about the reliability of the evidence, the case may be dismissed or result in an acquittal. Below are some methods of challenging the prosecution's evidence:

- **Questioning the Chain of Custody**: If the stolen property was seized by law enforcement, the defense can challenge whether it was properly handled and whether it can be reliably traced back to the defendant.
- **Challenging Eyewitness Testimony**: Eyewitnesses can be mistaken, and the defense can argue that the witnesses misidentified the defendant or made inaccurate observations.
- **Forensic Evidence**: The defense may challenge forensic evidence, such as fingerprints or DNA, by showing that it was improperly collected or does not conclusively link the defendant to the theft.

4. Plea Bargaining and Reduced Charges

In some cases, the evidence against the defendant may be overwhelming, but the defendant may still have an opportunity to negotiate a plea deal. A skilled defense attorney can help the defendant achieve a more favorable outcome through plea bargaining.

- **Plea to Lesser Charges**: If the evidence of grand theft is strong, the defense may negotiate for the defendant to plead guilty to a lesser offense, such as petty theft. Petty theft carries less severe penalties, and this can significantly reduce the defendant's sentence.
- **Sentencing Negotiations**: In cases where a conviction is likely, the defense may seek a reduced sentence by negotiating with the prosecution. This can include probation, community service, or rehabilitation programs instead of jail time.

5. The Role of a Criminal Defense Attorney

Given the complexity of grand theft charges and the potential penalties involved, it is crucial to have an experienced criminal defense attorney to represent you. A skilled attorney will:

- Analyze the evidence and investigate the circumstances surrounding the theft.
- Identify weaknesses in the prosecution's case.
- Develop a strategic defense tailored to the facts of the case.
- Negotiate for reduced charges or a favorable plea deal if necessary.
- Protect the defendant's rights and ensure a fair trial.

6. Possible Outcomes

The possible outcomes of a grand theft case will depend on the strength of the defense, the evidence presented, and the circumstances surrounding the charge. Possible outcomes include:

- **Case Dismissal**: If the defense can show that there is no evidence to support the charges, the case may be dismissed.
- **Acquittal**: If the jury or judge finds that the prosecution has not proven the defendant's guilt beyond a reasonable doubt, the defendant may be acquitted.
- **Conviction with Reduced Sentences**: If the defendant is convicted, the defense may be able to negotiate for a lesser sentence or alternative sentencing options, such as probation.

7. Conclusion

A grand theft charge is serious, but with a comprehensive defense strategy, it is possible to beat the charge or have it reduced to a lesser offense. Whether the defense focuses on lack of intent, mistaken identity, insufficient evidence, or challenging the prosecution's case, there are multiple avenues to explore. Having an experienced criminal defense attorney is essential for navigating the complexities of grand theft charges and securing the best possible outcome.

CHAPTER THIRTY EIGHT.

APPEALING YOUR CASE: DIRECT AND POST-CONVICTION

INTRODUCTION

Being convicted of a crime is often just the beginning of a lengthy legal process. If you believe that your conviction was unjust or that errors were made during your trial, you have the right to appeal. An appeal is a legal process in which a higher court reviews the decisions made in your case to determine if there were legal errors that affected the outcome. This chapter will focus on the two main types of appeals in criminal cases: **direct appeals** and **post-conviction appeals**.

1. Understanding the Appeal Process

Before delving into the specifics of direct and post-conviction appeals, it's essential to understand the appeal process itself. An appeal does not involve a new trial with new evidence. Instead, it involves the review of legal procedures, decisions, and actions taken during the original trial. Appeals are based on legal arguments that the lower court made significant errors that impacted the fairness of the trial or conviction.

There are two primary types of appeals in criminal cases:

- **Direct Appeal**: This occurs after a conviction and challenges the judgment or legal procedures in the trial. It is typically filed immediately after sentencing.
- **Post-Conviction Appeal**: This occurs after a direct appeal has been denied, or if the defendant could not raise certain issues on appeal. Post-conviction relief may be sought through a motion to vacate the conviction, a writ of habeas corpus, or other methods.

2. Direct Appeal

A direct appeal is an appeal filed right after conviction and sentencing, challenging the legality of the trial itself. Direct appeals focus on whether the trial court made legal errors that significantly impacted the defendant's rights, resulting in an unfair conviction.

A. Grounds for Direct Appeal

There are several grounds on which you can base a direct appeal. Some of the most common include:

1. **Errors in Jury Instructions**: If the trial judge gave improper instructions to the jury, this can lead to a flawed verdict. For example, incorrect explanations about how to evaluate evidence or misunderstandings about the law can cause a conviction to be overturned.
2. **Errors in Admitting or Excluding Evidence**: If the trial court wrongly admitted or excluded certain evidence, it can influence the trial's outcome. Examples include the use of illegally obtained evidence (violating your Fourth Amendment rights) or the exclusion of crucial evidence that would have supported your defense.
3. **Ineffective Assistance of Counsel**: You have the right to competent legal representation during your trial. If your defense attorney's performance was inadequate, such as failing to call important witnesses or providing incorrect legal advice, you may be able to challenge your conviction on these grounds.
4. **Prosecutorial Misconduct**: If the prosecutor acted improperly, such as withholding evidence (Brady violation) or engaging in unethical behavior, the appeal may be based on prosecutorial misconduct.
5. **Errors in the Sentencing**: If the sentencing was too harsh, violated sentencing laws, or involved a miscalculation of your sentence, this can be grounds for an appeal. For example, if you were sentenced to a

penalty beyond the legal limits for the offense, the appeal could seek to reduce the sentence.

6. **Violation of Constitutional Rights**: Any violations of your constitutional rights during the trial—such as unlawful search and seizure, coerced confessions, or double jeopardy—can form the basis for a direct appeal.

B. The Process of a Direct Appeal

- **Filing the Notice of Appeal**: The first step is to file a "notice of appeal," which must be done within a specific time frame after sentencing (often 30 days). Failure to file within the designated time frame could forfeit the right to appeal.
- **Appellate Brief**: After the notice of appeal is filed, the appellant (the party filing the appeal) must submit a written brief. This brief presents the legal arguments for why the conviction or sentence should be overturned, supported by citations to the law and the trial record.
- **The Response**: The prosecution will typically file a response brief arguing why the conviction should be upheld. Both sides may also file reply briefs addressing the other's arguments.
- **Oral Argument**: Some appeals may involve oral arguments before a panel of judges. During this stage, the defendant's attorney and the prosecutor have the opportunity to present their arguments directly to the appellate court. The judges may ask questions to clarify points raised in the briefs.
- **The Appellate Court Decision**: After reviewing the briefs and hearing oral arguments (if applicable), the appellate court will issue its decision. This decision may result in:
    - **Affirmation**: The conviction is upheld.
    - **Reversal**: The conviction is overturned, and a new trial or different outcome may occur.

- **Remand**: The case is sent back to the lower court for further proceedings or reconsideration.

C. Timeliness and Legal Representation

It's crucial to have legal representation from an experienced appellate attorney when filing a direct appeal. Appellate lawyers are familiar with the legal standards and procedural requirements involved in the appeal process. Timeliness is critical; if an appeal is not filed on time, the defendant may lose the opportunity to appeal the case.

3. Post-Conviction Appeal

A post-conviction appeal is filed after a direct appeal has been denied, or if certain issues were not raised during the direct appeal. These appeals focus on new evidence, legal errors not previously considered, or claims that the defendant's rights were violated after the trial was concluded.

A. Grounds for Post-Conviction Relief

Post-conviction relief typically involves raising new issues or challenges to the conviction. Some common grounds for post-conviction appeals include:

1. **Newly Discovered Evidence**: If new evidence has come to light that was not available during the trial and could have changed the outcome, you may file for post-conviction relief. This could include DNA evidence, new witness testimony, or other compelling proof that the defendant was wrongfully convicted.
2. **Ineffective Assistance of Counsel**: If your trial attorney was ineffective and this caused an unfair trial or conviction, you may raise this claim in a post-conviction motion. This could include failure to investigate certain aspects of the case or failure to object to critical errors in the trial.

3. **Innocence**: Some jurisdictions allow post-conviction relief based on claims of innocence. If new evidence proves that the defendant is innocent or that they did not commit the crime, this may lead to a new trial or a reversal of the conviction.
4. **Violation of Constitutional Rights**: If constitutional violations occurred during the trial that were not raised in the direct appeal, you may bring them up in post-conviction motions. Examples include issues with jury selection, racial discrimination, or improper conduct by the judge or prosecutor.
5. **Illegal Sentence**: If you believe the sentence imposed was illegal (e.g., it exceeds the statutory limits or violates double jeopardy), you may seek post-conviction relief to have the sentence reduced or vacated.

B. The Process of Post-Conviction Relief

The process for post-conviction relief differs from a direct appeal. The steps typically include:

1. **Filing a Motion**: The defendant files a motion for post-conviction relief, explaining the reasons why they believe the conviction should be overturned or the sentence reduced. This motion may be filed with the trial court or through a higher court, depending on the jurisdiction.

2. **Review of Motion**: The court will review the motion, and in some cases, a hearing may be held. The defense will present evidence supporting the claim, and the prosecution will respond.

3. **Possible Outcomes**: The court may grant the post-conviction relief, which could result in a new trial, a reduced sentence, or the vacating of the conviction. If the motion is denied, the defendant may have further options for appeal.

4. **Appeal**: If post-conviction relief is denied, the defendant may still have the option to appeal the decision to a higher court.

4. The Importance of Legal Representation

Whether you are filing a direct appeal or post-conviction motion, it is crucial to have skilled legal counsel. Appellate attorneys specialize in presenting cases before appellate courts and navigating the post-conviction process. They can identify legal errors, raise compelling arguments, and guide you through the complex appeal procedures.

5. Conclusion

Appealing a criminal conviction, whether through a direct appeal or post-conviction relief, offers a critical opportunity to challenge wrongful convictions and seek justice. While the process can be complex and time-consuming, with the right legal strategies and representation, there is a chance to reverse the conviction or reduce the sentence. Understanding your rights and having a skilled appellate attorney is key to increasing the likelihood of a favorable outcome.

CHAPTER THIRTY NINE

Beating a **trafficking in methamphetamine** charge is a difficult but not impossible task. The success of your defense strategy will depend on several factors, including the strength of the prosecution's case, the circumstances surrounding the arrest, and any potential legal or procedural issues in the case. Below are some potential legal defenses and strategies that could be used to fight or reduce charges in a **meth trafficking** case:

---

1. Challenging the Legality of the Search and Seizure

One of the most effective defenses in a drug trafficking case is to challenge the legality of the search and seizure that led to the discovery of the drugs. Under the **Fourth Amendment**, law enforcement officers are required to have a warrant or probable cause to conduct a search.

Case Law: *Mapp v. Ohio*, 367 U.S. 643 (1961)

- **Ruling**: The U.S. Supreme Court ruled that evidence obtained in violation of the Fourth Amendment is inadmissible in state courts. This ruling established the **exclusionary rule**, which can prevent illegally obtained evidence from being used against a defendant.
- **Defense**: If the police conducted a search without probable cause, without a warrant, or exceeded the scope of a valid search warrant, the evidence against you may be inadmissible. If the prosecution's evidence is suppressed, it could weaken their case significantly.

---

2. Lack of Knowledge or Intent

In a trafficking case, the prosecution must prove that you knew the methamphetamine was in your possession and that you intended to distribute or traffic the drug. If the prosecution cannot prove your knowledge or intent, the charges may be reduced or dismissed.

Key Case: *United States v. Lopez*, 514 U.S. 549 (1995)

- **Ruling**: The U.S. Supreme Court held that the government must prove that a defendant knowingly and intentionally engaged in criminal conduct, especially in drug-related cases.
- **Defense**: If you did not know about the methamphetamine or did not have the intent to distribute it, you could argue that you did not have the necessary mental state to be convicted of trafficking. For example, if the drugs were planted or if you were unaware of their presence in your vehicle or property, it could be used as a defense.

---

3. Challenging the Quantity of Methamphetamine

Drug trafficking charges often depend on the amount of the drug involved. In many states, the penalties for drug trafficking are based on specific weight thresholds. If the prosecution cannot prove that you were trafficking the requisite amount of methamphetamine, the charge could be reduced to a less severe drug possession charge.

Key Case: *United States v. Beasley*, 221 F.3d 1036 (9th Cir. 2000)

- **Ruling**: The court ruled that the government must provide sufficient evidence to establish the weight of the controlled substance involved in the trafficking charge. If the government cannot demonstrate that the weight exceeds the statutory threshold, the conviction for trafficking can be overturned or reduced.
- **Defense**: If the prosecution cannot prove the amount of methamphetamine exceeds the threshold for trafficking, the charge

may be reduced to possession with intent to distribute, which carries a lesser sentence. You may argue that the amount of methamphetamine found was not enough to qualify for trafficking.

4. Arguing Entrapment

Entrapment is a legal defense where you argue that law enforcement officers induced you to commit a crime you would not have otherwise committed. This defense is typically used when undercover officers or informants pressure or coerce the defendant into trafficking methamphetamine.

Key Case: *Jacobson v. United States,* 503 U.S. 540 (1992)

- **Ruling**: The Supreme Court ruled that a defendant cannot be convicted of a crime if they were entrapped by law enforcement. The court found that if the defendant was not predisposed to committing the crime, the government could not create the crime through entrapment.
- **Defense**: If you were persuaded or pressured by law enforcement officers, undercover agents, or informants to traffic methamphetamine when you otherwise had no intention of doing so, you may have an entrapment defense. This would require showing that law enforcement agents instigated the crime.

5. Challenging the Chain of Custody

In drug trafficking cases, the prosecution must establish that the drugs found in your possession were the same drugs that were seized and tested. If there is a break in the **chain of custody**, meaning the drugs were handled or stored improperly during the investigation, it could call into question the validity of the evidence.

Key Case: *State v. Hines*, 2006 WL 2536687 (Ark. 2006)

- **Ruling**: The court ruled that a failure to maintain an unbroken chain of custody of evidence could lead to the exclusion of that evidence.
- **Defense**: If the prosecution cannot demonstrate an unbroken chain of custody for the methamphetamine evidence, you can argue that the evidence should be excluded. Without this critical evidence, the case against you may collapse.

---

6. Insufficient Evidence of Intent to Distribute

In a trafficking case, the prosecution must prove not only that you possessed methamphetamine but that you intended to distribute it. If the prosecution cannot prove intent to distribute, the charge can be reduced to simple possession.

Key Case: *United States v. Johnson*, 61 F.3d 1493 (11th Cir. 1995)

- **Ruling**: The court held that the government must show more than mere possession of a controlled substance to convict a defendant of trafficking; the evidence must also demonstrate intent to distribute.
- **Defense**: If there is no evidence to suggest that you intended to distribute or sell the methamphetamine (e.g., no drug paraphernalia, large sums of cash, or involvement in a distribution network), you could argue that the charge should be reduced to possession, which carries a lesser penalty.

---

7. Cooperation with Authorities or Voluntary Surrender

If you voluntarily surrender to authorities or cooperate with law enforcement in the investigation, it may be possible to secure a favorable plea deal or reduced charges. Cooperation often leads to more lenient sentences in exchange for valuable information or assistance in the prosecution of others involved in the drug trade.

Key Case: *United States v. Koon*, 34 F.3d 1416 (9th Cir. 1994)

- **Ruling**: The court upheld a reduced sentence for a defendant who cooperated with law enforcement by providing information about a larger drug operation. Cooperation can sometimes result in a reduction in charges or a more lenient sentence.
- **Defense**: If you are facing a methamphetamine trafficking charge, cooperating with law enforcement or offering information about a larger drug operation might lead to a reduction in charges or a more favorable plea deal.

Conclusion

Successfully beating a **methamphetamine trafficking** charge is challenging, but a well-crafted defense strategy can make a significant difference. Key defenses include challenging the legality of the search and seizure, disputing the amount of drugs involved, arguing lack of knowledge or intent, raising an entrapment defense, challenging the chain of custody, and questioning whether the evidence supports an intent to distribute. Additionally, cooperating with authorities could potentially lead to a reduction in charges. A skilled defense attorney can tailor these strategies based on the specific facts of your case to maximize your chances of success.

CHAPTER FORTY.

BEATING ROBBERY AND ROBBERY BY SUDDEN SNATCHING.

These charges can be complex, but it is possible if you employ a sound legal defense strategy. The key is to challenge the evidence, argue lack of intent, or demonstrate that the actions did not meet the legal definitions of robbery or snatching. Here are several potential defenses to consider:

1. Challenging the Evidence (Lack of Identification)

In many robbery and robbery by sudden snatching cases, the prosecution's case heavily relies on the victim's identification of the defendant. If the victim is uncertain or makes a mistake during the identification process, or if there is no other evidence linking you to the crime, the case may be weak.

Case Law: *United States v. Wade*, 388 U.S. 218 (1967)

- **Ruling**: The Supreme Court held that the defendant's right to counsel is violated if the identification process is suggestive or conducted without their lawyer present.
- **Defense**: If the identification procedure was suggestive, such as a line-up or photo array that unfairly singled you out, you could challenge the identification and argue that the evidence should be excluded. Without a clear, reliable identification, the prosecution may not have a strong case.

---

2. Alibi Defense

If you can provide a credible alibi (i.e., you were elsewhere when the robbery occurred), you can argue that you could not have committed the crime. To strengthen this defense, you may need witnesses, surveillance footage, or other forms of proof to support your claim.

Key Case: *People v. Harris*, 1989 (California)

- **Ruling**: A defendant who presents a credible alibi, supported by witnesses or other evidence, can establish a reasonable doubt about their involvement in the robbery.
- **Defense**: If you have evidence that you were at a different location at the time of the robbery, such as phone records, video footage, or witness testimony, you can argue that you could not have committed the crime.

---

3. Lack of Intent (No Theft or Use of Force)

Robbery typically requires that the defendant used force, intimidation, or threats to take property from another person. **Robbery by sudden snatching** involves taking property from a person without consent, often by force or surprise.

If you can argue that there was no force used or that you did not take anything with the intent to permanently deprive the victim of it, you may be able to reduce the charge.

Key Case: *People v. Thomas*, 2007 (Michigan)

- **Ruling**: The court ruled that robbery requires evidence that the defendant used force, fear, or intimidation in taking the property. In the absence of force or fear, a robbery conviction may be reduced to theft.
- **Defense**: If the prosecution cannot prove that you used force or threats to take property or that you did not intend to permanently deprive the

victim of the property, you could argue that the charge should be reduced to **theft** or **petty theft**, which carries lesser penalties.

---

4. Disputing the Use of Force (Lack of Physical Confrontation)

In a **robbery by sudden snatching** case, it is essential that the prosecution proves that the defendant used force to take the property. If the prosecution cannot prove that you used physical force or violence against the victim, you may be able to challenge the charge.

Case Law: *State v. Duest*, 462 So. 2d 446 (1985)

- **Ruling**: The Florida Supreme Court clarified that **robbery by sudden snatching** involves using force to take property from another person, but that force does not need to involve physical violence. Even a light tugging of property can constitute force under this statute.
- **Defense**: You could argue that there was no sufficient "force" involved to constitute robbery or snatching. For example, if you grabbed an item that was easily snatched or were involved in an accidental incident, the force element may be insufficient for a conviction.

---

5. Mistaken Identity

Mistaken identity is another common defense in robbery cases. If there was a lack of clear physical description of the suspect or an error in how the victim or witnesses identified you, you could argue that you were wrongly accused.

Case Law: *State v. Robinson*, 1990 (Florida)

- **Ruling**: The court held that mistaken identification can be a valid defense when there is doubt about whether the defendant was the individual involved in the robbery.
- **Defense**: If the witness or victim did not have a clear view of the suspect during the robbery, or if there was a significant lapse of time between the crime and the identification, you could argue that the identification was faulty, and the case lacks sufficient evidence.

---

6. No Snatching (Property Never Taken)

In a **robbery by sudden snatching** case, the prosecution must prove that the property was taken from the victim's person, without consent, and by force or surprise. If the property was never successfully taken, or if the alleged victim was mistaken in claiming the property was snatched, it could undermine the charge.

Key Case: *People v. Horton*, 1956 (California)

- **Ruling**: The court ruled that no robbery can occur if the property is not physically taken from the victim or if there is no evidence that the property was forcibly removed.
- **Defense**: You could argue that the property was never taken from the victim's person, or if it was, it was not by means of force or snatching.

---

7. Self-Defense (Justification)

If you were acting in self-defense, or to protect yourself or others from imminent harm, you might be able to claim **justification** for your actions. If, for example, you were accused of using force in a robbery, but your intent was to prevent harm to yourself or others, self-defense may be a valid defense.

Case Law: *People v. Sawyer*, 1984 (California)

- **Ruling**: The court ruled that a defendant can raise the defense of self-defense if they can prove they acted in reasonable fear of imminent harm and used no more force than necessary to protect themselves.
- **Defense**: If you were involved in a confrontation where you acted to defend yourself or others, and the force used was reasonable under the circumstances, you could argue that the use of force was justified.

---

8. Reduced Charges (Plea Deal)

If the evidence against you is strong but you have mitigating factors, such as a lack of prior criminal history or a minor role in the crime, you may be able to negotiate a plea deal for a reduced charge, such as theft or simple assault.

Key Case: *Bordenkircher v. Hayes*, 434 U.S. 357 (1978)

- **Ruling**: The U.S. Supreme Court held that plea bargaining is a constitutional right, and defendants may accept offers to plead guilty to lesser charges.
- **Defense**: If you're facing a robbery charge, your attorney may be able to negotiate a plea deal with the prosecution to reduce the charge to theft or another lesser offense, which carries a lighter penalty.

Conclusion

Beating **robbery** or **robbery by sudden snatching** charges requires a strategic defense approach. Key defenses include challenging the evidence, disputing the use of force, arguing mistaken identity, presenting an alibi, or showing that there was no intent to permanently deprive the victim of property. Additionally, you may be able to negotiate a plea deal if the evidence against you is strong. A skilled criminal defense attorney will help assess your case, identify weaknesses in the prosecution's argument, and choose the best strategy for achieving a favorable outcome.

CHAPTER FORTY ONE.

BEAT THE FENTANYL CASE.

Beating charges related to **fentanyl** found in **pressed pills** is a difficult but not impossible task. The key to success lies in a variety of defense strategies that can be applied depending on the facts of the case, including challenging the evidence, disputing intent, and attacking the methods used in the investigation. Here are some possible defense strategies to consider:

1. Challenging the Identification of the Substance (Lack of Lab Testing)

One of the most critical elements in a fentanyl-related charge is proving that the substance in question is, in fact, fentanyl or a fentanyl analog. If the prosecution cannot provide reliable testing to confirm that the substance is fentanyl, then they may not have the necessary evidence to convict you.

Key Case: *Davis v. United States,* 2019

- **Ruling**: The Supreme Court ruled that for convictions based on controlled substances, the government must prove through testing that the substance is indeed the one alleged.
- **Defense**: If the substance in the pressed pills has not been tested by a certified lab, you can challenge the evidence. This would undermine the prosecution's case, as they would fail to establish that the substance was fentanyl beyond a reasonable doubt.

---

2. Lack of Knowledge (Ignorance of Contents)

One of the most common defenses in cases involving illicit drugs like fentanyl in pressed pills is the argument that the defendant did not know the pills contained fentanyl. If the pills were bought or obtained under the belief that they were something else (e.g., a different drug), this could create reasonable doubt.

Key Case: *Rico v. State*, 2017 (Florida)

- **Ruling**: The court found that knowledge of the specific drug was a necessary element for a conviction in drug trafficking cases.
- **Defense**: You can argue that you did not know the pills contained fentanyl, especially if you can show that the pills were sold to you as a different substance. For example, if you bought what you believed were prescription pills or counterfeit pills with a different substance, this lack of knowledge can be a valid defense.

---

3. Improper or Unlawful Search and Seizure (Violation of Constitutional Rights)

If the fentanyl-laced pills were found during an illegal search or seizure—one that violated your constitutional rights—you may be able to have the evidence excluded in court under the **Exclusionary Rule**.

Key Case: *Mapp v. Ohio*, 1961

- **Ruling**: The Supreme Court ruled that evidence obtained from an illegal search and seizure is inadmissible in court.
- **Defense**: If law enforcement conducted a search without a valid warrant or probable cause, you could argue that the evidence (pressed fentanyl pills) was obtained illegally. If the evidence is excluded, the prosecution may be left without key evidence to prove the charge.

---

4. Insufficient Evidence of Intent to Distribute (Possession vs. Trafficking)

Fentanyl possession with intent to distribute is a serious charge, but **intent** is an element that the prosecution must prove beyond a reasonable doubt. If you can demonstrate that the fentanyl-laced pills were not intended for distribution or were intended for personal use, this could lead to a lesser charge or even a dismissal.

Key Case: *United States v. Jackson*, 2012

- **Ruling**: The court ruled that possession alone is not enough to convict someone of trafficking or distribution unless the prosecution proves intent through additional evidence, such as the quantity of the substance, packaging, or paraphernalia.
- **Defense**: You can argue that the quantity of the pills found on you or at your residence was for personal use and not intended for distribution. For instance, if there are no scales, baggies, or other distribution-related paraphernalia, you can argue that you didn't have the intent to sell the pills.

---

5. Challenging the Pressed Pills as Counterfeit

Pressed pills often resemble legitimate prescription medications, which could lead to a claim that the pills in question were counterfeit or mixed with fentanyl. If the pills appear to be "counterfeit" or were made to resemble a different substance (such as oxycodone), this could provide a defense that you didn't know they contained fentanyl.

Key Case: *United States v. Thomas,* 2015

- **Ruling**: The court found that evidence showing the defendant knowingly possessed counterfeit pills with fentanyl or other controlled substances is essential for a conviction.
- **Defense**: You can argue that the pills were counterfeit or that they were unknowingly purchased as something else (like oxycodone). If you can prove that you were unaware that fentanyl was in the pills and that they were misrepresented as something else, this could weaken the prosecution's case.

---

6. Mistaken Identity (Possession of Someone Else's Pills)

Sometimes, drugs found in your possession are not actually yours, and you may be able to argue that they were planted or mistakenly attributed to you. If you can provide evidence or a plausible explanation that the pills did not belong to you, you might be able to have the charges dismissed or reduced.

Case Law: *People v. Garcia,* 2014 (California)

- **Ruling**: In cases where the drugs found were not the defendant's, the court ruled that it is crucial for the prosecution to prove ownership and knowledge of the drugs.
- **Defense**: If you were in a situation where the pills belonged to someone else (e.g., you were with a friend who had the pills, and they were found in your bag or car), you could argue that the drugs were not yours and that you had no knowledge of them.

---

7. Motion to Suppress (Unlawful Arrest)

If you were arrested without probable cause or without a proper warrant, you can file a motion to suppress the evidence, arguing that the arrest violated your constitutional rights. If the arrest was illegal, any evidence found during the arrest, including fentanyl-laced pills, may be inadmissible in court.

Key Case: *Terry v. Ohio*, 1968

- **Ruling**: The U.S. Supreme Court ruled that searches and seizures must be based on reasonable suspicion and probable cause to be constitutional.
- **Defense**: If the arrest was made without probable cause or without a valid warrant, you can file a motion to suppress the evidence obtained during the arrest. If the court agrees, it may lead to the charges being dropped.

---

8. Diversion Programs (For First-Time Offenders or Minor Charges)

If this is your first offense, or if you can show that you were caught in possession of fentanyl-laced pills under extenuating circumstances (such as addiction or peer pressure), you may qualify for diversion programs or rehabilitation options rather than a lengthy prison sentence.

Key Case: *State v. Green*, 2007

- **Ruling**: The court allowed for diversion programs for first-time drug offenders, particularly those with substance abuse issues.
- **Defense**: If this is your first offense or if you were dealing with an addiction, your attorney may be able to argue for you to enter a

rehabilitation program instead of facing incarceration. These programs are often available in lieu of serving time for drug charges.

Conclusion

Fighting a **fentanyl** charge involving **pressed pills** requires a multifaceted approach. Key defenses include challenging the evidence (such as the substance not being properly identified as fentanyl), disputing the intent to distribute, arguing lack of knowledge of the pills' contents, and showing that the search or arrest was unlawful. Additionally, if you can demonstrate that you were dealing with an addiction or mitigating circumstances, you may qualify for diversion programs. Consulting with an experienced criminal defense attorney who specializes in drug charges is crucial for exploring all available defenses and determining the best strategy for your case.

CHAPTER FORTY TWO.

BEATING CHARGES RELATED TO MARIJUANA POSSESSION, TRAFFICKING, MANUFACTURING, AND CULTIVATION.

This requires a detailed approach that focuses on challenging key aspects of the prosecution's case. Since marijuana laws vary from state to state, the defense strategies you choose will depend on the jurisdiction and the specifics of your case. Below are several defense strategies that can be used to fight these charges effectively:

1. Lack of Probable Cause for Search or Arrest

The most fundamental defense in any drug-related case is whether the police had a valid reason to search you, your property, or your vehicle. If the search or arrest was made without probable cause or a proper warrant, it could be grounds for a **motion to suppress** the evidence.

Key Case: *Mapp v. Ohio*, 1961

- **Ruling**: The Supreme Court held that evidence obtained through an illegal search and seizure cannot be used in court.
- **Defense**: If you can prove that the police violated your Fourth Amendment rights by searching you or your property without a warrant, consent, or probable cause, you can file a motion to suppress any evidence found. If the court agrees, it can lead to the dismissal of the charges.

2. Lack of Knowledge or Intent (Unaware of Marijuana Presence)

Another strong defense is claiming **lack of knowledge** or **lack of intent**. For example, if marijuana plants were found on your property and you had no knowledge of their existence, or if you were not aware that the plants were marijuana, you can argue that you did not possess or manufacture marijuana intentionally.

Key Case: *United States v. Ziegler*, 1989

- **Ruling**: The court ruled that in drug cases, the prosecution must prove beyond a reasonable doubt that the defendant knew they were in possession of drugs.
- **Defense**: If the prosecution cannot prove that you knew the marijuana was present, or if you can show that someone else was responsible for it (e.g., a family member or housemate), it can weaken their case. For manufacturing or trafficking, lack of knowledge can be a defense if you didn't know the marijuana was being cultivated or distributed.

3. Invalid or Incomplete Marijuana Testing

In some cases, marijuana may be misidentified, especially if it's found in a form that is not immediately identifiable. If the substance is not properly tested or the results of the test are inconclusive, you may be able to argue that the prosecution cannot prove the substance was actually marijuana.

Key Case: *Davis v. United States*, 2019

- **Ruling**: The court ruled that if the government does not have reliable and valid testing results that prove the substance is marijuana, they cannot convict the defendant.
- **Defense**: If the testing of the marijuana was not performed properly or by an accredited laboratory, you can challenge the accuracy of the evidence. If the prosecution cannot prove that the substance is marijuana beyond a reasonable doubt, you can request a dismissal of charges.

4. Mistaken Identity or Ownership (No Knowledge of Marijuana Plants or Trafficking Activities)

In some situations, you may not have been aware of the marijuana plants or trafficking activities taking place. If you can show that the plants or trafficking activities were under the control of someone else, you can argue that you were falsely accused.

Key Case: *People v. Robinson*, 2010

- **Ruling**: The court found that a defendant was not responsible for possession or trafficking if they were unaware that the drugs were present.
- **Defense**: If the marijuana was found in a property you own but was cultivated or trafficked by someone else (such as a roommate, guest, or another individual), you can argue that you were unaware of the illegal activities and should not be held accountable.

5. Challenging the Evidence of Trafficking or Manufacturing

For charges of **marijuana trafficking** or **manufacturing**, the prosecution must prove that you had the intent to distribute or that you were involved in large-scale cultivation. If they cannot prove this beyond a reasonable doubt, you may be able to have the charges reduced or dismissed.

Key Case: *United States v. Tenth Circuit Court*, 1999

- **Ruling**: The court held that to convict someone of trafficking or manufacturing marijuana, there must be evidence of large-scale cultivation, distribution, or intent to sell.
- **Defense**: If the amount of marijuana found on your property or in your possession does not meet the threshold for trafficking (depending on your jurisdiction), you can argue that the charges should be reduced to simple possession or cultivation for personal use. Additionally, if

there are no sales materials or packaging related to distribution, it could weaken the trafficking argument.

6. Violation of State Medical Marijuana Laws (In States Where Legal)

If you are in a state where **medical marijuana** is legal, and you have a medical marijuana card or prescription, you may have a defense based on the violation of your rights under state law. Many states have medical marijuana statutes that allow for personal cultivation or possession within certain limits.

Key Case: *People v. Beach*, 2011 (California)

- **Ruling**: The court ruled that in California, patients with medical marijuana cards can cultivate a certain amount of marijuana for personal use.
- **Defense**: If you were cultivating marijuana for medical use, and your state allows personal cultivation with a medical marijuana card, you may be able to argue that you were within your legal rights. However, the cultivation must be within the legal limits of the state.

7. Lack of Sufficient Evidence to Prove Cultivation or Manufacturing

To convict someone of manufacturing or cultivating marijuana, the prosecution must prove that you actively participated in growing or producing the drug. If the marijuana plants were found in a space that did not have the necessary tools or equipment to indicate large-scale cultivation, you may be able to argue that the marijuana was grown for personal use, not trafficking or manufacturing.

Key Case: *State v. Young*, 2005

- **Ruling**: The court ruled that to prove manufacturing, there must be evidence that the defendant was involved in activities such as growing, processing, or packaging marijuana in a manner consistent with trafficking.

- **Defense**: If the police found marijuana plants, but there was no evidence of sophisticated cultivation techniques (e.g., industrial lights, grow tents, large amounts of fertilizer, packaging), you can argue that the marijuana was for personal use and not for manufacturing or trafficking.

8. Substance Not Under Your Control (Co-Defendant or Unrelated to You)

If the marijuana plants or trafficking materials were found in a shared space (e.g., a home or vehicle you shared with someone else), you can argue that the marijuana was not under your control. If you were unaware of its presence, or if it belonged to a co-defendant, this can create reasonable doubt.

Key Case: *United States v. McGlothin*, 1999

- **Ruling**: The court found that a defendant was not responsible for possession or cultivation of drugs found in shared spaces unless they had exclusive control over the area.
- **Defense**: You can argue that you did not have control over the area where the marijuana was found, and thus were not responsible for its cultivation or possession.

Conclusion

Beating marijuana possession, trafficking, manufacturing, or cultivation charges requires a combination of tactics. Key defenses include challenging the legality of searches and seizures, disputing knowledge or intent, questioning the sufficiency of the evidence, and taking advantage of medical marijuana laws where applicable. Each case is unique, so it is critical to consult with an experienced criminal defense attorney who can develop a strategy tailored to the facts of your case and the laws in your jurisdiction.

CHAPTER FORTY THREE.

BEATING SALES AND DELIVERY OF A CONTROLLED SUBSTANCE.

These charges involve challenging the prosecution's evidence, questioning the legality of the search and seizure, and demonstrating that you did not engage in any criminal activities. Below are key defense strategies you could employ to fight these charges, with relevant case law to support each strategy:

1. Challenge the Legality of the Search or Seizure (Fourth Amendment Violation)

One of the most common and effective defenses is to challenge whether the search and seizure that led to the discovery of controlled substances was lawful. If the police conducted the search without a warrant or probable cause, you can file a **motion to suppress** the evidence, which may lead to the charges being dropped.

Key Case: *Mapp v. Ohio*, 1961

- **Ruling**: The Supreme Court ruled that evidence obtained through an illegal search or seizure cannot be used in court.
- **Defense**: If law enforcement officers violated your Fourth Amendment rights by searching your property, car, or person without a valid warrant, probable cause, or your consent, the evidence gathered during that search may be inadmissible in court. If the evidence is excluded, the prosecution may not have enough evidence to prove the case.

2. Lack of Knowledge or Intent to Sell or Deliver Controlled Substances

To be convicted of **sales or delivery** of a controlled substance, the prosecution must prove not only that you had possession of the substance but also that you **intended to sell or deliver** it. If you did not have the intent to sell or distribute, this can serve as a strong defense.

Key Case: *United States v. Bailey*, 1980

- **Ruling**: The court ruled that in order to convict a defendant of drug trafficking, there must be evidence of the defendant's intent to distribute or sell.
- **Defense**: If you were merely in possession of the controlled substance for personal use, and there is no evidence (e.g., packaging, scales, large sums of money, or drug distribution paraphernalia) showing an intent to sell or deliver, you can argue that you did not have the requisite intent to commit the crime. Without proving intent to distribute, the prosecution may fail to meet the burden of proof.

---

3. Challenging the Evidence of Sales or Delivery

In cases of **sales** or **delivery**, the prosecution must show actual evidence of a transaction (e.g., money exchanged for drugs, witness testimony, or intercepted communication). If the prosecution cannot show that a sale or delivery occurred, you may be able to have the charges dismissed.

Key Case: *United States v. Jenkins*, 2005

- **Ruling**: The court ruled that to convict someone of the sale or delivery of a controlled substance, there must be clear evidence of the exchange of the drug for money or some other form of compensation.

- **Defense**: If no actual sale or delivery occurred, or if the police cannot provide clear evidence of the transaction, you can argue that there was no crime. For instance, if the police only found drugs in your possession but no money or evidence of a sale, there may be reasonable doubt about whether you intended to deliver the substance.

---

4. Entrapment Defense

If law enforcement officers induced or coerced you into selling or delivering a controlled substance, you may be able to assert an **entrapment** defense. Entrapment occurs when law enforcement officials persuade or pressure someone into committing a crime they would not have committed otherwise.

Key Case: *Jacobson v. United States*, 1992

- **Ruling**: The Supreme Court ruled that entrapment occurs when law enforcement officers encourage a defendant to commit a crime they were not otherwise predisposed to commit.
- **Defense**: If you were coerced or persuaded by law enforcement to participate in a drug sale or delivery, and you can demonstrate that you were not predisposed to commit the crime, you may be able to argue entrapment as a defense. Law enforcement cannot create a crime that would not have occurred otherwise.

---

5. Mistaken Identity or False Accusations

If you are being falsely accused or the police mistakenly identified you as the person involved in drug sales, you may be able to argue **mistaken**

identity. This defense is often used if the drug transaction was made by someone else, or if there is a mix-up in the investigation.

Key Case: *United States v. Wade*, 1967

- **Ruling**: The court ruled that identification procedures must be fair and not suggestive to avoid wrongful convictions based on mistaken identity.
- **Defense**: If the police made an error in identifying you, or if there was a miscommunication during an undercover operation, you can challenge the identification. This can be crucial in cases where you were caught on surveillance or through witness testimony but were not actually the person involved in the drug transaction.

---

6. Lack of Sufficient Evidence to Prove Delivery or Sale

The prosecution is required to prove **delivery** or **sale** beyond a reasonable doubt. This means they must show more than just the possession of drugs; they must provide evidence that the drugs were going to be distributed or sold to another individual.

Key Case: *People v. Beamon*, 2015

- **Ruling**: The court ruled that mere possession of a controlled substance does not automatically equate to intent to sell or deliver.
- **Defense**: If the prosecution cannot show that the drugs were meant for delivery or sale, it can result in the charges being reduced to **possession** rather than trafficking, sales, or delivery. For example, if the drugs were found on your person but there is no evidence of an exchange, you can argue that there was no intent to sell or deliver the substance.

7. Violation of Informant or Undercover Operation Protocols

If the sale or delivery was set up through an undercover operation or confidential informant, you could challenge the **reliability** or **credibility** of the informant or undercover officer. If the informant's testimony is unreliable or the officer violated protocol, this could affect the prosecution's case.

Key Case: *United States v. Sykes*, 2001

- **Ruling**: The court ruled that a defendant could challenge the evidence obtained through an unreliable confidential informant.
- **Defense**: If the informant has a questionable history or if there is evidence that the officer violated proper procedures in making the arrest or obtaining the evidence, it can weaken the prosecution's case. For instance, if the informant had a history of dishonesty or if the officers failed to follow legal procedures during the operation, you can argue that the evidence is tainted.

---

8. Challenge the Drug's Classification (Testing Issues)

In some cases, the drug involved in the case may be misidentified or inaccurately classified. The substance must be **properly tested** and identified by a credible expert. If the substance was not accurately identified as a controlled substance, the prosecution's case could fall apart.

Key Case: *Harrison v. United States*, 1993

- **Ruling**: The court ruled that if the government does not provide accurate and reliable drug testing, the evidence cannot be used to convict the defendant.

- **Defense**: If the testing process was flawed, if the drug was not tested by an accredited laboratory, or if the substance was not properly identified as a controlled substance, you can challenge the prosecution's evidence. Without reliable evidence that the substance is illegal, the charges may be dismissed.

Conclusion

Fighting charges for **sales and delivery of a controlled substance** requires a strategic approach. Common defense strategies include challenging the legality of searches and seizures, disputing intent to sell or deliver, questioning the sufficiency of evidence, and showing violations of protocol during undercover operations. It’s critical to work with an experienced criminal defense attorney to develop a tailored defense strategy that addresses the unique facts of your case and the laws in your jurisdiction.

CHAPTER FORTY FOUR.

BEATING CONSTRUCTIVE POSSESSION CHARGES.

This involves challenging the prosecution's ability to prove that you had control over the contraband in question, even if it wasn't directly in your possession at the time of arrest. Constructive possession means that the government must show that you had the **intent** and **ability** to control the item, even if it wasn't on your person.

Here are effective strategies to fight **constructive possession** charges:

1. Challenge the Evidence of Control

In a constructive possession case, the prosecution has to prove that you knew about the item, had access to it, and had the ability to control it. If the prosecution cannot establish that you had control over the contraband, it will be difficult for them to meet their burden of proof.

Key Case: *United States v. Lopez*, 1999

- **Ruling**: The court ruled that to prove constructive possession, the government must show that the defendant had knowledge of the item and the ability to exercise control over it.
- **Defense**: Challenge the evidence of control. If the contraband was found in a place where multiple people had access to it (e.g., a shared vehicle or house), or if there was no direct evidence that you knew about the contraband, the prosecution may fail to prove constructive possession. You could argue that the contraband could have belonged to someone else, and that you didn't have dominion or control over it.

---

2. Lack of Knowledge or Awareness of the Contraband

For a conviction of constructive possession, the prosecution must show that you knew about the existence of the contraband. If you can prove that you were unaware of the item or that it was placed where you would not reasonably know about it, it may be difficult for the prosecution to meet their burden of proof.

Key Case: *Sullivan v. United States*, 1969

- **Ruling**: The court ruled that constructive possession requires the defendant to have knowledge of the item, and that mere proximity to contraband is not enough to establish constructive possession.
- **Defense**: Argue that you did not have knowledge of the contraband's presence. For example, if drugs or weapons were found in a car you were riding in or a room you were staying in, you could argue that you were unaware of their presence. The prosecution cannot convict you based on proximity alone, especially if you were not aware of the illegal items.

---

3. Challenge the Location or Nature of the Find

If the contraband was discovered in a place where multiple people could have had access (e.g., a shared apartment or a vehicle with multiple passengers), you could argue that the prosecution cannot definitively prove that you had control over it.

Key Case: *People v. Medina*, 2016

- **Ruling**: The court ruled that when drugs are found in a location that could be accessed by multiple people, the prosecution must present

specific evidence that ties the defendant to the contraband in a way that eliminates reasonable doubt.
- **Defense**: Challenge the fact that the contraband was found in a location where it could have belonged to someone else. If the drugs were in a common area, such as a living room, a kitchen, or a vehicle, argue that you did not have exclusive access to the area, and therefore, the prosecution cannot prove constructive possession beyond a reasonable doubt.

---

4. Lack of Intent to Control or Distribute

The prosecution must prove not only that you had the ability to control the contraband but also that you **intended** to do so. If there's no evidence that you had any intent to exercise control over the contraband, this can be a key defense.

Key Case: *United States v. Foster*, 2010

- **Ruling**: The court ruled that constructive possession requires proof of both knowledge of the contraband and the intention to control it.
- **Defense**: Argue that even if you had access to the contraband, there was no intent to control it. For example, if drugs were found in a shared apartment or a car you were in, and there's no evidence you intended to possess or distribute them, this can be used to cast doubt on the prosecution's theory of constructive possession.

---

5. Provide Evidence of an Alternative Explanation

Another way to defeat a constructive possession charge is to provide a plausible alternative explanation for the presence of the contraband. This could involve showing that another person had control over the contraband or that it was planted by someone else.

Key Case: *United States v. Thomas*, 2014

- **Ruling**: The court held that presenting evidence of an alternative explanation for the contraband can create reasonable doubt in a constructive possession case.
- **Defense**: Present an alternative explanation for why the contraband was where it was found. For example, if drugs were found in your home but you can show that a roommate or visitor had access to that space, you can argue that they were the ones responsible for the contraband, not you.

---

6. Disputing the Chain of Custody

The prosecution must demonstrate that the contraband was not tampered with and that the evidence is what it claims to be. If the chain of custody is broken, it can cast doubt on whether the evidence presented in court is reliable.

Key Case: *State v. Jackson*, 2004

- **Ruling**: The court ruled that a broken chain of custody could lead to the exclusion of evidence.
- **Defense**: Argue that the evidence presented in court is unreliable due to a broken chain of custody. If the police failed to properly document or store the contraband, it could undermine the credibility of the evidence, making it harder for the prosecution to prove constructive possession.

---

7. Show That the Contraband Was Not Yours (Denial of Ownership)

One of the most direct defenses is to deny ownership or control of the contraband, especially if there is no clear connection between you and the contraband. If the prosecution cannot establish that the contraband was yours, it may be unable to prove constructive possession.

Key Case: *United States v. Blake*, 2003

- **Ruling**: The court ruled that a defendant can argue that the contraband belonged to someone else if the prosecution cannot establish clear evidence of the defendant's control or knowledge of it.
- **Defense**: Deny ownership or knowledge of the contraband, particularly if it was found in a shared location. For example, if drugs or weapons were found in a backpack that was not yours or in a vehicle you were merely a passenger in, you can argue that they did not belong to you and that you had no control over them.

---

8. Improper Jury Instructions

If the case goes to trial, improper jury instructions can be used as a defense if the jury is not properly instructed on the legal standard for constructive possession.

Key Case: *United States v. Davis*, 2011

- **Ruling**: The court ruled that improper jury instructions regarding the law of constructive possession could lead to a wrongful conviction.
- **Defense**: If the jury was not properly instructed about the elements of constructive possession—such as the necessity of proving knowledge, access, and control—you can argue that the conviction should be overturned on appeal due to these errors.

Conclusion

To successfully **beat constructive possession** charges, it's crucial to challenge the evidence the prosecution presents. Defenses such as lack of knowledge, lack of control or intent, alternative explanations, and questioning the chain of custody can all be effective. Working with a skilled defense attorney who can tailor these strategies to the specifics of your case is key to successfully fighting these charges.

Beating a **driving on a suspended license (DWLS)** charge can be challenging, but there are several legal defenses and strategies you can use to contest the charge, potentially getting it reduced or dismissed. Below are key strategies and considerations for fighting a DWLS charge:

CHAPTER FORTY FIVE.

CHALLENGE THE SUSPENSION NOTICE AND KNOWLEDGE

For a conviction of DWLS, the prosecution must prove that you were aware that your license was suspended. If you never received proper notice from the Department of Motor Vehicles (DMV) or other relevant agency, you can argue that you were not aware of the suspension.

Key Considerations:

- **Failure to Notify**: If the DMV failed to properly notify you of the suspension or if the notice was not sent to your correct address, this could be a solid defense.
- **Notice Requirements**: In many states, the law requires the DMV to send a notice of suspension to the driver. If the notice was sent to an incorrect address, or if the DMV did not follow proper procedures, you may be able to argue that you did not know your license was suspended.

Case Law Example:

- **Case:** ***People v. O'Neill***, 2013
    - **Ruling**: The court ruled that if a driver can demonstrate they were not properly notified about their suspension, they may have a viable defense.
    - **Defense**: You can argue that the suspension was invalid due to improper notice and therefore you were unaware of the suspension.

---

2. Argument of No Knowledge or Intent

Even if your license was suspended, you can argue that you did not know it was suspended or that you were not intentionally violating the law by driving. For example, you may have had a reasonable belief that your license was valid based on mistaken information or assumptions.

Key Considerations:

- **Honest Mistake**: If you were not aware of the suspension because you believed it had been lifted or that you were still within your driving privileges, you might be able to argue it was an honest mistake.
- **Confusion Over License Status**: If there were issues with your paperwork or if you were under the impression that your license had been reinstated, you could argue that you were confused about the status.

---

3. Fighting the Basis of the Suspension

If you believe the suspension was issued in error or that it should not have occurred in the first place, you may be able to challenge the legality of the suspension. This may involve showing that the suspension was based on incorrect information or was imposed under unjust circumstances.

Examples of Legal Grounds to Challenge Suspension:

- **Clerical Error**: If there was an administrative error or clerical mistake leading to your suspension, you may have grounds to challenge the suspension itself.
- **Improper Procedure**: If the suspension was imposed without following the proper legal procedure, you could argue that the suspension was invalid.

4. Defenses Based on the Necessity to Drive

In some cases, individuals may face a DWLS charge because they had to drive to prevent a more significant harm, such as getting to a job, seeking medical attention, or responding to an emergency. While this defense is rarely successful, it can be used in some situations.

Key Considerations:

- **Emergency Situations**: If you were driving to respond to a genuine emergency or to avoid a more serious harm, you could argue that the necessity of the situation justified your actions.
- **Hardship Defense**: In some states, you can argue that the suspension imposes an undue hardship on you and that you need your license to work or for essential daily activities. If this is the case, you may be able to apply for a hardship license.

---

5. Requesting a Trial

If you believe you were wrongfully charged with DWLS or there is insufficient evidence, you have the right to request a trial. At trial, the prosecution must prove beyond a reasonable doubt that you were driving with a suspended license. You can cross-examine witnesses, challenge the evidence, and present your defense.

Key Considerations:

- **Burden of Proof**: The prosecution has the burden to prove you were driving with knowledge that your license was suspended. You can challenge the sufficiency of the evidence and point out weaknesses in the case against you.

- **Cross-Examination**: You can cross-examine the arresting officer or any witnesses to highlight inconsistencies or errors in their testimony.

---

6. Filing a Motion to Dismiss

In some cases, you may file a **motion to dismiss** the charge based on legal deficiencies, such as lack of evidence or improper procedure. For example, if the prosecution fails to provide adequate proof that you were knowingly driving with a suspended license, a judge may dismiss the case.

---

7. Show That Your License Was Reinstated

If your license was suspended but you have since paid fines, completed required courses, or fulfilled other conditions for reinstatement, you may be able to show that your license is no longer suspended. If you can prove that your suspension was lifted prior to the date of the offense, the charge may be dropped.

Key Considerations:

- **Reinstatement of License**: Gather evidence that your suspension was lifted or that your license was valid at the time of your arrest. This could include documentation such as proof of payment of fines, reinstatement letters from the DMV, or confirmation that you completed any required classes.

---

8. Use of Legal Counsel

A strong defense against a DWLS charge requires thorough knowledge of both the law and your specific circumstances. Consulting with an experienced criminal defense attorney is critical, as they will be able to:

- Review all documentation related to your suspension.
- Investigate whether any errors or mistakes were made in the suspension process.
- Help you determine the best defense strategy, whether that's challenging the suspension, arguing a lack of knowledge, or showing that your suspension was invalid or improperly imposed.

---

9. Negotiating a Plea Bargain

If you are unable to successfully beat the DWLS charge, you may be able to negotiate a plea bargain with the prosecution. Depending on your criminal record and the circumstances, the prosecution may be willing to reduce the charge to a less severe offense or offer a more lenient sentence in exchange for your guilty plea.

Conclusion

To successfully **beat a driving wh**ile **suspended license** charge, you must carefully examine the facts of your case and consider possible defenses, such as lack of knowledge of the suspension, challenging the legality of the suspension itself, or presenting alternative explanations for your driving. Working with an experienced attorney is key to finding the most effective defense and ensuring the best possible outcome for your case.

CHAPTER F0RTY SIX.

BEATING A WIRETAP.

This involves challenging the legality of the wiretap itself, questioning the evidence obtained through the wiretap, and asserting potential violations of constitutional rights. Wiretap cases typically involve surveillance of phone calls, electronic communications, or conversations, and the government must comply with strict legal requirements to conduct such surveillance. Below are some common strategies to challenge and potentially defeat a wiretap case:

1. Challenge the Wiretap Authorization Process

The government is required to obtain a court order or authorization before conducting a wiretap, and the application for the wiretap must meet certain legal criteria. If the wiretap was improperly authorized or the process was flawed, it could result in the evidence being excluded from trial.

Key Legal Points:

- **Fourth Amendment Violation**: The Fourth Amendment of the U.S. Constitution protects individuals from unreasonable searches and seizures. Wiretapping without proper authorization or probable cause can be argued as an unreasonable search.
- **Lack of Probable Cause**: The government must demonstrate probable cause that a crime is being committed and that the wiretap will provide relevant evidence. If the application for the wiretap did not establish this probable cause, the wiretap may be illegal.
- **Failure to Exhaust Other Methods**: The law requires that before resorting to a wiretap, the government must show that other investigative methods, such as surveillance or informants, have been

exhausted or are unlikely to succeed. If this requirement is not met, the wiretap may be challenged.

Case Law Example:

- **Katz v. United States**, 389 U.S. 347 (1967): This landmark case established the principle that wiretapping must comply with the Fourth Amendment, and any interception of communication without proper judicial authorization can be deemed unlawful.

2. Challenge the Scope of the Wiretap

Even if the wiretap was authorized, it must adhere to strict limitations. The government cannot listen to communications that go beyond the scope of the authorized investigation. If the wiretap was too broad or exceeded the scope of the approval, the evidence obtained could be inadmissible.

Key Considerations:

- **Overbroad Authorization**: If the wiretap authorized surveillance of a specific phone number or set of communications but the wiretap ended up monitoring unrelated conversations, this could be grounds for challenging the evidence.
- **Duration**: Wiretaps are typically only authorized for a limited time, and the government must demonstrate that the wiretap is still necessary. If the wiretap continued longer than authorized or if surveillance was extended without justification, it could be considered unlawful.

Case Law Example:

- **United States v. Giordano**, 416 U.S. 505 (1974): The Court ruled that a wiretap could be invalidated if it was authorized improperly or if the wiretap's duration exceeded what was reasonable under the law.

3. Violation of Statutory Procedures

In addition to constitutional requirements, wiretap investigations must follow the procedures set forth in **Title III of the Omnibus Crime Control and Safe Streets Act of 1968** (the Wiretap Act). If these procedures were violated in any way, such as improper documentation or failure to notify the individuals involved, it could result in the wiretap being deemed unlawful.

Key Violations:

- **Improper Application**: The government must follow specific steps when applying for a wiretap, including detailing the suspected criminal activity and the communications to be intercepted. If the application was not completed properly, it could lead to the exclusion of evidence.
- **Failure to Notify**: In some cases, the individuals whose communications were intercepted must be notified within a certain period. Failure to provide this notice can lead to suppression of the wiretap evidence.

Case Law Example:

- **United States v. Chavez**, 416 U.S. 562 (1974): The Court found that the failure to follow procedural requirements when obtaining wiretap authorization led to the suppression of evidence.

4. Challenge the Evidence Obtained from the Wiretap

Once a wiretap is in place, the evidence gathered from the surveillance can be contested. This can involve arguing that the evidence was obtained in violation of the law, was misinterpreted, or was too remote from the alleged crime.

Key Considerations:

- **Improper Interception**: The wiretap may have involved the interception of communications that were not related to the suspected criminal activity, such as personal, privileged, or confidential conversations.
- **Chain of Custody Issues**: If there were any issues with the chain of custody of the intercepted communications, such as tampering or improper handling, it can weaken the credibility of the evidence.

Case Law Example:

- **Franks v. Delaware**, 438 U.S. 154 (1978): This case established that the defense can challenge the validity of evidence obtained through wiretap if they can demonstrate that false statements or omissions were made in the application for the wiretap.

5. Argue a Lack of Evidence Linking the Defendant to the Wiretap

Even if the wiretap itself is legal, the prosecution must show that the evidence gathered directly implicates the defendant. If the wiretap evidence does not actually tie the defendant to the criminal activity or cannot prove the charges beyond a reasonable doubt, you can argue that the evidence is insufficient.

Key Considerations:

- **Weak Connections**: If the wiretap revealed conversations that mention the defendant but do not provide direct evidence of their involvement in the crime, the defense can argue that the evidence is circumstantial at best.
- **Implicating Third Parties**: In some cases, the wiretap may involve conversations with other individuals that do not link the defendant to

the criminal enterprise or activity. If this is the case, the evidence should be challenged as not relevant to the defendant's actions.

---

6. File a Motion to Suppress the Evidence

If the wiretap was illegal or violated any of the requirements mentioned above, the defense can file a **motion to suppress** the evidence. If the court grants the motion, the wiretap evidence cannot be used in trial, which may lead to the dismissal of charges.

Key Considerations:

- **Fourth Amendment Challenge**: If the wiretap violated the defendant's Fourth Amendment rights, the defense may argue that the evidence should be suppressed under the exclusionary rule, which prevents illegally obtained evidence from being used in court.
- **Filing Before Trial**: It's important to file the motion to suppress before trial, typically in the pre-trial phase, to have a chance to exclude the wiretap evidence.

Conclusion

Beating a wiretap case requires thorough legal analysis of the procedures followed, the scope of the wiretap, and the evidence it produced. If any irregularities or violations occurred in the wiretap process, you can challenge its legality and seek to have the evidence suppressed. Working with an experienced criminal defense attorney is crucial to identifying the best strategy, whether challenging the wiretap on constitutional grounds, procedural violations, or insufficient evidence linking the defendant to the crime.

CHAPTER FORTY SEVEN.

BEATING THE SPEEDING TICKET

Beating a speeding ticket typically involves challenging the evidence presented against you, questioning the methods used to determine your speed, and potentially proving that the ticket was issued in error. Below are several strategies that can be used to fight and potentially dismiss a speeding ticket:

1. Challenge the Accuracy of the Speed Measurement

Most speeding tickets are issued based on radar or lidar (laser) readings, but these devices can sometimes be inaccurate due to a variety of factors. You can challenge the accuracy of the measurement in the following ways:

Radar and Lidar Calibration:

- **Device Calibration**: Radar and lidar devices must be calibrated regularly to ensure accuracy. If the device was not properly calibrated, the reading may be invalid. Request the maintenance and calibration records of the device used to measure your speed. If the records are incomplete or unavailable, you can argue that the device may not have been functioning correctly.
- **Operator Training**: The officer who operated the radar or lidar device must be properly trained. If the officer was not trained or did not follow the proper procedures, you can argue that the measurement may not have been accurate.

Case Law Example:

- **People v. Brumback**: A case where the court found the radar device to be improperly calibrated and ruled in favor of the defendant, dismissing the ticket.

2. Question the Officer's Method of Speed Measurement

- **Visual Estimation**: Some tickets are issued based on the officer's visual estimation of speed, particularly if no radar or lidar is used. However, visual estimation is highly subjective and prone to error. The officer must be able to testify that they had a clear, unobstructed view of the vehicle and were properly trained to estimate speed. If the officer fails to establish these elements, you can argue that the ticket is based on an unreliable estimation.

- **Pacing**: In some cases, officers may follow behind a vehicle to measure its speed (pacing). You can challenge the accuracy of pacing by questioning whether the officer maintained a consistent speed while following you or whether any traffic conditions affected their ability to accurately gauge your speed.

Case Law Example:

- **People v. Morrow**: The court ruled that the officer's visual estimation was not sufficient to prove the defendant's speed, as there was no radar or other evidence.

3. Dispute the Posted Speed Limit

You can argue that the posted speed limit was not clearly visible or was incorrectly marked, especially if there were signs that were obstructed by foliage or if there was a change in the speed limit that you were unaware of.

Key Arguments:

- **Obscured Signage**: If the speed limit sign was obscured or difficult to see, you can argue that you were not given a clear indication of the speed limit, which would make it unreasonable to issue a ticket for speeding.

- **Inaccurate Speed Limit**: In some cases, the speed limit may have been set too low for the type of road or conditions. You could argue that the posted speed limit was unreasonable for the area or road type.

Case Law Example:

- **People v. Fox**: The court ruled that the defendant was not guilty of speeding because the speed limit signs were not clearly visible at the location where they were ticketed.

4. Challenge the Officer's Presence and Legal Authority

In some cases, the officer who issued the ticket may not have been in a legal position to measure your speed. For example:

- **Unmarked Vehicle**: If the officer was driving an unmarked vehicle and did not have proper training or authorization to pull you over, you can challenge the ticket.

- **Lack of Proper Observation**: If the officer did not have a clear line of sight or did not have sufficient time to observe your vehicle before issuing the ticket, you can argue that the ticket was issued without proper grounds.

5. Present Evidence of Necessity or Emergency

If you were speeding for an emergency situation (e.g., rushing someone to the hospital), you may be able to argue that speeding was necessary under the circumstances.

Key Considerations:

- **Emergency**: You must present evidence that you were acting in response to an emergency and that the speed was necessary to avoid harm. Having documentation or witness testimony about the emergency situation can help support your claim.

- **No Recklessness**: Even in an emergency, you must demonstrate that you were not driving recklessly or dangerously. Simply being in a rush is not a valid excuse for speeding.

6. Use the "No Speeding" Defense

In some cases, you can argue that you were not speeding at all. This can involve:

- **Witness Testimony**: If someone else was in the car with you, they could testify that you were driving within the speed limit.
- **GPS Data**: If you have a GPS system in your vehicle, it may provide data about your speed at the time of the alleged violation. Some vehicles also have speed tracking devices that can provide evidence of your speed.

Case Law Example:

- **People v. Gaspard**: A case where the defendant used GPS data to prove that their speed was below the speed limit, and the court ruled in their favor.

7. Challenge the Timing of the Ticket

Sometimes, the timing of the ticket can work in your favor. For example, if the officer took too long to issue the ticket or if there was a discrepancy between the time the alleged offense occurred and the time the ticket was issued, you may be able to raise doubts about the accuracy of the officer's records.

8. Present Character Evidence

If you have a clean driving record and can demonstrate that you are a careful driver, this might help your case, especially if you can show that speeding is not typical for you. This may not directly lead to the dismissal of the ticket but can influence the judge or jury's perception of your credibility.

Steps to Take When Fighting a Speeding Ticket

1. **Review the Ticket**: Make sure all the information on the ticket is accurate, including your vehicle information, the location, and the date of the violation.
2. **Request the Officer's Evidence**: You have the right to request any evidence the officer may use against you, such as calibration records for radar or lidar equipment, dashcam footage, and any written reports from the officer.
3. **Prepare Your Defense**: Gather evidence that supports your case, including witness statements, GPS data, photographs, and maintenance records for radar or lidar devices.
4. **Attend the Hearing**: Present your case clearly and calmly. If you're unsure of how to proceed, consider hiring an attorney who specializes in traffic law.
5. **Negotiate a Settlement**: In some cases, you may be able to negotiate with the prosecutor for a reduced fine or penalty, particularly if it is your first offense or if there are mitigating factors.

Conclusion

Beating a speeding ticket requires presenting a solid defense based on the facts of the case. Whether you challenge the accuracy of the speed measurement, question the officer's methods, dispute the speed limit, or provide evidence of an emergency, there are many ways to fight a speeding ticket. By thoroughly reviewing the case and gathering evidence, you increase your chances of having the ticket dismissed or reduced.

CHAPTER FORTY EIGHT.

DEFENDING AGAINST AGGRAVATED CHILD ABUSE CHARGES IN FLORIDA

Aggravated child abuse is a severe criminal charge in Florida, carrying significant legal consequences, including lengthy prison sentences and a lasting criminal record. If you or a loved one is facing such charges, it is critical to understand the nature of the offense, possible defenses, and the legal strategies available to protect your rights and freedom.

Understanding Aggravated Child Abuse Under Florida Law

Under Florida Statutes § 827.03(2), aggravated child abuse is defined as any of the following acts committed against a child:

- Willfully torturing, maliciously punishing, or willfully and unlawfully caging a child.
- Knowingly or willfully abusing a child in a manner that causes great bodily harm, permanent disability, or permanent disfigurement.

Because of the serious nature of these allegations, a conviction can lead to a first-degree felony charge, punishable by up to 30 years in prison and hefty fines.

Legal Defenses Against Aggravated Child Abuse Charges

If you have been accused of aggravated child abuse, it is crucial to build a strong defense. Several legal strategies can be used depending on the circumstances of your case:

1. Lack of Intent

Aggravated child abuse charges require that the prosecution prove intent. If the injury was accidental rather than willful, it may serve as a strong defense. Proving that the harm resulted from an accident rather than malicious intent can lead to a reduction or dismissal of charges.

Case Example: In State v. Johnson (2018), a Florida father was charged with aggravated child abuse after his toddler fell from a high chair and sustained a head injury. The defense successfully argued that the injury was accidental, and medical expert testimony supported the claim. The charges were ultimately dropped.

2. False Allegations

False accusations are not uncommon in child abuse cases, particularly in contentious custody battles or situations involving personal vendettas. Your defense attorney can gather evidence, such as witness testimonies, medical reports, and psychological evaluations, to challenge the credibility of the accuser and expose inconsistencies in their claims.

Case Example: In Smith v. Florida (2020), a mother accused her ex-husband of child abuse in an attempt to gain full custody of their children. However, forensic analysis of phone records and recorded conversations revealed that the allegations were fabricated. The court dismissed the case, and the mother faced perjury charges.

3. Insufficient Evidence

The prosecution must prove beyond a reasonable doubt that you committed aggravated child abuse. If there is a lack of medical documentation, inconsistent witness testimonies, or unreliable evidence, your attorney can argue that the case does not meet the legal burden of proof.

Case Example: In Florida v. Martinez (2019), a babysitter was charged after a child suffered unexplained bruises. The defense presented expert testimony that the child had a medical condition causing easy bruising. Due to insufficient evidence linking the bruises to abuse, the defendant was acquitted.

4. Parental Right to Discipline

Florida law permits reasonable discipline, including corporal punishment, provided it does not lead to serious harm. If your actions were part of lawful discipline, demonstrating that they were reasonable and did not result in great bodily harm can be a valid defense.

Case Example: In State v. Carter (2017), a stepfather disciplined his teenage stepson by restricting access to electronics and giving him light physical punishment. The child's biological father filed abuse charges, but the court ruled that the discipline was lawful and dismissed the case.

5. Mistaken Identity

In some cases, authorities may arrest the wrong person based on misidentification or misleading statements. Establishing an alibi or presenting evidence that someone else committed the alleged abuse can be key to your defense.

Case Example: In Florida v. Delgado (2021), a school employee was mistakenly charged after a child accused the wrong individual. Surveillance footage later revealed that another person was responsible. The case was dismissed, and the actual perpetrator was later arrested.

Steps to Take If You Are Accused

If you are facing aggravated child abuse charges in Florida, take the following steps to protect yourself:

1. **Remain Silent:** Do not make statements to law enforcement without legal counsel.

2. **Hire an Experienced Attorney:** Retaining a lawyer with expertise in Florida criminal defense is crucial to building a strong case.
3. **Gather Evidence:** Collect medical records, witness statements, and any other documents that can support your defense.
4. **Avoid Contact with the Accuser:** Engaging with the accuser could be used against you in court.
5. **Follow Legal Advice:** Comply with all legal proceedings and court orders to avoid further complications.

Conclusion

Aggravated child abuse charges in Florida carry life-altering consequences, but a strong legal defense can help mitigate the damage. By understanding the law, recognizing possible defenses, and hiring an experienced attorney, you can fight these allegations and work toward the best possible outcome in your case. The key to success lies in early action and a well-prepared defense strategy.

CHAPTER FORTY NINE.

DEFENDING AGAINST TRESPASSING CHARGES IN FLORIDA

Trespassing is a common criminal charge in Florida, but it can carry serious legal consequences depending on the circumstances. Whether you have been accused of trespassing on private property, a business, or government land, it is crucial to understand your rights and the legal defenses available to fight the charges.

Understanding Trespassing Under Florida Law

Trespassing in Florida is governed by Florida Statutes §§ 810.08 and 810.09, which define trespassing as the unauthorized entry onto another person's property. There are two main types of trespassing offenses:

1. **Trespass in a Structure or Conveyance (§ 810.08)** - Entering or remaining in a building, home, or vehicle without authorization.
2. **Trespass on Property Other than a Structure or Conveyance (§ 810.09)** - Entering or remaining on land after being warned to leave or without permission.

Trespassing can be charged as either a misdemeanor or a felony, depending on factors such as the presence of a weapon, prior warnings, or intent to commit another crime.

Legal Defenses Against Trespassing Charges

If you are facing trespassing charges in Florida, several defenses may apply to your case. The right defense can result in reduced charges, case dismissal, or acquittal at trial.

1. Lack of Intent

A key element of trespassing is intent. If you did not knowingly enter or remain on the property without permission, the charges may not hold up in court.

Case Example: In Florida v. Johnson (2019), a delivery driver was charged with trespassing after mistakenly entering a private driveway. The court dismissed the case, ruling that there was no intent to trespass.

2. Lack of Notice or Warning

Trespassing charges often require that the property owner or an authorized individual gave clear notice that entry was prohibited. If there were no visible signs, verbal warnings, or other indicators, this could be a strong defense.

Case Example: In State v. Rodriguez (2020), a man was arrested for trespassing at a public park after hours. However, his attorney proved that the park had no clear signage indicating it was closed. The charges were dropped.

3. Rightful Presence on the Property

If you had permission or a legal right to be on the property, you cannot be convicted of trespassing.

Case Example: In Florida v. Miller (2021), a tenant was accused of trespassing after entering his former apartment. The defense presented a lease agreement showing that he still had legal access. The case was dismissed.

4. Necessity Defense

Under Florida law, if you trespassed due to an emergency, such as seeking shelter from a storm or avoiding imminent danger, you may have a valid legal defense.

Case Example: In State v. Carter (2018), a woman entered an abandoned building to escape a severe thunderstorm. The court ruled that the necessity defense applied, and the charges were dismissed.

5. Mistaken Identity

Law enforcement may arrest the wrong person based on misleading witness statements or poor surveillance footage.

Case Example: In Florida v. Simmons (2022), a man was arrested after being misidentified as a trespasser at a shopping mall. His attorney presented alibi evidence proving he was elsewhere at the time, leading to a full acquittal.

Steps to Take If You Are Accused of Trespassing

If you are facing trespassing charges, take these steps to protect yourself:

1. **Remain Silent:** Do not admit to anything or explain your actions without an attorney present.
2. **Hire an Experienced Attorney:** A criminal defense lawyer can assess your case and develop the best defense strategy.
3. **Gather Evidence:** Collect any documents, witness statements, or photos that prove your right to be on the property.
4. **Challenge the Evidence:** If law enforcement lacks proof of intent or warning, your lawyer can push for a case dismissal.
5. **Attend All Court Hearings:** Failing to appear can result in additional charges or a warrant for your arrest.

Conclusion

Trespassing charges in Florida can often be challenged successfully with the right legal strategy. Whether the case involves a misunderstanding, lack of notice, or rightful presence, an experienced defense attorney can help protect your rights. By understanding the law and taking immediate legal action, you can improve your chances of beating a trespassing charge and avoiding criminal penalties.

CHAPTER FIFTY.

BEATING TRESPASSING, LOITERING, AND PROWLING CHARGES IN FLORIDA

Trespassing, loitering, and prowling are common criminal charges in Florida, but they are often misunderstood. Many people face these charges due to misunderstandings, unclear property boundaries, or false accusations. If you have been charged, it is essential to understand the law, potential defenses, and legal strategies that can help you beat the charges.

Understanding Trespassing Under Florida Law

Florida law classifies trespassing into two main categories:

1. **Trespass in a Structure or Conveyance (Florida Statute § 810.08)** – Occurs when a person enters or remains in a building, home, or vehicle without authorization.
2. **Trespass on Property Other Than a Structure or Conveyance (Florida Statute § 810.09)** – Occurs when a person enters or remains on private land without permission, particularly after being warned to leave.

Trespassing charges can be classified as either a misdemeanor or a felony, depending on circumstances such as whether the accused was armed, whether the property was occupied, and whether any damage was caused.

Understanding Loitering and Prowling Under Florida Law

Loitering and prowling are criminal offenses under Florida Statute § 856.021. A person commits this offense when they:

- Are in a place, at a time, or in a manner that is unusual or suspicious.
- Engage in behavior that suggests an immediate threat to public safety or property.

Unlike trespassing, loitering and prowling do not require unauthorized entry onto private property. However, law enforcement officers must have reasonable suspicion that criminal activity was about to occur.

Common Legal Defenses Against Trespassing, Loitering, and Prowling Charges

There are several strong defenses that can be used to fight these charges in Florida. Here are some of the most effective strategies:

1. Lack of Intent

Trespassing, loitering, and prowling charges often require proof that the defendant knowingly engaged in prohibited behavior. If the actions were accidental or unintentional, the charges may not stand.

Case Example: In *State v. Thompson (2021)*, a man was arrested for trespassing in a gated community. His defense showed that he had entered mistakenly while looking for a friend's house. The case was dismissed due to lack of intent.

2. Lack of Proper Notice or Warning

Property owners must provide clear notice that entry is prohibited, and for loitering and prowling, law enforcement must issue a warning before making an arrest. If there were no such warnings, you might have a valid defense.

Case Example: In *Florida v. Garcia (2019)*, a woman was charged with trespassing in a vacant lot. Her attorney argued that there were no "No Trespassing" signs, and the judge dismissed the case due to insufficient notice.

3. No Reasonable Suspicion (for Loitering and Prowling)

For a loitering and prowling charge to be valid, law enforcement must prove that a person's behavior posed an immediate threat. Simply standing in a public place without engaging in criminal activity is not enough to support a conviction.

Case Example: In *Florida v. White (2021)*, a man was arrested for loitering near a convenience store. His attorney argued that he was waiting for a ride and had not engaged in any suspicious activity. The case was dismissed due to a lack of reasonable suspicion.

4. Rightful Presence on the Property

If you had permission or a legal right to be on the property, you cannot be convicted of trespassing.

Case Example: In *Smith v. Florida (2020)*, a maintenance worker was arrested for trespassing on an apartment complex property. His employer provided documentation proving that he was authorized to be there, leading to the dismissal of the charges.

5. Public Property Defense

If the location where the alleged offense occurred is public property, the prosecution must prove that you were unlawfully restricted from being there.

Case Example: In *State v. Johnson (2022)*, a man was accused of trespassing in a public park after dark. The defense showed that he was unaware of the park's closing hours and that signs were not clearly posted. The case was dropped.

6. Necessity Defense

If you entered the property or remained in a location due to an emergency, such as seeking shelter from severe weather or avoiding a dangerous situation, you may have a valid defense.

Case Example: In *State v. Carter (2018)*, a homeless man entered an abandoned building during a hurricane. His attorney successfully argued the necessity defense, and the charges were dismissed.

7. Mistaken Identity

In some cases, law enforcement arrests the wrong person based on misidentification. Establishing an alibi or proving that another individual was responsible can be crucial to your defense.

Case Example: In *Florida v. Davis (2023)*, a man was arrested for trespassing at a shopping mall. His attorney presented security footage proving he was at another location, leading to his acquittal.

Steps to Take If You Are Charged With Trespassing, Loitering, or Prowling

If you are facing these charges in Florida, take these steps to protect your rights:

1. **Remain Silent** – Do not provide statements to law enforcement without an attorney present.
2. **Hire a Skilled Criminal Defense Lawyer** – An experienced attorney can help you build the best defense strategy.
3. **Gather Evidence** – Collect any documents, witness statements, or video footage that supports your case.
4. **Challenge the Evidence** – Your lawyer can examine whether the prosecution has enough evidence to prove intent or proper notice.

5. **Attend All Court Hearings** – Failing to appear can result in additional legal consequences.

Conclusion

Trespassing, loitering, and prowling charges in Florida can often be beaten with the right legal defense. Whether your case involves lack of intent, insufficient notice, rightful presence, or necessity, an experienced defense attorney can help protect your rights. If you are facing any of these charges, acting quickly and securing legal representation can greatly improve your chances of a favorable outcome.

CHAPTER FIFTY ONE.

BEATING WRITTEN THREAT TO KILL CHARGES IN FLORIDA

In Florida, making a written threat to kill or cause bodily harm is a serious criminal offense under Florida Statute § 836.10. This law criminalizes threats made in writing, whether through letters, emails, text messages, or social media. Being accused of this crime can have severe legal consequences, including felony charges, potential imprisonment, and a permanent criminal record. However, various legal defenses may be available to challenge these charges and secure a favorable outcome.

Understanding Florida Statute § 836.10

Florida law defines written threats as any communication that explicitly or implicitly threatens to kill, injure, or commit an act of mass violence against a person or group. The key elements of the offense include:

1. The threat must be **in writing** (electronic communications are included).
2. The threat must be directed **at a specific person or group**.
3. The accused must have **knowingly** made the threat.
4. The message must be **transmitted** to the alleged victim or made publicly available.

A conviction for making a written threat is classified as a **second-degree felony**, punishable by up to **15 years in prison**, **15 years of probation**, and a **$10,000 fine**.

Common Legal Defenses Against Written Threat Charges

If you are facing charges for making a written threat to kill, the prosecution must prove each element of the crime beyond a reasonable doubt. Several legal defenses can challenge these allegations and potentially result in a dismissal or acquittal.

1. Lack of Intent

A critical aspect of the law is proving that the accused **intended** for the written communication to be perceived as a genuine threat. If the statement was made jokingly, sarcastically, or without any real intent to harm, this defense can be effective.

Case Example: In *State v. Carter (2021)*, a teenager posted a violent rap lyric on social media, leading to his arrest for making a written threat. His defense successfully argued that the statement was artistic expression rather than an actual threat. The case was dismissed.

2. No True Threat (Protected Free Speech)

Under the **First Amendment**, not all offensive or violent statements are criminal. The courts have ruled that only **"true threats"**—statements meant to instill fear—are punishable. If the prosecution cannot prove the statement was a true threat, the case may be dismissed.

Case Example: In *Florida v. Johnson (2020)*, a man sent an angry email to a local politician but later argued that it was political hyperbole, not a genuine threat. The court ruled in his favor, citing First Amendment protections.

3. No Transmission of the Threat

To be convicted under § 836.10, the written threat must be **sent, published, or shared** with another person. If the alleged threat was found in a private journal, draft email, or unsent message, it does not meet the legal standard.

Case Example: In *State v. Williams (2019)*, a college student wrote violent thoughts in his private notebook, which was later discovered by a roommate. The court ruled that because the writing was never communicated, it did not constitute a crime.

4. Ambiguous Language

The law requires that the statement be a clear and unambiguous threat. If the message can be interpreted in multiple ways, the defense can argue that the statement does not meet the legal threshold of a threat.

Case Example: In *State v. Rivera (2022)*, a social media post stating, “I’d love to see my enemies disappear,” was challenged as being too vague to constitute a true threat. The court agreed and dismissed the charges.

5. Mistaken Identity or False Allegation

Many written threat cases arise from **hacked accounts, mistaken identity, or false accusations**. If there is no solid proof linking the accused to the message, the case can be challenged.

Case Example: In *Florida v. Martinez (2023)*, a man was charged with sending a threatening email, but his lawyer proved that his email account had been hacked. The charges were dropped.

Steps to Take If You Are Accused of Making a Written Threat

If you are facing charges under Florida’s written threat law, taking the right steps can make a significant difference in your case:

1. **Do Not Speak to Law Enforcement Without a Lawyer** – Anything you say can be used against you in court.
2. **Preserve Evidence** – Save all messages, emails, and communications that may support your defense.
3. **Identify Witnesses** – Anyone who can testify about your intent or context of the statement can help.

4. **Hire an Experienced Criminal Defense Attorney** – A skilled lawyer can analyze the evidence, challenge the prosecution's case, and develop a strong defense strategy.
5. **Avoid Further Communication About the Case** – Refrain from discussing the case on social media or with anyone except your attorney.

Conclusion

Being accused of making a written threat to kill in Florida is a serious matter, but there are many ways to challenge the charge. Whether arguing lack of intent, free speech protections, lack of transmission, or mistaken identity, an aggressive legal defense can significantly improve your chances of avoiding a conviction. If you or a loved one is facing these charges, seeking immediate legal assistance is crucial to protecting your future.

CHAPTER FIFTY TWO.

BEATING AGGRAVATED ASSAULT WITH WEAPONS OR FIREARMS IN FLORIDA

INTRODUCTION

In Florida, aggravated assault is a serious criminal offense that involves the intentional threat of harm to another person with a weapon or firearm. When a weapon or firearm is used in the commission of assault, the charges can escalate significantly. The legal consequences for aggravated assault with a weapon or firearm can be severe, but it is possible to defend against these charges, depending on the circumstances. This chapter will explore the elements of aggravated assault with a weapon or firearm in Florida, potential defenses, and strategies to beat such charges.

---

1. Understanding Aggravated Assault with a Weapon or Firearm

Aggravated assault in Florida is defined under **Florida Statute 784.021**. The statute categorizes aggravated assault as an intentional threat or act of violence toward another person with the use of a deadly weapon. A "deadly weapon" could be any object capable of causing death or serious bodily injury, including firearms, knives, or other dangerous items.

The key elements of aggravated assault with a weapon or firearm in Florida are:

- **Intentional Threat**: The accused must have intentionally threatened another person with the weapon or firearm.
- **Weapon or Firearm**: The assault must involve the use of a weapon or firearm. Even if the weapon is not used to physically harm the victim, its mere presence can lead to aggravated assault charges.

- **Fear of Harm**: The victim must have reasonably feared that the weapon or firearm could cause harm.
- **No Physical Injury Required**: Unlike battery charges, where physical injury is often required, in aggravated assault, the victim does not need to be physically harmed—just put in fear of imminent harm.

Penalties for Aggravated Assault with a Firearm

Aggravated assault with a firearm is a second-degree felony in Florida. A conviction can result in:

- Up to **15 years in prison**
- **$10,000 in fines**
- Mandatory **3 years of probation**

If the assault involves the discharge of the firearm, the penalties may be enhanced.

---

2. Common Defenses Against Aggravated Assault with a Weapon or Firearm

When charged with aggravated assault in Florida, several defenses may be raised to contest the allegations. The most common defenses include:

A. Self-Defense

Florida law allows individuals to use force, including deadly force, if they believe it is necessary to defend themselves from imminent bodily harm. Under **Florida's Stand Your Ground Law** (section 776.013), an individual does not have a duty to retreat and can use force in situations where they fear harm or death. Key points include:

- The defendant must have been in reasonable fear of harm.

- The threat must have been imminent and serious.
- The defendant must have used only the amount of force reasonably necessary to protect themselves.

B. Lack of Intent

For an aggravated assault conviction, the prosecution must prove that the defendant intentionally threatened the victim with the weapon or firearm. A strong defense could be that the defendant did not have the requisite intent to commit the crime. For example:

- The defendant may have been acting in self-defense or protecting property but did not intend to create a fear of imminent harm.
- The weapon or firearm may not have been aimed directly at the victim, which could undermine the claim that the victim reasonably feared for their safety.

C. False Allegations

Another defense may be that the accusations are false. This could be due to personal conflict, misunderstanding, or mistaken identity. Evidence such as witness testimony, video footage, or inconsistencies in the victim's account can be used to challenge the prosecution's version of events.

D. Weapon Not Involved in the Threat

In some cases, the weapon or firearm may not have been used in a threatening manner, or it may not have been present at all. For example:

- The defendant may have been holding the weapon but did not intend to use it in a threatening manner.
- The victim may have misinterpreted the defendant's actions.

If the prosecution cannot prove that the weapon or firearm was used in a threatening way, the charge may be reduced or dismissed.

3. Key Legal Strategies for Beating the Charge

A. Challenge the Victim's Credibility

In many cases, the outcome of an aggravated assault case comes down to which version of events the jury believes. If the defense can cast doubt on the victim's testimony, it may be enough to raise reasonable doubt. Possible approaches include:

- Showing inconsistencies in the victim's statements.
- Proving that the victim had a motive to lie or exaggerate the threat.
- Bringing forward evidence that the victim had a history of false reporting.

B. Negotiate for Lesser Charges

While aggravated assault with a weapon or firearm is a serious offense, a skilled defense attorney may be able to negotiate a plea deal with the prosecution for a lesser charge, such as simple assault or battery. In exchange for a guilty plea to a lesser offense, the defendant may receive a reduced sentence, probation, or other favorable outcomes.

C. File Pre-Trial Motions

Pre-trial motions, such as motions to dismiss or suppress evidence, can be powerful tools in the defense strategy. For example, if the evidence against the defendant was gathered improperly (e.g., through an illegal search), it may be possible to have that evidence excluded from the trial.

---

4. Understanding the Role of an Experienced Defense Attorney

Given the serious consequences of a conviction for aggravated assault with a weapon or firearm, it is critical to seek representation from a criminal defense attorney experienced in handling violent crime cases in Florida. A competent attorney will:

- Review the details of the case to identify weaknesses in the prosecution's evidence.
- Investigate the circumstances surrounding the alleged assault, including gathering witness statements and surveillance footage.
- Advise on the best defense strategy based on the specific facts of the case.
- Negotiate with the prosecution to seek a reduction in charges or penalties, if applicable.

An attorney with experience in Florida's self-defense laws, as well as the Stand Your Ground statute, will be invaluable in assessing whether these defenses apply to the case at hand.

---

5. Conclusion

Beating a charge of aggravated assault with a weapon or firearm in Florida is a complex and challenging task, but it is not impossible. Defendants must challenge the elements of the crime, the evidence, and the credibility of the witnesses. Whether through asserting self-defense, proving a lack of intent, or highlighting false allegations, a skilled defense attorney can significantly improve the chances of a favorable outcome.

Given the serious nature of the charge, it is essential for anyone facing aggravated assault charges to take immediate action by seeking legal counsel. With the right strategy, it is possible to defend against these charges and avoid the severe penalties associated with a conviction.

CHAPTER FIFTY THREE

BEATING COUNTERFEIT CURRENCY CHARGES IN FLORIDA

INTRODUCTION

Counterfeiting currency is a federal crime, but it is also taken seriously under Florida state law. Being accused of passing or possessing counterfeit currency in Florida can carry severe consequences, including hefty fines and imprisonment. However, there are various defenses available to those facing counterfeit currency charges, depending on the specifics of the case. This chapter will provide an overview of the offense of counterfeiting in Florida, examine potential defenses to such charges, and explore strategies for successfully defending against these serious allegations.

---

1. Understanding Counterfeit Currency Charges in Florida

Under both federal and state law, counterfeit currency refers to any form of fake or fraudulent money that is intentionally created to deceive others into accepting it as genuine. In Florida, counterfeit currency charges typically fall under **Florida Statutes 831.01 to 831.08**, which govern the possession, manufacture, and passing of counterfeit money.

Key Elements of the Offense

The following are the primary elements that prosecutors must prove in a counterfeit currency case in Florida:

- **Possession of Counterfeit Currency**: The defendant must have knowingly possessed counterfeit money.
- **Intent to Defraud**: The defendant must have had the intent to pass the counterfeit currency as genuine, or to use it to defraud someone.

- **Knowledge of the Counterfeit Nature**: The defendant must have known that the currency was counterfeit. If a person is unaware that they are in possession of fake currency, they may not be guilty of this crime.

Types of Counterfeit Currency Offenses in Florida

Florida law distinguishes between different types of counterfeit currency offenses:

- **Possession of Counterfeit Currency** (Florida Statute 831.03): Simply possessing counterfeit currency is illegal, and it is a third-degree felony in Florida. A conviction can result in up to 5 years in prison and fines up to $5,000.
- **Passing Counterfeit Currency** (Florida Statute 831.02): This offense involves knowingly using counterfeit currency to purchase goods or services, or to give the fake money to someone else. This is a second-degree felony, punishable by up to 15 years in prison and fines of up to $10,000.
- **Manufacturing Counterfeit Currency** (Florida Statute 831.01): The act of producing counterfeit money, whether it is intended to pass as legitimate currency or not, is a third-degree felony in Florida.

---

2. Common Defenses Against Counterfeit Currency Charges

A defense against counterfeit currency charges in Florida can be based on a variety of factors, including a lack of intent, lack of knowledge, or mistakes in identification. The following are some of the most common defenses to be used in such cases:

A. Lack of Knowledge

One of the most common defenses in counterfeit currency cases is that the defendant was unaware that the currency was counterfeit. This is particularly relevant if the defendant received the counterfeit money from someone else and had no reason to believe it was not legitimate. To successfully raise this defense, the defendant may present evidence showing that they were duped by someone else and had no intent to defraud.

For example:

- The defendant may have received counterfeit money as change in a transaction.
- The defendant may have been unaware that the money was fake when it was passed to them, and they had no knowledge that the money was counterfeit at the time it was used.

If the defense can show that the defendant did not know the currency was counterfeit and had no intent to defraud, this may lead to a dismissal or reduction of the charges.

B. Lack of Intent to Defraud

Even if the defendant is aware that they possess counterfeit currency, they may not have had the intent to defraud anyone. Under Florida law, intent is a crucial element of the offense. A defendant could argue that their actions were unintentional or accidental.

For example:

- The defendant may have tried to use the counterfeit money in good faith but without an intent to deceive or defraud anyone. They may have believed the currency was genuine and may have acted in a reckless or careless manner rather than intentionally intending to pass fake money.

- In other situations, the defendant may have been unknowingly involved in a larger scheme of fraud but did not have direct intent to defraud the recipient.

Proving that the defendant did not have the intent to defraud can help in reducing the charges or getting the case dismissed.

C. Mistake of Fact

Mistake of fact is a legal defense where the defendant asserts that they acted based on a mistaken understanding of the facts. In the case of counterfeit currency, this might involve the defendant receiving or passing counterfeit money by mistake. The defendant may have believed the money was real, based on the circumstances or their prior experiences.

For example:

- The defendant might argue that they received the counterfeit money from a legitimate source, such as a store or another individual, and had no reason to question its authenticity.
- If the counterfeit money was very well-made and appeared genuine, the defendant may argue that they made a mistake in believing the money was valid.

A mistake of fact defense can be used to establish that the defendant was not intentionally involved in any criminal activity.

D. Improper Law Enforcement Procedure or Evidence Handling

If the counterfeit currency was obtained through an unlawful search or seizure, or if the police did not follow proper procedure in collecting or handling evidence, this could serve as the basis for a defense. In such a case, the defendant might file a motion to suppress the evidence, arguing that the counterfeit currency should not be admissible in court.

For example:

- If the currency was seized without a warrant or probable cause, the defendant can argue that the seizure was illegal.
- If the counterfeit currency was mishandled or tampered with by law enforcement, the defendant may challenge the evidence's integrity.

In such cases, if the defense can prove procedural errors or improper handling of evidence, the counterfeit currency charge could be dismissed or the evidence excluded.

---

3. Key Legal Strategies for Beating the Charge

A. Challenge the Authenticity of the Evidence

A defense attorney might seek to challenge the authenticity of the counterfeit currency itself. For example, the currency may not meet the legal definition of "counterfeit" as specified under Florida law. A forensic expert or expert witness may be used to examine the currency and testify that it does not meet the necessary criteria to be considered counterfeit.

B. Negotiating with Prosecutors for Reduced Charges

In some cases, a defense attorney may be able to negotiate with prosecutors to reduce the charges to a less severe offense. For example, a defendant charged with manufacturing counterfeit currency might agree to a plea deal for possession or passing counterfeit currency. This could result in a lesser sentence or reduced fines.

C. Gathering Exculpatory Evidence

Gathering evidence that supports the defendant's version of events is critical to winning a counterfeit currency case. This may include:

- Witnesses who can testify that the defendant received the counterfeit money without knowing it.
- Documentation showing that the defendant did not intentionally pass fake currency.
- Video footage or transaction records that can corroborate the defendant's story.

Such evidence can bolster the defense's case and potentially lead to a favorable outcome.

---

4. The Importance of Legal Representation

Because counterfeit currency charges carry serious penalties, it is essential to work with an experienced criminal defense attorney who understands Florida's laws and has experience defending clients against similar charges. A skilled attorney will be able to:

- Investigate the facts of the case thoroughly.
- Identify weaknesses in the prosecution's case.
- Raise valid legal defenses based on the facts and circumstances.
- Negotiate for reduced charges or alternative sentencing options.

An attorney experienced in handling counterfeit currency cases will also be familiar with federal laws, as counterfeiting is typically prosecuted at the federal level, which could bring additional complexity to the case.

---

5. Conclusion

Being charged with counterfeit currency offenses in Florida can be daunting, but it is important to remember that several defenses may be available to challenge these charges. Whether through demonstrating a lack of knowledge, lack of intent, or highlighting procedural issues with the case, a skilled criminal defense attorney can often provide a strong defense against counterfeit currency charges.

Anyone facing these charges should consult with an experienced defense attorney who can provide expert legal counsel and increase the chances of a favorable outcome. With the right defense strategy, it is possible to avoid the harsh penalties associated with counterfeit currency offenses.

CHAPTER FIFTY FOUR.

BEATING BANK FRAUD CHARGES IN FLORIDA

INTRODUCTION

Bank fraud is a serious financial crime in Florida, and it involves illegal actions designed to deceive financial institutions and gain unauthorized financial benefits. Whether it's through falsifying documents, misrepresenting information, or using fraudulent methods to gain access to a bank account, bank fraud charges carry severe consequences. In Florida, bank fraud is prosecuted aggressively, and a conviction can lead to significant prison time, hefty fines, and long-term damage to one's reputation. However, it is possible to beat bank fraud charges through various legal defenses, depending on the circumstances. This chapter will outline the elements of bank fraud, discuss potential defenses, and provide strategies to fight these charges effectively.

---

1. Understanding Bank Fraud in Florida

Bank fraud in Florida is primarily governed by **Florida Statutes Chapter 817**, which outlines various crimes related to fraud, including crimes involving financial institutions. Bank fraud itself involves using deceitful practices to obtain money, assets, or property from a bank or other financial institution. It can include a variety of fraudulent acts such as identity theft, check fraud, credit card fraud, and loan fraud.

Key Elements of Bank Fraud

To secure a conviction for bank fraud in Florida, the prosecution must prove the following elements beyond a reasonable doubt:

- **Intent to Defraud**: The defendant must have knowingly and intentionally attempted to deceive the bank or financial institution with fraudulent intent. This means the person must have been aware of the fraud and acted deliberately to deceive the institution.
- **False Representation or Falsified Information**: The defendant must have used false representations, statements, or documents to carry out the fraudulent activity. This could involve submitting fake paperwork, altering financial documents, or providing incorrect information to obtain loans, credit, or funds.
- **Connection to a Bank or Financial Institution**: The fraud must involve a bank, credit union, or other financial institution. This is a key element, as non-bank frauds may fall under different laws, and the institution must be directly affected by the fraudulent activity.

Penalties for Bank Fraud

Bank fraud is a **third-degree felony** in Florida, punishable by up to **5 years in prison, $5,000 in fines**, and possible probation. However, if the fraud involves larger amounts or is part of a larger criminal scheme, the penalties may be significantly increased. In cases where the fraud is committed through the use of interstate commerce or mail, federal charges could apply, carrying even harsher penalties.

---

2. Common Defenses Against Bank Fraud Charges

There are several defenses that can be raised against bank fraud charges in Florida. These defenses vary depending on the specific facts of the case, but the following are some of the most commonly used:

A. Lack of Intent to Defraud

A critical element in a bank fraud case is the defendant's intent. To be guilty of bank fraud, the prosecution must prove that the defendant had the specific intent to defraud the bank or financial institution. If the defendant lacked the intent to deceive or defraud, they cannot be convicted.

Common scenarios where this defense may apply include:

- **Mistake or misunderstanding**: The defendant may have made an error in submitting information to the bank, but there was no intent to deceive.
- **Inadvertent error**: If the defendant made an honest mistake, such as misinterpreting the terms of a loan or failing to understand the implications of certain financial actions, they may argue that there was no fraudulent intent.

If the defense can show that the defendant did not intend to defraud the bank or mislead the institution, the case may be dismissed or result in a reduced charge.

B. Lack of False Representation or Falsified Information

For a bank fraud conviction, the prosecution must prove that false information was intentionally submitted. If the defendant did not make any false statements or provide fraudulent documents, this can serve as a strong defense.

Examples of this defense include:

- The defendant may have provided truthful or accurate information but was accused of providing false documentation.

- The defendant may have been the victim of another party's fraudulent actions, in which case they may not be liable for the fraudulent acts of others.

A thorough investigation into the evidence can reveal inconsistencies or lack of proof that the defendant falsified information, which could lead to the charges being dropped or reduced.

C. Entrapment

Entrapment occurs when law enforcement officers or government agents induce a person to commit a crime they would not have otherwise committed. If the defendant can prove they were coerced or manipulated by law enforcement into committing fraudulent acts they would not have otherwise engaged in, they may have a valid entrapment defense.

In bank fraud cases, this could include situations where an undercover agent encouraged the defendant to falsify documents or misrepresent their financial status in a way they wouldn't have done under normal circumstances.

D. Involuntary Action

If the defendant did not voluntarily or knowingly engage in fraudulent behavior, they might be able to argue that their actions were involuntary. This defense could apply in cases where the defendant was acting under duress, coercion, or extreme pressure and was not fully aware of the nature of their actions.

For example:

- The defendant could have been coerced into committing fraudulent actions by another party who threatened them with harm.

- The defendant may have been influenced by extreme personal circumstances or mental health issues that affected their ability to understand the actions they were taking.

Involuntary action may be difficult to prove but can be a valid defense when supported by evidence.

E. Insufficient Evidence

In any criminal case, the burden of proof lies with the prosecution. The defendant is not required to prove their innocence; instead, the prosecution must prove the defendant's guilt beyond a reasonable doubt. If the prosecution fails to provide sufficient evidence to support all elements of the bank fraud charge, the defense can argue that the case should be dismissed due to lack of evidence.

Examples include:

- Incomplete or contradictory financial records.
- Lack of clear evidence that the defendant knowingly submitted false information.
- Failure to prove that the bank or financial institution was directly impacted by the alleged fraudulent activities.

---

3. Key Legal Strategies for Beating Bank Fraud Charges

A. Challenging the Fraudulent Documents or Evidence

Bank fraud charges often rely heavily on documents that may have been altered, forged, or misrepresented. A strong defense strategy can involve challenging the authenticity of the documents presented as evidence. For instance:

- **Forensic document experts** can be used to examine signatures, alterations, and other aspects of the documents to demonstrate they were not falsified or were mistakenly created.
- **Digital evidence** such as email correspondence, transaction logs, or computer records can be scrutinized to show that no fraudulent acts occurred or that the defendant was not responsible for the discrepancies.

By casting doubt on the evidence, the defense may be able to weaken the prosecution's case.

B. Negotiating a Plea Bargain

In some cases, it may be in the best interest of the defendant to negotiate a plea deal with the prosecution. While this may result in a reduced charge or sentence, a plea bargain could help avoid a lengthy trial and the risk of a harsh conviction.

A skilled attorney can negotiate with the prosecutor for a reduction in charges or a more lenient sentence, such as probation, community service, or restitution instead of imprisonment.

C. Reviewing the Financial Institution's Practices

It may be beneficial to examine the policies and practices of the financial institution involved in the fraud. In some cases, banks may not have followed proper procedures when handling accounts, loans, or documents, and this can be used as a defense. For instance:

- The financial institution may have failed to properly verify the information provided by the defendant, leading to confusion or errors.
- The defendant may have been a victim of the bank's negligence in its handling of financial transactions.

If the defense can demonstrate that the bank or financial institution failed to follow proper procedures, the defendant may not be liable for the alleged fraud.

---

4. The Importance of Skilled Legal Representation

Given the serious nature of bank fraud charges in Florida, it is essential to retain experienced legal counsel if you are facing such allegations. A skilled criminal defense attorney specializing in financial crimes will be able to:

- Thoroughly review the case and develop an effective defense strategy.
- Negotiate with prosecutors for a favorable plea deal or reduced charges.
- Challenge the prosecution's evidence and build a case for the defense.
- Provide guidance throughout the legal process, from pre-trial motions to trial proceedings.

A strong legal defense is crucial in avoiding severe penalties and ensuring the best possible outcome in a bank fraud case.

---

5. Conclusion

Bank fraud charges are serious offenses in Florida, but they are not insurmountable. By leveraging various defenses such as lack of intent, lack of false representation, or challenging the evidence, defendants may be able to avoid conviction or reduce their charges. The key to beating bank fraud charges is early legal intervention, gathering strong evidence, and working with a skilled defense attorney who can mount a strategic defense. With the right legal approach, it is possible to effectively fight these charges and protect your future.

CHAPTER FIFTY FIVE

FIGHTING CREDIT CARD FRAUD CHARGES IN FLORIDA

Mark sat in his attorney's office, his mind racing. Just a week ago, he had been living his normal life—working his job, paying his bills, and taking care of his family. Now, he was facing felony credit card fraud charges that could send him to prison for years.

"This has to be a mistake," he told his lawyer, Alex Carter, a seasoned defense attorney with a reputation for dismantling financial crime cases.

"It might be," Alex said, "but the prosecution isn't in the business of assuming mistakes. They're here to convict."

Mark had never been arrested before. His supposed crime? A series of unauthorized credit card transactions linked to his account—purchases he swore he didn't make. But proving that in a courtroom? That was another matter entirely.

Understanding the Charges

Florida's credit card fraud laws are strict, outlined under Florida Statute 817.61. The state considers fraud to be the unlawful use of a credit card to obtain money, goods, or services. The severity of the charges depends on the amount allegedly stolen:

- Less than $300: Misdemeanor, punishable by up to one year in jail and a $1,000 fine.
- More than $300 (within six months): Third-degree felony, punishable by up to five years in prison and a $5,000 fine.
- More than $20,000: Second-degree felony, with a 15-year prison sentence possible.

The burden of proof rested on the prosecution. To convict Mark, they needed to show:

1. That he knowingly used a credit card fraudulently.
2. That he intended to commit a crime.
3. That his actions resulted in financial loss to a victim.

Mark had one advantage—he had a strong defense attorney who knew how to fight these cases.

Building the Defense

Alex leaned back in his chair, studying the case file. "We have options," he said. "The prosecution has to prove intent. If they can't, we can beat this."

1. Lack of Intent

Mark insisted that he never intended to commit fraud. Alex planned to argue that Mark was simply the victim of identity theft—perhaps a stolen card number, or a case of account compromise.

"We'll subpoena the bank records and the retailer's security footage," Alex said. "If there's no proof that you personally made these purchases, the case weakens."

2. Mistaken Identity

Prosecutors often rely on electronic evidence—transaction timestamps, IP addresses, or security footage. But those can be misleading.

"Do you ever let someone else use your card?" Alex asked.

Mark shook his head. "No. But I was at a bar a few weeks ago, and I used my card at an ATM. Someone could have skimmed it."

That was critical. Card skimming and hacking are common defenses in credit card fraud cases. If Alex could introduce reasonable doubt that Mark's card had been cloned, it would force the prosecution to rethink their stance.

3. Insufficient Evidence

A strong defense often comes down to evidence—or lack thereof. In many fraud cases, prosecutors rely on circumstantial connections rather than direct proof.

Alex planned to challenge the state's case by requesting:

- Surveillance footage from stores where the transactions occurred.
- IP address tracking for online purchases.
- Forensic analysis of Mark's devices to show he never accessed the fraudulent accounts.

If the prosecution couldn't definitively tie Mark to the transactions, they would struggle to convince a jury.

4. Procedural Violations

"Did the police search your house or phone?" Alex asked.

Mark nodded. "They went through my laptop."

That was a potential Fourth Amendment violation. If law enforcement hadn't obtained the right warrants, any evidence they found could be thrown out.

Alex filed a motion to suppress the illegally obtained evidence. If granted, it would cripple the prosecution's case.

Pretrial Negotiations & Strategy

Before trial, Alex worked on two strategies—pushing for dismissal or negotiating a plea deal.

- Motion to Dismiss: If the prosecution's evidence was weak, Alex would argue for a full dismissal.
- Plea Bargain: If dismissal wasn't possible, Alex could negotiate for a misdemeanor charge with no jail time.

"Your clean record works in your favor," Alex said. "If we play this right, you could walk away with no conviction at all."

Courtroom Battle

The trial day arrived. The prosecution presented bank records, claiming they linked Mark to the fraud.

But Alex countered with expert testimony from a digital forensics investigator, who showed that the transactions originated from an IP address in another state—one that Mark had never visited.

When the judge reviewed the evidence, it became clear: there was too much reasonable doubt.

"Case dismissed," the judge ruled.

Aftermath

Mark walked out of the courtroom a free man, his life intact. He had faced a terrifying ordeal but, with the right defense, had beaten the charges.

"I still don't know how this happened," he said.

Alex nodded. “These cases happen more than you think. What matters is that we fought back—and won.”

CHAPTER FIFTY SIX.

BEATING CARJACKING CHARGES IN FLORIDA

INTRODUCTION

Carjacking is one of the most serious criminal offenses in Florida, involving the forceful or violent taking of a vehicle from another person. This crime is heavily penalized due to its violent nature, with convictions leading to long prison sentences and significant fines. Florida law treats carjacking as a first-degree felony, which can result in severe consequences for those convicted. However, it is important to understand that being charged with carjacking does not automatically mean conviction. There are various legal defenses available to challenge these charges. This chapter will explore the elements of carjacking under Florida law, the potential defenses available to those accused of this crime, and strategies to effectively fight carjacking charges.

---

1. Understanding Carjacking in Florida

Under **Florida Statute 812.133**, carjacking is defined as the taking of a motor vehicle from another person, either by force, violence, or the threat of force or violence. The key element that distinguishes carjacking from other theft-related crimes is the use of force or intimidation to take the vehicle directly from the victim.

Key Elements of Carjacking

For a person to be convicted of carjacking, the prosecution must prove the following elements beyond a reasonable doubt:

- **Taking a Vehicle**: The defendant must have taken or attempted to take a motor vehicle from another person. This includes physically removing the victim from the vehicle or forcing them to give up control of it.

- **Use of Force or Threat of Force**: The defendant must have used force, violence, or threats of violence to take the vehicle. This includes physical force or the threat of harm to the victim if they do not comply.

- **The Victim's Presence**: The victim must have been present during the carjacking. The crime involves direct confrontation or interaction between the defendant and the victim, not simply stealing a car that is unoccupied.

Penalties for Carjacking in Florida

Carjacking in Florida is a **first-degree felony**, punishable by:

- Up to **life in prison**.
- A minimum sentence of **10 years in prison** if a firearm was used during the commission of the crime.
- **Fines** of up to **$10,000**.

If the carjacking involves the use of a firearm, the penalties can be even more severe, and the defendant may face additional charges related to the use of the firearm.

---

2. Common Defenses Against Carjacking Charges

There are several defenses that can be raised against carjacking charges in Florida, which can potentially result in a dismissal of the charges or a reduction in penalties. The most common defenses include:

A. Lack of Intent or Knowledge

Carjacking charges require proof of the defendant's intent to take the vehicle using force or the threat of force. If the defendant did not have the intent to steal the vehicle or use violence, this can be a strong defense.

For example:

- The defendant may have been involved in a situation where the alleged "taking" of the vehicle was not intentional. Perhaps the defendant mistakenly believed that they were allowed to drive the vehicle or had permission to take it.
- The defendant may have been attempting to flee a dangerous situation, such as being chased or attacked, and took the vehicle in a moment of panic without intending to commit a carjacking.

A lack of intent to commit the crime may be enough to raise reasonable doubt in the prosecution's case, leading to a dismissal or reduction of charges.

B. Self-Defense

In some cases, a defendant may claim that they were acting in self-defense when taking the vehicle. This defense could apply if the defendant was facing a real and imminent threat of harm and took the vehicle to escape the situation.

For example:

- The defendant may have been threatened with violence by the car's owner or another person, leading them to take the vehicle to avoid serious harm or death.
- If the defendant can prove that they were acting in self-defense, the charges could be reduced or dropped entirely.

It is essential that the defendant shows they were in immediate fear for their safety and that their response (taking the vehicle) was proportional to the threat they faced.

C. False Allegations or Mistaken Identity

Carjacking cases often come down to the credibility of the victim and witness testimony. If the defendant can show that they were not the person who committed the crime, or that the victim's identification of them was inaccurate, this can lead to the charges being dropped.

Common scenarios where mistaken identity or false allegations can be used as a defense include:

- The victim mistakenly identified the defendant in a police lineup or during a show-up.
- The defendant has a strong alibi or can prove that they were somewhere else when the carjacking occurred.
- The defendant may have been wrongly accused due to personal animosity, a misunderstanding, or other reasons unrelated to the crime.

The defense can investigate the circumstances of the accusation and highlight inconsistencies or flaws in the victim's testimony.

D. Insufficient Evidence

In any criminal case, the prosecution must prove its case beyond a reasonable doubt. If there is insufficient evidence to prove the defendant's involvement in the carjacking, this can be grounds for a dismissal or acquittal.

Examples of insufficient evidence include:

- Lack of physical evidence linking the defendant to the crime, such as fingerprints, DNA, or surveillance footage.
- No credible witnesses who saw the defendant commit the carjacking.
- The defendant's lack of motive or opportunity to commit the crime.

If the prosecution cannot establish a clear connection between the defendant and the carjacking, the case may be dismissed or result in a not guilty verdict.

E. Entrapment

Entrapment occurs when law enforcement officers or agents induce a person to commit a crime they would not have otherwise committed. In a carjacking case, the defendant could argue that they were coerced or manipulated by law enforcement to take the vehicle.

For example:

- Law enforcement officers may have set up a sting operation where they encouraged the defendant to take a car under circumstances that would not have occurred naturally.
- The defendant may have been pressured or threatened by law enforcement into committing the crime.

If the defense can prove entrapment, the charges may be dismissed or the defendant may be acquitted.

---

3. Key Legal Strategies for Beating the Charge

A. Challenging the Credibility of Witnesses

In many carjacking cases, the outcome depends on witness testimony, including the victim's version of events. The defense can attack the credibility of these witnesses by:

- Presenting evidence that contradicts the victim's testimony.
- Highlighting inconsistencies in the victim's statements or actions.
- Presenting alternative witnesses or evidence that cast doubt on the accuracy of the victim's account.

Inconsistent or unreliable witness testimony can weaken the prosecution's case and help the defense create reasonable doubt.

B. Negotiating a Plea Deal

If the evidence against the defendant is strong and the risk of conviction is high, negotiating a plea deal with the prosecution may be a strategic option. In exchange for a guilty plea to a lesser charge or a reduced sentence, the defendant may avoid the harsh penalties associated with a carjacking conviction.

A skilled defense attorney can work with the prosecution to secure a plea deal that minimizes the defendant's exposure to prison time and may offer a more favorable outcome, such as probation or a reduced charge.

C. Pre-Trial Motions

A defense attorney may file pre-trial motions to challenge the evidence before the trial begins. Some motions that could be filed include:

- **Motion to Suppress Evidence**: If evidence was obtained illegally (such as through an unlawful search or seizure), the defense can file a motion to exclude that evidence.
- **Motion to Dismiss**: If there is insufficient evidence to support the carjacking charge, the defense can file a motion to dismiss the case before it goes to trial.

Filing pre-trial motions can be a way to eliminate evidence or even secure a dismissal of the charges before trial.

---

4. The Importance of Legal Representation

Carjacking charges are extremely serious, and defending against such charges requires a skilled and experienced criminal defense attorney. A knowledgeable lawyer can:

- Investigate the facts of the case to uncover any inconsistencies or weaknesses in the prosecution's evidence.
- Develop a tailored defense strategy based on the defendant's specific circumstances.
- Negotiate with the prosecution for a reduced sentence or alternative punishment if appropriate.
- Represent the defendant in court, challenging the prosecution's case and presenting a compelling defense.

Having an experienced attorney can significantly improve the chances of obtaining a favorable outcome in a carjacking case.

---

5. Conclusion

Carjacking charges in Florida carry severe penalties, but a conviction is not guaranteed. With the right legal strategy, defendants can challenge the charges through defenses such as lack of intent, self-defense, mistaken identity, insufficient evidence, and entrapment. It is essential for anyone facing carjacking charges to consult with an experienced criminal defense attorney to help build a strong defense and protect their rights. With effective representation, it is possible to fight carjacking charges and avoid the harsh consequences associated with a conviction.

CHAPTER FIFTY SEVEN.

BEATING HOME INVASION CHARGES IN FLORIDA

INTRODUCTION

Home invasion is one of the most severe crimes in Florida. The state treats it as an extremely serious offense due to its violent nature and the threat it poses to individuals in their own homes. Home invasion charges can carry significant penalties, including long prison sentences and hefty fines. Florida law defines home invasion as the unlawful entry into a dwelling with the intent to commit a crime, often involving violence, and it can lead to charges that may be difficult to fight without skilled legal representation. However, facing home invasion charges does not necessarily mean a conviction is inevitable. There are various defenses and strategies that can be employed to challenge the accusations. This chapter will provide an overview of home invasion charges in Florida, outline the key legal defenses that can be used to fight these charges, and offer strategies for defending against home invasion allegations.

---

1. Understanding Home Invasion in Florida

Under **Florida Statute 810.011**, home invasion is a first-degree felony involving the unlawful and forceful entry into a dwelling with the intent to commit a crime, such as robbery, assault, or theft. A home invasion becomes particularly serious if the defendant uses a weapon or commits violence against the occupants of the dwelling.

Key Elements of Home Invasion

For a conviction of home invasion in Florida, the prosecution must prove the following elements beyond a reasonable doubt:

- **Unlawful Entry**: The defendant must have entered or attempted to enter a dwelling without the owner's consent. This can involve breaking and entering, entering through an open door, or entering by other unauthorized means.

- **Intent to Commit a Crime**: The defendant must have entered the dwelling with the intent to commit a crime, such as theft, assault, or battery. If the defendant entered with no criminal intent (for example, as a guest or by mistake), the charge of home invasion would not apply.

- **Use of Force, Violence, or Threat of Force**: If the defendant was armed or threatened the occupants of the dwelling with force, this would elevate the charges and penalties, especially if a weapon (such as a firearm) was involved. If the defendant was unarmed and did not use violence or threats, this could weaken the prosecution's case.

Penalties for Home Invasion

Home invasion in Florida is a **first-degree felony**, which can lead to:

- Up to **life imprisonment**.
- **Minimum mandatory sentences** if a firearm or other weapon was used during the crime.
- **Fines** of up to **$10,000**.
- Possible **enhanced penalties** if the crime involved a firearm or resulted in serious bodily injury.

A conviction for home invasion with a firearm could lead to a **minimum mandatory sentence of 10 years in prison**, and using a firearm or other weapon could further increase the severity of the penalties.

2. Common Defenses Against Home Invasion Charges

There are several defenses that can be raised in a home invasion case. These defenses often depend on the facts of the case, but the following are some of the most common and effective defenses against home invasion charges in Florida:

A. Lack of Intent to Commit a Crime

One of the key elements of home invasion is that the defendant entered the dwelling with the intent to commit a crime. If the defendant did not have this intent, they cannot be convicted of home invasion.

Possible scenarios where lack of intent could be used as a defense include:

- The defendant may have entered the dwelling without the intention to commit a crime, perhaps as a result of confusion or misunderstanding. For example, they could have entered the wrong house or thought they had permission to enter.
- The defendant could have entered the dwelling to retrieve something or to speak with someone, without any intention of committing a crime.

If the defendant can demonstrate that they did not have the intent to commit a crime, this could weaken the prosecution's case and result in a dismissal of the charges or a reduction in charges.

B. Consent to Enter the Dwelling

If the defendant had permission or consent from the owner or occupant of the dwelling to enter, there is no unlawful entry, and the charge of home invasion would not apply. This defense can be particularly useful if the defendant is a visitor or someone who had legitimate access to the dwelling.

For example:

- The defendant may have been invited into the home by the resident or occupant and did not have any intention of committing a crime.
- If the defendant can provide evidence that they were welcome in the home, this could be a strong defense against the charge.

This defense relies on showing that the entry was consensual and not unauthorized, which can be a key factor in defeating the charge.

C. Mistaken Identity or False Accusations

In cases where the defendant is wrongly identified or falsely accused, challenging the identity of the perpetrator can be an effective defense. The defendant may argue that they were not the individual who committed the home invasion or that they were mistakenly identified by the victim or witnesses.

Scenarios where mistaken identity or false accusations may arise include:

- The victim or witnesses may have been too scared or confused to accurately identify the perpetrator.
- The defendant may have an alibi or be able to demonstrate that they were not at the scene of the crime when the home invasion occurred.
- The victim may have made a mistake in identifying the defendant, or they may have falsely accused the defendant due to a personal dispute or other reasons.

A strong alibi, witness testimony, or evidence proving that the defendant was not involved in the crime can lead to a dismissal of charges or an acquittal.

D. Lack of Use of Force or Violence

Another possible defense is that the defendant did not use force, violence, or the threat of violence while entering the dwelling. If the defendant entered the home without engaging in violent behavior or threatening the occupants, this could reduce the severity of the charge and penalties.

Examples of this defense include:

- The defendant did not engage in any violent behavior, such as physically attacking the occupants or threatening them with harm.
- The defendant did not carry a weapon or use force to break into the home.

By demonstrating that there was no violence or threat of violence involved, the defendant may be able to reduce the charges or avoid enhanced penalties.

E. Self-Defense

In certain cases, the defendant may argue that they entered the dwelling in self-defense or to avoid harm. If the defendant was in danger or felt threatened, they may have entered the home to seek refuge or to protect themselves from immediate harm.

This defense might apply in situations such as:

- The defendant was fleeing from an assailant or dangerous situation and took refuge in the home, believing they were in danger.
- The defendant was attempting to defend themselves from a violent attack by an occupant of the dwelling.

To succeed with this defense, the defendant must show that they had a reasonable belief that they were in imminent danger and that their actions were proportional to the threat they faced.

F. Insufficient Evidence

The prosecution bears the burden of proving the defendant's guilt beyond a reasonable doubt. If there is insufficient evidence to prove that the defendant committed a home invasion, the charges should be dropped or the defendant should be acquitted.

Weaknesses in the prosecution's evidence could include:

- Lack of physical evidence linking the defendant to the crime, such as fingerprints, DNA, or surveillance footage.
- Inconsistencies in the victim's testimony or contradictions in witness statements.
- No credible eyewitnesses who can definitively identify the defendant as the perpetrator.

If the defense can highlight the lack of convincing evidence, it may be possible to have the case dismissed or to secure a not guilty verdict.

---

3. Key Legal Strategies for Beating Home Invasion Charges

A. Challenging the Prosecution's Evidence

A skilled defense attorney will thoroughly examine the evidence presented by the prosecution to find inconsistencies or weaknesses. This may include:

- Reviewing physical evidence, such as fingerprints, DNA, and any items recovered from the crime scene.
- Investigating witness testimony for contradictions or unreliable statements.
- Examining surveillance footage or other video evidence to determine if the defendant's involvement can be proven.

By identifying weaknesses in the prosecution's case, the defense can create reasonable doubt and increase the chances of a favorable outcome.

B. Negotiating a Plea Bargain

In cases where the evidence is strong, a plea bargain may be an effective strategy. A plea deal could involve the defendant pleading guilty to a lesser charge in exchange for a reduced sentence or other favorable terms, such as probation or community service. A skilled defense attorney can negotiate with the prosecution for a more lenient outcome.

C. Pre-Trial Motions

A defense attorney may file pre-trial motions to challenge certain aspects of the case before the trial begins. Some examples of pre-trial motions include:

- **Motion to Suppress Evidence**: If the evidence was obtained unlawfully, such as through an illegal search or seizure, it may be excluded from the trial.
- **Motion to Dismiss**: If there is insufficient evidence to support the charges, the defense can file a motion to dismiss the case.

These motions can be crucial in weakening the prosecution's case and securing a favorable result for the defendant.

---

4. The Importance of Skilled Legal Representation

Home invasion charges in Florida are serious and carry severe consequences. Therefore, it is essential for anyone facing such charges to retain an experienced criminal defense attorney who specializes in violent crimes. A skilled lawyer will:

- Investigate the facts of the case and develop an effective defense strategy.
- Challenge the prosecution's evidence and witness testimony.
- Negotiate plea deals or alternative sentencing options if appropriate.
- Provide expert legal representation throughout the trial process.

A strong defense can make the difference between a conviction and a favorable outcome, so seeking the help of an experienced attorney is critical when facing home invasion charges.

---

5. Conclusion

Home invasion charges are among the most serious criminal charges in Florida, carrying significant penalties and long-lasting consequences. However, being charged with home invasion does not guarantee a conviction. There are several legal defenses that can be raised to challenge these charges, including lack of intent, mistaken identity, lack of force or violence, and self-defense. With the help of an experienced defense attorney, it is possible to fight home invasion charges and avoid a conviction or reduce the penalties associated with the offense. Legal strategies such as challenging the prosecution's evidence, filing pre-trial motions, and negotiating plea deals can also play a significant role in securing a favorable outcome.

CHAPTER FIFTY EIGHT.

BEATING FELONY MURDER CHARGES IN FLORIDA

INTRODUCTION

Felony murder is one of the most serious charges in Florida, carrying severe penalties, including life imprisonment or even the death penalty. Florida law treats felony murder as a first-degree felony, punishable by life in prison without the possibility of parole for those convicted under certain circumstances. In a felony murder case, the prosecution does not have to prove that the defendant intended to kill the victim. Instead, if the defendant was involved in the commission of a felony that led to someone's death, they can be charged with felony murder. This charge can be devastating, but there are legal defenses and strategies that can help defendants fight these charges. This chapter will explain felony murder in Florida, provide an overview of the potential defenses available, and discuss strategies for fighting felony murder allegations.

---

1. Understanding Felony Murder in Florida

Under **Florida Statute 782.04(1)(a)**, felony murder occurs when a person commits a killing during the commission of certain felonies, even if the killing was unintentional. The key factor in felony murder is that the killing occurred during the commission of a qualifying felony, not necessarily due to an intentional act of violence or malice.

Key Elements of Felony Murder

To secure a conviction for felony murder, the prosecution must prove the following elements beyond a reasonable doubt:

- **Commission of a Felony**: The defendant must have been engaged in the commission of a serious felony. Florida law lists several felonies that can lead to felony murder charges, including but not limited to:
    - **Robbery**
    - **Burglary**
    - **Arson**
    - **Sexual battery**
    - **Kidnapping**
    - **Aggravated assault**
- **Death of a Person**: The defendant's actions must have resulted in the death of another person. The death can be the result of direct actions (e.g., shooting someone during a robbery) or indirect actions (e.g., a co-felon unintentionally kills someone during a robbery or burglary).
- **Causation**: The killing must have occurred as a direct result of the felony. This means the prosecution must prove that the felony was a proximate cause of the death. If the death was caused by something unrelated to the felony, the felony murder charge may not apply.

Penalties for Felony Murder

Felony murder in Florida is classified as **first-degree murder**, which is a **capital felony**. A conviction for felony murder can result in:

- **Life imprisonment** without the possibility of parole (if not sentenced to death).
- The **death penalty**, if aggravating factors apply and the defendant is sentenced to capital punishment.

Given the severity of these penalties, defending against felony murder charges is crucial to avoid life-altering consequences.

2. Common Defenses Against Felony Murder Charges

While felony murder charges are serious, defendants do not automatically face conviction. There are several defenses that can be used to fight felony murder allegations in Florida. The specific defense will depend on the circumstances of the case, but the following are common strategies:

A. Lack of Participation in the Underlying Felony

One of the most straightforward defenses to felony murder is to argue that the defendant was not involved in the underlying felony that led to the death. If the prosecution cannot prove that the defendant was engaged in the commission of a felony, the felony murder charge may be dismissed or reduced.

Examples include:

- The defendant was not part of the robbery, burglary, or other felony being committed at the time of the death.
- The defendant can demonstrate that they had no knowledge of the felony being committed, such as being an innocent bystander or a person who was not directly involved in the criminal act.

If the defendant was not an active participant in the underlying felony, they cannot be held liable for felony murder.

B. No Causation Between the Felony and the Death

In felony murder cases, the prosecution must prove that the death was caused by the felony. If the defendant can show that the death was not caused by the felony or was the result of some independent action, this can be an effective defense.

Possible scenarios include:

- The victim's death was caused by something unrelated to the felony (for example, a pre-existing medical condition or a separate accident).
- The defendant can argue that the victim's death occurred because of the actions of a third party, not because of the felony.

If the defense can establish that the death was not a proximate result of the felony, the felony murder charge may not apply.

C. The Death Was Not Foreseeable

Under Florida law, a defendant may be charged with felony murder even if they did not directly cause the death, as long as the death occurred during the commission of a felony. However, if the defendant can show that the death was not foreseeable given the nature of the felony, they may be able to argue that felony murder does not apply.

For example:

- If the victim's death was caused by an unpredictable or unforeseen event (such as an accidental death), the defense could argue that it was not a foreseeable consequence of the felony.

This defense focuses on the argument that the defendant could not have anticipated that the felony would result in death and that the killing was an outlier event in the course of the crime.

D. Withdrawal from the Felony

If the defendant can prove that they withdrew from the felony before the death occurred, they may be able to avoid felony murder charges. Withdrawal means that the defendant voluntarily disengaged from the criminal activity before the death happened, thus breaking the chain of causality between their actions and the victim's death.

For example:

- The defendant might have started to participate in a robbery but then withdrew from the scene before the victim was killed, indicating that they were not involved in the fatal act.
- The defense could present evidence that the defendant took reasonable steps to stop the commission of the felony or to leave the scene, breaking any connection between their actions and the death.

If successful, this defense could reduce the severity of the charges or result in the dismissal of felony murder charges.

E. Co-Felon Defense (Fellow Felon Rule)

Under Florida's **fellow felon rule**, a defendant may be liable for felony murder if they were involved in a felony where someone else (such as an accomplice) caused the death of the victim. However, the defendant can argue that they should not be held responsible if the death was caused by an act that was not part of the original felony plan or was entirely outside of their control.

For example:

- If the co-felon intentionally kills the victim during a robbery, but the defendant did not plan or intend for violence to occur, they may be able to argue that they are not responsible for the murder, only for the underlying felony.
- The defense can argue that the death was an unforeseeable act by the co-felon, not a necessary or foreseeable consequence of the felony that was being committed.

This defense seeks to limit the scope of liability for a co-felon involved in a crime where another individual is responsible for the victim's death.

F. Self-Defense or Defense of Others

In some cases, a defendant may argue that they were acting in self-defense or in defense of others when the death occurred. For example, if the defendant was engaged in a robbery and the victim or someone else posed a threat, and the defendant acted to protect themselves or others, they may argue that the killing occurred in a context of justified defense.

For example:

- If the defendant shot and killed the victim in response to the victim drawing a weapon or threatening violence, the defendant may argue that the killing was a result of self-defense rather than the commission of a felony.

While it can be difficult to succeed with this defense in a felony murder case, it may be effective if the defendant can prove that their actions were motivated by fear of harm or immediate threat to their safety.

---

3. Key Legal Strategies for Beating Felony Murder Charges

A. Challenging the Prosecution's Evidence

The defense will often begin by carefully reviewing all the evidence presented by the prosecution. Common strategies for challenging the evidence include:

- Disputing witness testimony and presenting alternative accounts of the events.
- Questioning the validity or reliability of physical evidence (e.g., forensic evidence, DNA, or ballistics reports).
- Identifying inconsistencies in police reports or investigative methods that could undermine the prosecution's case.

If the defense can show that the prosecution's evidence does not conclusively prove the defendant's involvement in the felony or the murder, the charges may be dropped or reduced.

B. Negotiating a Plea Deal

In some cases, the defense may seek to negotiate a plea deal with the prosecution to reduce the severity of the charges. A plea agreement could involve pleading guilty to a lesser charge, such as manslaughter, in exchange for a reduced sentence or more lenient terms of punishment.

C. Filing Pre-Trial Motions

A skilled defense attorney may file pre-trial motions to exclude certain evidence or challenge the legality of the investigation. Key motions include:

- **Motion to Suppress Evidence**: If evidence was obtained through illegal means (e.g., an unlawful search or seizure), it may be excluded from the trial.
- **Motion to Dismiss**: If there is insufficient evidence to charge the defendant with felony murder, the defense can seek to have the case dismissed before trial.

---

4. The Importance of Legal Representation

Felony murder charges are incredibly serious, and the consequences of a conviction are severe. Having experienced legal representation is critical to building a strong defense and challenging the prosecution's case. A skilled criminal defense attorney will:

- Investigate the facts of the case thoroughly to identify weaknesses in the prosecution's argument.

- Develop a defense strategy tailored to the specific circumstances of the case.
- Negotiate plea deals or work to have charges reduced.
- Represent the defendant in court and advocate for the best possible outcome.

---

5. Conclusion

Felony murder charges in Florida are among the most serious charges a person can face, with life-altering consequences. However, a conviction is not automatic. There are several strong defenses that can be raised, including lack of participation in the felony, no causation between the felony and the death, and the death being unforeseeable. With the right legal strategy, a defendant may be able to fight these charges and avoid the severe penalties associated with felony murder. Seeking the help of an experienced defense attorney is crucial in navigating this complex area of law and ensuring that the defendant's rights are protected throughout the process.

CHAPTER FIFTY NINE

BEATING PROSTITUTION CHARGES IN FLORIDA

INTRODUCTION

Prostitution charges in Florida can carry serious legal consequences, including fines, imprisonment, mandatory counseling, and damage to one's reputation. Under Florida law, both those who engage in sex for money and those who solicit or offer sex for money are subject to prosecution. However, being charged with prostitution does not guarantee a conviction. With effective defense strategies, defendants may be able to avoid or minimize the penalties associated with these charges. This chapter will explore prostitution laws in Florida, provide an overview of potential defenses, and outline key legal strategies for beating prostitution charges.

---

1. Understanding Prostitution Laws in Florida

Florida law criminalizes prostitution under **Florida Statutes 796.07**. Prostitution encompasses engaging in, offering, or soliciting sexual activity for money or other forms of compensation. The law makes it clear that both parties involved in the exchange—those offering sexual services and those soliciting sex—can face criminal charges.

Key Elements of Prostitution Charges

To be convicted of prostitution under Florida law, the prosecution must prove the following elements beyond a reasonable doubt:

- **Engagement in Sexual Activity for Money or Compensation**: The defendant must have engaged in sexual activity with another person in exchange for money, goods, or services. This includes both the act of prostitution itself and soliciting or offering to engage in such activity.

- **Intent to Engage in Prostitution**: The defendant must have had the intent to engage in prostitution. If a defendant was unaware that sexual activity was being offered for money, this could potentially provide a defense.

- **Solicitation or Offer**: If the defendant is accused of soliciting prostitution, the prosecution must prove that the defendant made an offer to engage in sex in exchange for money. This could involve direct communication or implied solicitation.

Types of Prostitution-Related Charges

Prostitution-related charges in Florida can include:

- **Prostitution**: Engaging in sexual activity for money or goods.
- **Solicitation**: Offering or attempting to offer sexual services for compensation.
- **Pandering**: Encouraging or inducing someone to engage in prostitution or to operate as a prostitute.
- **Lewdness or Lascivious Behavior**: Publicly engaging in sexual acts or lewd conduct, which may overlap with prostitution offenses.

Penalties for these offenses can vary based on the nature of the charge and whether the defendant has any prior convictions. Convictions for prostitution can result in fines, jail time, probation, mandatory counseling, and community service.

2. Common Defenses Against Prostitution Charges

There are several potential defenses available to challenge prostitution charges in Florida. The viability of each defense will depend on the specific facts and circumstances of the case. Below are some of the most common defenses used in prostitution cases:

A. Lack of Intent to Engage in Prostitution

One of the most effective defenses against prostitution charges is proving that the defendant did not have the intent to engage in prostitution. The prosecution must prove that the defendant knowingly and intentionally participated in the act of prostitution. If the defendant can show that they did not have the intention to offer sexual services for money, the charge may be dismissed or reduced.

Examples where lack of intent could be relevant:

- The defendant may have been talking to someone or engaging in conversation but had no intention of accepting money in exchange for sexual activity.
- The defendant might argue that they were misled or manipulated into an encounter, believing it was a different kind of arrangement (e.g., dating or socializing) rather than prostitution.

B. Entrapment

Entrapment occurs when law enforcement officers induce or coerce a person into committing a crime they would not have otherwise committed. In prostitution cases, this typically happens when an undercover officer poses as a potential customer and convinces the defendant to offer sexual services.

To successfully argue entrapment, the defense must show that:

- Law enforcement officers initiated the interaction and encouraged the defendant to engage in prostitution.
- The defendant was not predisposed to commit prostitution but was induced or coerced by law enforcement into doing so.

If the defense can prove that the defendant was entrapped by law enforcement, the charges could be dropped or dismissed.

C. Mistaken Identity or False Accusations

In some cases, defendants may be falsely accused of engaging in prostitution or soliciting sex. This could happen due to mistaken identity or malicious intent on the part of another person (e.g., a disgruntled former partner or acquaintance).

Mistaken identity defenses can include:

- The defendant was misidentified by the arresting officer or the accuser.
- The defendant was not present at the scene of the alleged prostitution event and has an alibi to support their claim.

If the defendant can demonstrate that they were wrongly accused or that the accusation is based on a misunderstanding, this could lead to a dismissal or acquittal.

D. Lack of Evidence

In many cases, the prosecution's case will depend heavily on circumstantial evidence. The defense may argue that there is insufficient or no direct evidence to prove that the defendant engaged in prostitution or solicited sex for money.

The defense may point out weaknesses such as:

- No physical evidence or documentation proving the exchange of money for sexual services.
- Lack of corroborating witness testimony to confirm the defendant's involvement in prostitution.
- Inconsistencies in the alleged victim's testimony or law enforcement reports.

If the prosecution fails to present enough convincing evidence, the defendant may be acquitted or have the charges reduced.

E. Coercion or Duress

In some situations, a defendant might argue that they were forced or coerced into engaging in prostitution. For example, if the defendant was threatened or manipulated by someone else to offer sexual services, this could form the basis of a defense.

Defendants may argue that they engaged in prostitution under duress, such as:

- Being pressured by a controlling or abusive partner or associate.
- Facing threats of violence or harm if they did not comply with demands to engage in prostitution.

If the defense can demonstrate that the defendant was under duress and had no choice but to engage in the illegal act, this could reduce or eliminate liability.

F. Violation of Rights During the Arrest or Investigation

If law enforcement violated the defendant's constitutional rights during the investigation or arrest, it could be grounds for challenging the charges. Common violations include:

- **Unlawful search and seizure**: If evidence was obtained without a warrant or probable cause, it may be inadmissible in court.
- **Failure to read Miranda rights**: If the defendant was not informed of their right to remain silent and to have an attorney present during questioning, statements made during the arrest may be inadmissible.

In such cases, the defense can file a motion to suppress evidence or request that the case be dismissed due to the violation of the defendant's rights.

---

3. Key Legal Strategies for Beating Prostitution Charges

A. Challenge the Prosecution's Evidence

A critical part of defending against prostitution charges is challenging the evidence presented by the prosecution. The defense attorney may examine the following:

- **Witness testimony**: Are the police officers or witnesses reliable? Are there inconsistencies in their statements?
- **Physical evidence**: Is there any physical proof that the defendant engaged in prostitution (such as money exchanged, texts, or photos)?
- **Surveillance footage**: Was there any video or audio evidence obtained by law enforcement during the operation, and does it actually show the defendant engaging in prostitution?

By pointing out the weaknesses in the prosecution's case, the defense can raise reasonable doubt and seek an acquittal.

B. Negotiating a Plea Deal

In some cases, the evidence against the defendant may be strong, but there are still options for reducing the severity of the penalties. The defense may negotiate a plea deal with the prosecution, in which the defendant agrees to plead guilty to a lesser charge in exchange for a reduced sentence or other concessions.

For example:

- A defendant might plead guilty to a charge of **lewdness** rather than prostitution, which may carry a lighter sentence.
- The prosecution might offer probation or mandatory counseling in place of jail time.

A skilled attorney can negotiate a plea agreement that minimizes the consequences for the defendant.

C. File Pre-Trial Motions

Before the trial begins, the defense can file pre-trial motions to challenge certain aspects of the case. These may include:

- **Motion to Suppress Evidence**: If the evidence was obtained illegally, such as through an unlawful search or without a warrant, the defense can request that it be excluded from the trial.
- **Motion to Dismiss**: If the prosecution's evidence is insufficient to support a conviction, the defense may seek to have the charges dismissed before the trial begins.

Successfully filing pre-trial motions can significantly weaken the prosecution's case.

---

4. The Importance of Legal Representation

Prostitution charges in Florida can have lasting consequences, including fines, criminal records, and damage to one's personal and professional reputation. As such, it is crucial to have skilled legal representation when facing such charges. An experienced defense attorney can:

- Investigate the case thoroughly, gathering evidence and interviewing witnesses.
- Challenge the prosecution's evidence and identify weaknesses in the case.
- Negotiate with the prosecution for a reduced sentence or more favorable terms.
- Represent the defendant in court, advocating for the best possible outcome.

A strong defense strategy tailored to the specific facts of the case can make a significant difference in the outcome of the case.

---

5. Conclusion

Being charged with prostitution in Florida is a serious matter, but a conviction is not inevitable. With a skilled attorney and a strong defense strategy, it is possible to fight these charges effectively. The most common defenses to prostitution charges include lack of intent, mistaken identity, entrapment, coercion, and lack of evidence. By challenging the prosecution's case, filing pre-trial motions, or negotiating a plea deal, defendants may be able to reduce or avoid the penalties associated with prostitution charges. Legal representation is essential to ensuring that one's rights are protected and that the best possible defense is mounted.

CHAPTER SIXTY.

BEATING DISCHARGING A FIREARM CHARGES IN FLORIDA

INTRODUCTION

Discharging a firearm in Florida is a serious offense, and individuals charged with violating laws related to gunfire can face significant legal consequences, including imprisonment, fines, and a permanent criminal record. Under Florida law, discharging a firearm recklessly or in certain prohibited areas can lead to felony or misdemeanor charges, depending on the circumstances. However, like many criminal charges, a conviction is not inevitable. Defendants may have several legal avenues for defending themselves against accusations of discharging a firearm. This chapter will explore the key elements of discharging a firearm in Florida, potential defenses to the charge, and strategies for beating the charge.

---

1. Understanding the Law on Discharging a Firearm in Florida

In Florida, the laws governing the discharge of firearms are primarily set forth in **Florida Statute 790.15**. This statute prohibits the discharge of a firearm in certain situations and outlines the penalties for doing so.

Key Elements of Discharging a Firearm Charges

To understand how to beat a charge of discharging a firearm, it's essential to understand the elements the prosecution must prove in order to convict a defendant:

1. **Discharge of a Firearm**: The defendant must have intentionally fired a gun. This can include firing a weapon either directly at a target, into

the air, or in a general direction, regardless of whether anyone is injured or property is damaged.

2. **Location**: The law specifically prohibits the discharge of a firearm in certain places, such as:
    - In public or residential areas where it could endanger people or property.
    - Near schools or other prohibited locations.
    - In a manner that could reasonably be expected to cause harm to others, even if no one was harmed.

3. **Recklessness or Negligence**: The discharge of a firearm may be considered illegal if it is done recklessly or negligently, even if no harm or injury occurs. Florida law takes into account whether the shooting was done in a careless or dangerous manner.

Types of Charges for Discharging a Firearm

There are several types of charges associated with discharging a firearm in Florida, including:

- **Reckless Discharge of a Firearm**: Florida law criminalizes the reckless or careless firing of a firearm that endangers the safety of others or property. This is usually classified as a **third-degree felony** and carries serious penalties, including up to five years in prison and significant fines.

- **Discharge of a Firearm in Public or Residential Areas**: If a firearm is discharged in a public place or a residential area, it may result in a **second-degree misdemeanor** charge, which could carry up to 60 days in jail and fines.

- **Discharge of a Firearm Near Schools**: Discharging a firearm near a school, or within 1,000 feet of a school, is a **third-degree felony** under

Florida law. This is a more serious charge and can lead to harsher penalties, especially if it is determined that the discharge was done intentionally or recklessly.

Penalties

- **Misdemeanor Conviction**: A misdemeanor charge for discharging a firearm in a public or residential area carries a maximum penalty of up to 60 days in jail and a fine of up to $500.
- **Felony Conviction**: A felony conviction for reckless discharge or discharging a firearm near a school can result in up to five years in prison, substantial fines, and a permanent criminal record.

Because of the serious consequences associated with firearm-related charges, it is critical to understand the legal defenses available and how to contest the charges.

---

2. Common Defenses to Discharging a Firearm Charges

Several defenses can be raised to contest a charge of discharging a firearm in Florida. A successful defense may result in a dismissal of the charges, a reduction in the severity of the offense, or an acquittal. Below are some of the most common defenses that may be raised in cases involving firearm discharges.

A. Self-Defense or Defense of Others

In cases where the defendant discharged a firearm because they felt threatened or were acting in self-defense, they may raise a **self-defense** argument. Florida has **Stand Your Ground** laws, which allow individuals to use force, including deadly force, if they reasonably believe they are in imminent danger of harm.

If the defendant was legally justified in using a firearm to defend themselves or others, the discharge of the firearm may not constitute a crime. The defense may argue that the discharge was a response to an immediate threat of death or serious bodily injury.

For example:

- A defendant may argue that they fired a weapon to defend themselves against an attacker who was threatening their life.
- If the defendant was protecting someone else from harm, this defense could also apply.

To succeed with this defense, the defendant must provide evidence that their actions were reasonable and necessary in the context of the situation.

B. Accidental Discharge

If the defendant's firearm was discharged accidentally, they may argue that it was unintentional. Firearms can discharge accidentally if the safety is not engaged, or if the trigger is pulled accidentally. However, under Florida law, even accidental discharges in public areas can result in charges if the discharge endangers others.

However, if the defense can show that the discharge was truly an accident and did not endanger public safety, the charges could potentially be reduced or dropped. For example:

- The firearm was improperly handled, and the defendant had no intention of firing it.
- The discharge was due to a malfunction or defect in the firearm.

This defense can be bolstered by evidence such as the defendant's statements or testimony from firearm experts.

C. Lack of Evidence of Recklessness

To secure a conviction for reckless discharge of a firearm, the prosecution must prove that the defendant acted recklessly and endangered others. If the defendant can argue that they did not act recklessly and that their actions were within the bounds of lawful behavior, this can be a powerful defense.

The defense may argue that:

- The defendant fired the weapon in a controlled or safe manner, such as at a shooting range or on private property, where there was no risk to public safety.
- The discharge was not intentional and did not create a foreseeable danger.

If the defense can create doubt as to whether the defendant acted recklessly or negligently, it may be possible to have the charges reduced or dismissed.

D. Constitutional Violations (Search and Seizure)

If the firearm was discovered as a result of an unlawful search or seizure, the defense could challenge the charges based on constitutional violations. Under the **Fourth Amendment** of the U.S. Constitution, individuals are protected from unreasonable searches and seizures by law enforcement.

If the defendant was arrested without probable cause or a proper search warrant, any evidence obtained as a result of the unlawful search may be excluded from trial. This could weaken the prosecution's case and potentially result in the charges being dropped or dismissed.

E. Lack of Proximity to Schools

If the charge involves discharging a firearm near a school, the defense may argue that the discharge did not occur within the prohibited area or that the defendant was not aware of their proximity to the school. Florida law prohibits the discharge of a firearm within **1,000 feet of a school**, and the defense may seek to challenge this element if the prosecution cannot prove that the defendant was within this distance.

The defense could argue:

- The defendant was not near a school when the firearm was discharged.
- There was no indication that the defendant was aware that they were near a school, especially if the location was not clearly marked.

This defense may involve presenting evidence of the defendant's location at the time of the incident, such as GPS data, surveillance footage, or witness testimony.

---

3. Key Legal Strategies for Beating Discharging a Firearm Charges

A. Challenge the Evidence

One of the most important steps in defending against charges of discharging a firearm is challenging the evidence presented by the prosecution. This may include:

- Disputing the testimony of law enforcement officers or witnesses who claim to have seen the defendant discharge the firearm.
- Questioning the chain of custody of physical evidence, such as the firearm or shell casings.
- Challenging the results of any forensic analysis, such as gunshot residue tests, if the tests were conducted improperly or if the results are inconclusive.

By undermining the prosecution's evidence, the defense can raise reasonable doubt and work toward a favorable outcome for the defendant.

B. File Pre-Trial Motions

Pre-trial motions can be used to challenge aspects of the case before it even goes to trial. Some potential motions include:

- **Motion to Suppress Evidence**: If the firearm or other evidence was obtained through unlawful means, the defense can file a motion to suppress the evidence.
- **Motion to Dismiss**: If the prosecution's case is weak or lacks sufficient evidence, the defense may file a motion to dismiss the charges entirely.

These motions can be effective in reducing the chances of a conviction before the trial even begins.

C. Plea Negotiation

In cases where the evidence against the defendant is strong, the defense may seek to negotiate a plea deal with the prosecution. A plea deal could involve the defendant pleading guilty to a lesser charge, such as **disorderly conduct** or **reckless behavior**, in exchange for a reduced sentence or alternative penalties, such as probation or community service.

A plea deal can help avoid the uncertainty of a trial and may result in a more lenient sentence for the defendant.

---

4. Conclusion

Being charged with discharging a firearm in Florida is a serious matter, but a conviction is not inevitable. By utilizing strong legal defenses, including challenging the evidence, raising constitutional violations, or arguing lack of recklessness or intent, a defendant may be able to avoid the severe penalties associated with this charge. Skilled legal representation is crucial in navigating firearm-related offenses and ensuring that a fair defense is mounted. Through a strategic defense approach, it is possible to achieve a favorable outcome in a discharging a firearm case in Florida.

CHAPTER SIXTY ONE

BEATING RECKLESS DRIVING CHARGES IN FLORIDA

INTRODUCTION

Reckless driving is a serious offense in Florida, carrying the potential for significant consequences, including fines, license suspension, and even jail time. Reckless driving refers to operating a vehicle in a manner that demonstrates a willful disregard for the safety of people or property. While the penalties can be severe, there are numerous legal defenses that can be used to fight a reckless driving charge. This chapter will explore what constitutes reckless driving in Florida, potential defenses to this charge, and the best strategies to beat it in court.

---

1. Understanding Reckless Driving Laws in Florida

In Florida, reckless driving is defined under **Florida Statute 316.192**. According to this statute, reckless driving occurs when a person operates a vehicle in a way that shows a "willful or wanton disregard for the safety of persons or property." The law focuses on the driver's behavior and the risk their actions pose to others.

Key Elements of Reckless Driving

To convict someone of reckless driving, the prosecution must prove the following elements beyond a reasonable doubt:

1. **Operation of a Vehicle**: The defendant must have been driving a motor vehicle at the time of the alleged offense.
2. **Recklessness**: The defendant's driving behavior must demonstrate a willful or wanton disregard for the safety of others or property.

Recklessness is different from simple negligence in that it involves conscious disregard of the risk of harm.

3. **Endangerment**: The defendant's driving must have created a significant risk of injury or damage. It is not necessary for an actual accident to occur for someone to be convicted of reckless driving, only that their actions could have caused harm.

Types of Reckless Driving Charges

Reckless driving in Florida can be charged as:

- **First Offense**: If convicted of reckless driving for the first time, it is generally classified as a **second-degree misdemeanor**, punishable by up to 90 days in jail, fines, and the possibility of a driver's license suspension.

- **Second Offense**: If someone is convicted of reckless driving for a second time, the charge may be upgraded to a **first-degree misdemeanor**, which could result in up to 1 year in jail, higher fines, and additional penalties.

- **Reckless Driving with Serious Injury or Death**: If reckless driving results in serious injury or death to another person, it could be elevated to a **third-degree felony**, which carries more severe penalties, including prison time and long-term consequences.

---

2. Common Defenses Against Reckless Driving Charges

Reckless driving charges are often based on the subjective judgment of law enforcement officers, which can leave room for reasonable doubt. There are several possible defenses to reckless driving charges in Florida, and a skilled defense attorney will evaluate the specific facts of each case to determine which defense strategy is most appropriate.

A. Lack of Recklessness

One of the most effective defenses to reckless driving charges is to argue that the defendant's actions did not rise to the level of recklessness. While driving behaviors such as speeding, swerving, or driving aggressively may appear reckless at first glance, they may not necessarily demonstrate the "willful or wanton disregard for safety" required for a reckless driving conviction.

Examples where lack of recklessness could be argued include:

- **Unfamiliarity with the Area**: If the defendant was driving in an unfamiliar area and unintentionally made an error in judgment that did not endanger others, this could be used to argue that they were not acting recklessly.
- **Defensive Driving**: The defense may argue that the defendant was engaged in defensive driving (e.g., swerving to avoid an obstacle) rather than engaging in reckless behavior.

If the defense can show that the defendant's driving was simply an error or misunderstanding, it may be possible to get the charge reduced or dismissed.

B. Lack of Evidence of Endangerment

The prosecution must prove that the defendant's actions posed a risk to others or property. If no actual harm occurred or no one was endangered, the defense may argue that the driving was not reckless because it did not put anyone or anything at risk.

For example:

- **No Actual Injury**: If the defendant was charged with reckless driving but there was no collision or injury, the defense could argue that no harm came from the defendant's actions.

- **No Dangerous Conditions**: The defense could argue that there were no other drivers or pedestrians in the vicinity, meaning the actions did not create any significant risk of harm.

If the defense can show that the driving did not endanger others, this could lead to a reduction in charges or a dismissal.

C. Mistaken Identity or False Allegations

In some cases, individuals are wrongly accused of reckless driving. Mistaken identity or false allegations can occur, especially in situations where the police officer did not witness the event firsthand.

A defense based on mistaken identity or false allegations could be raised if:

- The defendant was not the person who engaged in the alleged reckless driving.
- The officer misidentified the defendant or misunderstood the situation.

If the defense can provide evidence, such as an alibi or contradictory witness testimony, that the defendant was not involved in reckless driving, the charges may be dismissed.

D. Emergency Situations (Necessity Defense)

If the defendant was driving recklessly in response to an emergency situation, they may have a **necessity defense**. This defense argues that the defendant's reckless actions were justified because they were necessary to avoid a greater harm or danger.

For example:

- The defendant may have swerved into another lane or driven at a higher speed to avoid a potential collision with a vehicle or pedestrian.
- The defendant may have been trying to get to a hospital quickly due to a medical emergency.

If the defense can show that the defendant's actions were motivated by a genuine emergency and were the only reasonable response to avoid a greater risk, the charges may be reduced or dismissed.

E. Improperly Calibrated Equipment (Speeding Radar or Dashcams)

Reckless driving charges are often based on evidence such as radar speed readings, dash cam footage, or other monitoring equipment. If the equipment used to measure the defendant's driving was improperly calibrated, faulty, or unreliable, the defense may be able to challenge the validity of the evidence.

For example:

- **Faulty Radar Gun**: If the officer used a radar gun to measure speed, but the radar gun was not properly calibrated, the defense may argue that the speed measurement is inaccurate and should be dismissed as evidence.
- **Inaccurate Dashcam Footage**: Dashcam or body cam footage that was improperly recorded or edited may be questioned for accuracy.

If the defense can demonstrate that the equipment was faulty or that the evidence is unreliable, the case against the defendant could be weakened, potentially leading to a dismissal or reduced charge.

3. Key Legal Strategies for Beating Reckless Driving Charges

A. Challenge the Officer's Observations and Testimony

In many cases, reckless driving charges are based on the subjective judgment of law enforcement officers. The defense can challenge the officer's observations and testimony, arguing that the officer misinterpreted the situation. For example:

- The officer may have misjudged the defendant's speed, especially if traffic conditions or weather were factors.
- The officer may have failed to witness key aspects of the incident that could suggest the defendant's actions were not reckless.

By questioning the credibility of the officer's observations, the defense can create reasonable doubt about the defendant's actions.

B. File Pre-Trial Motions

Before trial, the defense may file various pre-trial motions to challenge the evidence or the legality of the arrest. These motions might include:

- **Motion to Suppress Evidence**: If the evidence was obtained illegally, such as through an improper traffic stop or unlawful search, the defense can file a motion to suppress that evidence.
- **Motion to Dismiss**: If the defense can show that there is insufficient evidence to support a reckless driving charge, they may file a motion to dismiss the case entirely.

These motions can eliminate key evidence or even result in a dismissal of the case before trial.

C. Negotiating a Plea Deal

In some cases, the evidence against the defendant may be overwhelming, and the best option may be to negotiate a plea deal with the prosecution. The defendant could agree to plead guilty to a lesser charge, such as **careless driving**, in exchange for a reduced sentence or alternative penalties, such as probation or community service.

Plea deals can allow the defendant to avoid the harsher penalties associated with reckless driving, such as jail time or a lengthy license suspension.

D. Seek a Reduction to a Lesser Charge

In certain cases, the defense may be able to negotiate a reduction of the charge from **reckless driving** to a **careless driving** offense, which is a less severe charge. Careless driving involves driving without the same level of recklessness or disregard for safety, and the penalties for careless driving are typically less severe.

---

4. Conclusion

Reckless driving charges in Florida can have serious consequences, but with the right defense strategy, they can be successfully fought in court. The key to beating a reckless driving charge is to challenge the prosecution's evidence, question the officer's observations, and raise credible defenses such as lack of recklessness, necessity, or mistaken identity. Whether through pre-trial motions, negotiating a plea deal, or presenting strong evidence at trial, it is possible to reduce or eliminate the penalties associated with reckless driving. Legal representation from an experienced criminal defense attorney is crucial in navigating the complexities of reckless driving charges and achieving the best possible outcome.

CHAPTER SIXTY TWO.

BEATING LEAVING THE SCENE OF AN ACCIDENT CHARGES IN FLORIDA

INTRODUCTION

Leaving the scene of an accident in Florida is a criminal offense that can carry serious legal consequences, including fines, license suspension, and even imprisonment. The charge is often referred to as a "hit-and-run" offense, and the penalties depend on the severity of the accident and whether injuries or fatalities occurred. However, even if you are accused of leaving the scene of an accident, it is not a foregone conclusion that you will be convicted. There are several potential legal defenses that can be used to contest the charge. This chapter will explore what constitutes leaving the scene of an accident in Florida, possible defenses to the charge, and effective strategies for beating the charge.

---

1. Understanding the Law on Leaving the Scene of an Accident in Florida

The law on leaving the scene of an accident in Florida is governed by **Florida Statutes Section 316.061 and Section 316.027**. Under these laws, a person involved in an accident must stop and provide certain information or render aid, depending on the circumstances.

Key Elements of Leaving the Scene of an Accident

To convict someone of leaving the scene of an accident, the prosecution must prove the following elements beyond a reasonable doubt:

1. **Involvement in an Accident**: The defendant must have been involved in a motor vehicle accident. This includes hitting another vehicle, a

pedestrian, or property (such as a fence or a parked car).

2. **Failure to Stop**: The defendant must have failed to stop at the scene of the accident. The law requires that drivers stop and provide certain information to the other party involved or to law enforcement.

3. **Failure to Render Aid (if necessary)**: If the accident resulted in injury or death, the defendant must provide reasonable assistance, such as calling for medical help or offering aid to the injured party. If this is not done, the defendant could be charged with leaving the scene of an accident involving injury or death.

Penalties for Leaving the Scene of an Accident

The penalties for leaving the scene of an accident in Florida vary based on the circumstances of the accident:

- **Accident with Property Damage**: If the accident only involves property damage (e.g., hitting a parked car or a fence), leaving the scene is a **second-degree misdemeanor**. This charge can carry up to 60 days in jail, a fine of up to $500, and a potential license suspension.

- **Accident with Injury**: If the accident results in injury to another person, leaving the scene is a **third-degree felony**, punishable by up to 5 years in prison, fines, and a driver's license suspension.

- **Accident with Death**: If the accident causes a fatality and the defendant leaves the scene, it is a **first-degree felony**, which can carry a penalty of up to 30 years in prison and a lifetime driver's license suspension.

Given the severity of the penalties, defending against a charge of leaving the scene of an accident is critical to avoid long-lasting consequences.

---

2. Common Defenses to Leaving the Scene of an Accident Charges

There are several potential defenses that can be raised to challenge the charge of leaving the scene of an accident in Florida. A skilled defense attorney can assess the specific facts of the case and apply one or more of these defenses to help achieve a favorable outcome.

A. Lack of Knowledge of the Accident

A common defense to leaving the scene of an accident is the claim that the defendant did not know they were involved in an accident. In many hit-and-run cases, especially when there is minor damage or no visible injuries, the defendant may not realize that an accident occurred. This is particularly relevant in cases where:

- The accident was very minor, and the defendant did not feel an impact (such as when hitting a parked car or a minor collision).
- The defendant was unaware of damage to their own vehicle or did not hear the sound of an impact.

If the defense can show that the defendant did not know they were involved in an accident and thus did not leave the scene intentionally, this could lead to a dismissal or reduction of the charge.

B. Reasonable Fear for Safety

In some situations, the defendant may have left the scene because they feared for their own safety. If the defendant was involved in an accident but believed remaining at the scene would put them in danger (e.g., because of aggressive behavior from the other party or the risk of harm), this could be used as a defense.

For example:

- The defendant may have fled the scene to avoid being assaulted by another driver.
- The defendant may have been involved in an accident in a high-crime area and feared retaliation or harm.

While fleeing the scene may not be the best choice, if the defense can show that the defendant reasonably feared for their safety, the charges may be reduced or dismissed.

C. Attempt to Report the Accident

If the defendant left the scene but later attempted to report the accident to the authorities, this could be a defense to the charge. Florida law requires that drivers stop and provide information to the other party involved or law enforcement, but it also allows for a reasonable effort to return to the scene or notify authorities.

For example:

- If the defendant drove away due to panic but later returned to the scene or called the police to report the accident, the defense could argue that the defendant made a good-faith effort to comply with the law.
- The defendant may have left the scene because of confusion or disorientation (e.g., if they were involved in a hit-and-run accident involving multiple parties), but later tried to rectify the situation by contacting the authorities.

This defense works best when there is evidence showing that the defendant made efforts to return to the scene or contact law enforcement.

D. No Intentionality to Leave the Scene

In some cases, the defendant may argue that they did not intentionally leave the scene. For instance, if the defendant was confused about the nature of the accident or believed it was a minor incident, they might not have realized they were required to stop. This defense might be more effective in minor accidents where the defendant did not recognize the need to exchange information or render aid.

For example:

- The defendant may have believed the accident was so minor that there was no need to stop.
- The defendant might have been disoriented after the accident (e.g., due to a medical issue or distraction) and drove away without realizing they should have stopped.

By showing a lack of intent to evade responsibility, the defense could argue that the defendant did not knowingly violate the law.

E. The Accident Was Not Actually an Accident

In some situations, the defendant may argue that no accident occurred in the first place. For example:

- The defendant may have been falsely accused of being involved in an accident when, in fact, there was no collision.
- The vehicle involved may not have been the defendant's, or they may not have been the one driving the vehicle at the time of the alleged accident.

In these cases, the defense could argue that there was no legal basis for the charge of leaving the scene because there was no accident to begin with.

3. Key Legal Strategies for Beating Leaving the Scene of an Accident Charges

A. Challenge the Prosecution's Evidence

The prosecution must provide strong evidence that the defendant was involved in an accident and then intentionally left the scene. The defense can challenge the prosecution's evidence in several ways:

- **Disputing Identification**: The defense may argue that the defendant was not the person involved in the accident, especially if there are issues with witness identification or surveillance footage.
- **Lack of Proof of Intent**: The defense can argue that the defendant did not intentionally leave the scene or that there was a reasonable explanation for why they did not remain at the scene.

B. File Pre-Trial Motions

Before trial, the defense may file pre-trial motions to exclude certain evidence or seek a dismissal of the case. Some potential motions include:

- **Motion to Suppress Evidence**: If the evidence against the defendant was obtained unlawfully (e.g., through an illegal search or seizure), the defense can file a motion to suppress that evidence.
- **Motion to Dismiss**: If the prosecution cannot prove the defendant was involved in an accident or intentionally left the scene, the defense may file a motion to dismiss the charges.

C. Negotiating a Plea Deal

In some cases, a plea deal may be the best option. If the evidence against the defendant is strong, the defense may seek to negotiate a plea deal with the prosecution. The defendant could plead guilty to a lesser charge, such as **careless driving** or **failure to provide information**, in exchange for a reduced sentence, probation, or alternative penalties.

A plea deal can help avoid the harsh penalties associated with leaving the scene of an accident, especially if the defendant has no prior criminal record or if the accident was minor.

---

4. Conclusion

Leaving the scene of an accident in Florida is a serious charge, but it is not a conviction waiting to happen. There are several potential defenses that can be raised to contest the charge, including lack of knowledge of the accident, fear for safety, and efforts to report the accident. By challenging the evidence, filing pre-trial motions, and negotiating plea deals when necessary, the defendant can achieve a favorable outcome. A strong defense, combined with experienced legal representation, can help protect the defendant's rights and minimize the consequences of leaving the scene of an accident.

CHAPTER SIXTY THREE

BEATING RAPE CHARGES IN FLORIDA

INTRODUCTION

Rape is one of the most serious criminal offenses in Florida, carrying severe penalties, including lengthy prison sentences, significant fines, and lifelong consequences. A conviction for rape can drastically impact an individual's life, both legally and personally. However, the accusations of rape are often complex and based on subjective interpretations of events. In some cases, these accusations are false, misinterpreted, or based on incomplete evidence. This chapter will explore the elements of rape charges in Florida, potential defenses that can be raised in a rape case, and strategies to challenge the evidence and protect one's rights in such a serious legal situation.

---

1. Understanding the Law on Rape in Florida

In Florida, rape is typically charged under the crime of **sexual battery**, which is defined in **Florida Statutes Section 794.011**. Sexual battery is any intentional and non-consensual penetration of another person’s body, using a body part or an object. The offense of rape, or sexual battery, is classified into different degrees based on the severity of the crime, the use of force, and whether the victim sustained serious injury.

Key Elements of Rape (Sexual Battery)

To convict someone of rape or sexual battery in Florida, the prosecution must prove the following elements beyond a reasonable doubt:

1. **Non-Consensual Act**: The prosecution must prove that the sexual act was non-consensual. This means that the victim did not agree to engage in sexual activity, or that the consent was invalid (e.g., due to coercion, intoxication, or unconsciousness).

2. **Intentional Penetration**: The defendant must have intentionally penetrated the victim's body, either with a body part (such as the penis) or with an object.

3. **Lack of Consent**: The victim did not give legal consent to engage in the sexual activity. Consent is defined as a clear, voluntary, and conscious agreement to engage in the specific act.

4. **Force or Threat of Force**: If the victim was threatened or physically forced into the act, the charge will be classified as aggravated sexual battery, which carries even harsher penalties.

Penalties for Rape (Sexual Battery) in Florida

The penalties for a sexual battery conviction depend on the circumstances of the crime, such as whether the victim suffered injury, whether the defendant used a weapon, and whether the defendant has prior convictions. Penalties can range from 25 years to life in prison for the most severe cases, to probation and lesser sentences for cases with mitigating factors.

- **First-Degree Felony (Aggravated Sexual Battery)**: This includes situations where the victim was threatened with a weapon, sustained serious injury, or was a minor. Conviction may result in 25 years to life in prison.

- **Second-Degree Felony (Sexual Battery)**: This can occur if there was no use of a weapon, but the victim was physically forced or incapacitated. A conviction could result in up to 15 years in prison.

- **Life Sentences**: In some cases, such as sexual battery against a minor under 12 years old, the defendant could be sentenced to life in prison.

---

2. Common Defenses to Rape Charges in Florida

Rape cases often involve conflicting testimonies, as the defense may dispute the victim's account of events. There are several potential defenses that can be raised to challenge a rape charge in Florida, and an experienced criminal defense attorney will evaluate the circumstances to craft the most effective strategy.

A. Lack of Consent (Accusation of False Allegations)

One of the most common defenses in rape cases is that the sexual act was consensual. The defense may argue that the victim consented to the sexual activity, and the accusation of rape is based on a misunderstanding, regret, or false allegations.

Examples where this defense may be applicable:

- **Consensual Sex with No Clear Communication**: The defense might argue that both parties engaged in sexual activity consensually but that the victim later claimed otherwise, possibly due to regret or a change of heart.
- **Mistaken Identity**: In some cases, the accused may argue that the victim misidentified them or that there was some confusion about the identity of the person involved.
- **False Allegations**: The defense may argue that the accusation is entirely fabricated, possibly due to personal animosity, a desire for revenge, or other motives.

In many cases, witnesses, text messages, or prior relationships between the parties may be used to support this defense.

B. Consent Obtained Under False Pretenses or Coercion

In some cases, the defense may argue that while the victim appeared to consent, that consent was obtained under false pretenses, threats, or coercion. This could include:

- **Coercion or Manipulation**: If the victim was pressured or manipulated into consenting, the defense could argue that their consent was not voluntary and should not be considered legally valid.
- **False Pretenses**: If the defendant convinced the victim to engage in sexual activity under false pretenses (e.g., telling the victim they were married when they were not), the defense may argue that the consent was invalid.

This defense focuses on the nature of the consent, claiming that it was not freely given.

C. Mistaken Belief in Consent

The defense may argue that the defendant honestly and reasonably believed that the victim consented to the sexual activity, even if the victim later disagrees. This argument could be based on factors such as:

- **Prior Sexual Relationship**: If the defendant and the victim had an ongoing sexual relationship, the defendant might have reasonably believed that the victim consented, even if the victim later claimed otherwise.
- **Behavior and Communication**: The defense may argue that the victim's actions or words led the defendant to believe that consent was given (e.g., the victim did not resist or communicated consent through body language).

This defense seeks to demonstrate that the defendant did not act with criminal intent, and that any perceived lack of consent was the result of a misunderstanding.

D. Lack of Penetration or Physical Evidence

In some cases, the defense may argue that the act did not meet the legal definition of sexual battery. Florida law requires intentional penetration, and if the defense can demonstrate that penetration did not occur or that the physical evidence does not support the victim's version of events, the charge may be reduced or dismissed.

For example:

- **No Penetration**: If the defendant was accused of rape, but there was no actual penetration, the defense can argue that the charge does not meet the statutory definition of sexual battery.
- **Inconsistent or No Physical Evidence**: In many rape cases, physical evidence (e.g., DNA, bruising, or injury) plays a significant role. If there is no physical evidence or if the evidence is inconsistent with the victim's account, the defense can argue that the case should be dismissed or reduced.

E. False Confession or Improper Police Practices

Sometimes, individuals confess to crimes they did not commit due to pressure or coercion by law enforcement officers. If a confession was made under duress, threat, or manipulation, the defense may argue that the confession should be inadmissible in court.

Additionally, if the police mishandled the investigation, violated the defendant's rights, or engaged in improper practices (e.g., leading questions during an interrogation), this could be grounds for the charges to be dismissed.

3. Key Legal Strategies for Beating Rape Charges

A. Challenge the Credibility of the Accuser

In many rape cases, the defense may focus on the credibility of the accuser. By attacking the victim's account of events, the defense can create doubt in the minds of the jury. Some strategies include:

- **Inconsistencies in Testimony**: The defense may highlight contradictions or inconsistencies in the victim's testimony, as well as any prior false allegations of sexual assault.
- **Motive to Lie**: The defense may argue that the accuser has a motive to lie, such as revenge, regret, or gaining an advantage in a legal proceeding.

If the defense can demonstrate that the accuser's story is not credible, this could lead to a not guilty verdict or a reduction in charges.

B. Use of Expert Testimony

In some cases, expert testimony can be crucial to discrediting the prosecution's case. For example:

- **Sexual Assault Nurse Examiner (SANE) Testimony**: An expert can examine medical evidence and testify about the absence of physical injury, lack of DNA evidence, or other factors that undermine the victim's claims.
- **Psychological Expert**: A psychologist or psychiatrist may testify about the mental state of the defendant or the victim, explaining behavior patterns such as false memories, mistaken beliefs, or how trauma can affect a person's perception of an event.

Expert testimony can lend credibility to the defense's arguments and sway the jury.

C. File Pre-Trial Motions

Before trial, the defense may file various pre-trial motions to challenge the evidence against the defendant. These motions might include:

- **Motion to Suppress Evidence**: If the prosecution's evidence was obtained through unlawful methods, such as an improper search or coerced confession, the defense may file a motion to suppress that evidence.
- **Motion to Dismiss**: If the prosecution's evidence is insufficient or inconsistent, the defense may file a motion to dismiss the charges before trial.

These motions can be effective in weakening or eliminating the prosecution's case before it even reaches the courtroom.

---

4. Conclusion

Rape charges in Florida are extremely serious, and a conviction can have lifelong consequences. However, there are numerous potential defenses that can be raised in response to an accusation of rape, including claims of false allegations, lack of consent, mistaken identity, and issues with physical evidence. An experienced criminal defense attorney will analyze the facts of the case, challenge the prosecution's evidence, and employ legal strategies that can lead to a favorable outcome for the defendant. Whether the defense focuses on credibility, expert testimony, or pre-trial motions, there are several ways to fight rape charges and protect one's rights in a Florida court.

CHAPTER SIXTY FOUR

BEATING FALSE IDENTIFICATION TO LAW ENFORCEMENT CHARGES IN FLORIDA

INTRODUCTION

False identification to law enforcement is a serious criminal offense in Florida, with the potential to lead to significant legal penalties, including fines, imprisonment, and a criminal record. The crime typically involves providing a false name, date of birth, or other personal information to law enforcement officers when questioned during an investigation or arrest. While the penalties for this offense can be severe, it is important to recognize that there are various legal defenses available to individuals accused of providing false identification. This chapter will explore what constitutes false identification to law enforcement in Florida, the possible defenses to such charges, and the strategies that can be used to beat these charges.

---

1. Understanding the Law on False Identification to Law Enforcement in Florida

In Florida, the offense of providing false identification to law enforcement is defined under **Florida Statutes Section 843.08**. This statute makes it a crime to knowingly give false information about one's identity during a police investigation or when being arrested. It is important to understand that this charge applies not only to individuals who actively provide false information, but also to those who conceal their true identity or refuse to identify themselves when law enforcement has a legal right to ask.

Key Elements of False Identification to Law Enforcement

To convict someone of providing false identification to law enforcement in Florida, the prosecution must prove the following elements:

1. **The Defendant Provided False Information**: The individual must have knowingly provided false information, such as a fake name, false date of birth, or a fictitious address, to a law enforcement officer.

2. **The False Information Was Given to Law Enforcement**: The false information must have been given directly to law enforcement officers during an investigation, arrest, or stop. This could involve providing false information in response to questions or on documents such as driver's licenses or identification cards.

3. **Intent to Mislead**: The defendant must have had the intent to mislead law enforcement officers or to avoid identification. If the defendant did not knowingly provide false information, they may have a valid defense.

Penalties for Providing False Identification to Law Enforcement

The penalties for providing false identification to law enforcement in Florida depend on the specifics of the case, but generally, it is classified as a **third-degree felony**. This can result in:

- Up to **5 years in prison**
- Fines of up to **$5,000**
- A criminal record that could affect future employment, housing, and personal relationships

Additionally, if the defendant is already facing other charges, such as resisting arrest or other criminal charges, the penalties for providing false identification can be enhanced.

---

2. Common Defenses to False Identification to Law Enforcement Charges

While the consequences of providing false identification to law enforcement can be severe, there are several legal defenses that can be used to challenge the charge. Depending on the circumstances of the case, a skilled defense attorney can employ one or more of these defenses to protect the defendant's rights and potentially have the charges reduced or dismissed.

A. Lack of Knowledge or Intent

One of the primary defenses to a charge of providing false identification is the argument that the defendant did not knowingly provide false information, or that they did so unintentionally. For example, if the defendant gave incorrect information due to a misunderstanding or confusion, this may be grounds for a defense.

Possible scenarios where this might apply:

- **Confusion about Identity**: The defendant may have mistakenly given the wrong name or birthdate, such as if they were asked for identification during a stressful situation and confused their own details with those of someone else.
- **Miscalculation of Information**: In some cases, the defendant may have simply made an honest error, such as misremembering a date of birth or providing outdated identification without realizing it.

If the defense can show that the defendant did not have the intent to deceive law enforcement, this could result in the charges being dropped or reduced.

B. Involuntary Action or Coercion

In certain situations, the defendant may have been coerced or forced into providing false identification. If the defendant was under duress or threats of harm, they may not have acted voluntarily when providing false information to law enforcement.

For example:

- **Threat of Arrest**: The defendant may have been under pressure from law enforcement to provide identification quickly, leading them to make a false statement out of fear of further legal consequences.
- **Fear for Safety**: If the defendant was intimidated or felt unsafe during an encounter with law enforcement, they might have given false information out of fear, rather than a deliberate attempt to mislead.

The defense could argue that the defendant was not acting voluntarily but instead was under extreme stress or fear at the time of the incident, thus casting doubt on their intent.

C. False Identity as a Defensc to Another Crime

Sometimes, the defendant may have given a false identity to law enforcement in an attempt to avoid being arrested for another crime. While providing false information is still illegal, a defense could be built around the context of why the defendant lied. For example:

- **Avoiding Arrest for a Prior Warrant**: If the defendant was wanted for a previous crime, they may have given a false name to avoid arrest.
- **Avoiding Criminal Penalties**: The defendant may have provided false identification to avoid penalties or harsher charges in a different legal matter.

If the defendant can demonstrate that they were trying to avoid unfair legal consequences in another case, it might mitigate the seriousness of the charge of providing false identification.

D. Lack of Knowledge of Law Enforcement Inquiry

In some cases, the defendant may not have been aware that law enforcement officers were conducting an official investigation or inquiry when they provided false information. For example, the defendant may have been approached by police while they were not fully aware of the situation or did not understand the nature of the investigation.

If the defense can show that the defendant did not realize that law enforcement was trying to confirm their identity, they may argue that the defendant did not knowingly provide false information in a criminal context.

E. Mistaken Identity or Lack of Identification Requirement

Sometimes, the defense can argue that the defendant was not legally required to identify themselves to law enforcement in the first place. For instance, in Florida, the law only requires individuals to identify themselves when law enforcement has reasonable suspicion of criminal activity or when the individual is being lawfully arrested. If the law enforcement officers did not have a legal right to ask for identification or did not have probable cause, the defendant could argue that the charge of providing false identification is invalid.

For example:

- **Unlawful Detention**: If the defendant was unlawfully detained or stopped by law enforcement without reasonable suspicion, the defendant may not have been required to provide any identification at all.

- **Failure to State Lawful Authority**: If the police officer did not have lawful authority to demand identification from the defendant, the defense may argue that the defendant was under no obligation to comply with their request.

---

3. Key Legal Strategies for Beating False Identification Charges

A. Challenge the Evidence of False Identification

The defense can challenge the evidence that the defendant provided false identification. Some key strategies for this include:

- **Disputing the Accuracy of the Identification**: If the police officer made an error in recording the defendant's information, the defense can argue that the defendant's identification was never truly "false."
- **Witness Testimony**: Witnesses who were present during the interaction between the defendant and law enforcement may be able to testify that the defendant did not intentionally provide false information or that the incident was misunderstood.

B. File Pre-Trial Motions

The defense may file pre-trial motions to challenge the legitimacy of the charge or to exclude certain evidence. Some key motions might include:

- **Motion to Dismiss**: If the defendant can show that the charge was based on a misunderstanding or lack of evidence, they may file a motion to dismiss the case before it goes to trial.
- **Motion to Suppress**: If the defendant's identification was obtained illegally, such as through an unlawful search or seizure, the defense may file a motion to suppress evidence related to the false identification.

C. Negotiating a Plea Deal

In some cases, a plea deal may be an effective strategy for dealing with false identification charges. If the evidence against the defendant is strong but they do not have a prior criminal record, a plea deal may allow the defendant to plead guilty to a lesser charge in exchange for a reduced sentence or alternative penalties.

A plea deal could help the defendant avoid the more serious consequences of a felony conviction while still resolving the case efficiently.

---

4. Conclusion

False identification to law enforcement is a serious criminal offense in Florida, but it is not a charge that cannot be successfully challenged. There are several potential defenses to false identification charges, including lack of intent, coercion, mistaken identity, and lack of knowledge about the law enforcement inquiry. A skilled defense attorney can employ various legal strategies, such as challenging the evidence, filing pre-trial motions, or negotiating a plea deal, to help the defendant achieve the best possible outcome. Whether defending against the charge in court or negotiating with prosecutors, there are ways to beat false identification charges and protect one's future.

CHAPTER SIXTY FIVE.

BEATING ROBBERY WITH A MASK CHARGES IN FLORIDA

INTRODUCTION

Robbery is a serious crime in Florida, and when it involves wearing a mask or other forms of disguise, the charges become even more severe. Robbery with a mask or other disguise is a particularly aggravating offense under Florida law, as it can imply premeditation, an intent to conceal one's identity, and a heightened level of criminal intent. This chapter will delve into the legal definition of robbery with a mask in Florida, the potential penalties, common defenses, and strategies for challenging these charges.

---

1. Understanding the Law on Robbery with a Mask in Florida

In Florida, robbery is defined as the **taking of money or property** from another person with the use of force, violence, or fear. The crime is outlined in **Florida Statutes Section 812.13**. Robbery with a mask or disguise is a more severe version of this crime because the use of a mask or disguise during the commission of a robbery can indicate an intention to conceal one's identity and avoid detection.

Under **Florida Statutes Section 812.13(2)(b), robbery with a mask or disguise** is considered a **first-degree felony**. This means that if you are convicted of robbery with a mask or disguise, you could face up to **life in prison** depending on the circumstances of the crime.

Key Elements of Robbery with a Mask

To convict someone of robbery with a mask or disguise, the prosecution must prove the following elements beyond a reasonable doubt:

1. **Taking Property or Money**: The defendant must have taken property or money from another person.
2. **Use of Force, Violence, or Intimidation**: The defendant must have used force, violence, or intimidation to commit the robbery. The threat of harm or actual harm is necessary to elevate the crime to robbery (rather than theft).
3. **Wearing a Mask or Disguise**: The defendant must have been wearing a mask or other disguise while committing the robbery, making the crime "aggravated" robbery under the law. This element distinguishes robbery with a mask from simple robbery.
4. **Intent**: The defendant must have had the intent to commit robbery while wearing the mask or disguise.

Penalties for Robbery with a Mask in Florida

As a **first-degree felony**, robbery with a mask carries severe penalties. If convicted, the defendant could face:

- **Up to 30 years in prison**
- **Fines up to $10,000**
- **Probation** following release
- **Restitution** to the victim

In cases where a firearm or deadly weapon is used during the robbery, additional charges may apply, and penalties can increase significantly.

---

2. Common Defenses to Robbery with a Mask Charges

Although robbery with a mask is a serious offense, it is not uncommon for defendants to be falsely accused or for there to be weaknesses in the prosecution's case. A skilled criminal defense attorney can raise various defenses to challenge the charge of robbery with a mask. Some of the most common defenses include:

A. Lack of Identity

One of the most effective defenses to a robbery charge is **lack of identification**. If the prosecution cannot prove beyond a reasonable doubt that the defendant was the person who committed the robbery while wearing a mask, the case may fail. The defense could argue that the defendant was mistaken for someone else or that there was a lack of reliable identification evidence.

In cases where the defendant's identity is in question, the defense may argue:

- **Mistaken Identity**: The defendant may not have been involved in the robbery at all but was incorrectly identified by witnesses or law enforcement.
- **Alibi**: The defendant may provide evidence that they were somewhere else at the time of the robbery, such as through surveillance footage, witness testimony, or phone records.

If there is no solid evidence linking the defendant to the crime, the case could be dismissed or result in an acquittal.

B. No Intent to Commit Robbery

In some cases, the defendant may admit to being involved in an incident but may not have had the intent to commit robbery. For example, the defendant may have been wearing a mask for reasons unrelated to committing a robbery, or the act was an unintentional crime of passion.

The defense might argue:

- **No Intent to Steal**: The defendant may have engaged in a confrontation with the victim, but without the intent to steal property. If the defendant did not have the specific intent to take money or property by force, they may not be guilty of robbery.
- **No Use of Force or Fear**: If the defendant did not use force or intimidation to take property, the charge may be reduced to a lesser offense, such as theft.

In such cases, the defense could argue that the incident was a misunderstanding or a situation that did not meet the legal definition of robbery.

C. Coercion or Duress

If the defendant was forced or coerced into committing the robbery under duress, they may have a valid defense. Duress occurs when a person commits a crime because they were threatened with serious harm if they did not comply. In the context of robbery with a mask, the defense might argue that the defendant was compelled to participate in the robbery by someone else, such as an accomplice or criminal mastermind.

Possible scenarios for duress may include:

- **Threat of Harm**: The defendant was threatened with violence or harm by another person if they did not participate in the robbery.
- **Fear of Retaliation**: The defendant was afraid for their life or the safety of loved ones and acted under duress.

If the defense can prove that the defendant committed the crime because they were under threat of serious harm, this could reduce or eliminate their criminal liability.

D. Insufficient Evidence or Lack of Corroboration

In many robbery cases, the evidence presented by the prosecution is circumstantial. If there is no direct evidence linking the defendant to the crime—such as surveillance footage, fingerprints, or DNA evidence—the defense can argue that the prosecution has failed to prove the case beyond a reasonable doubt.

For example:

- **No Physical Evidence**: If no physical evidence ties the defendant to the scene of the robbery or to the mask, the defense could argue that the prosecution's case is weak.
- **Inconsistent Testimony**: If the victim or eyewitnesses provide conflicting accounts of the incident, the defense can point out these discrepancies to undermine the prosecution's case.

If the prosecution cannot present strong evidence of the defendant's involvement in the robbery with a mask, the charges may be reduced or dropped.

E. The Mask or Disguise Was Not Used to Facilitate the Robbery

Another potential defense could be that the mask or disguise was not worn for the purpose of committing robbery. The defense may argue that the mask was used for another reason, such as to protect the defendant's identity in a different context (e.g., during a protest or for another legitimate reason).

The defense could assert that the presence of the mask was coincidental, or that the defendant was engaged in a different activity that did not involve robbery.

3. Key Legal Strategies for Beating Robbery with a Mask Charges

A. Challenge the Evidence of the Mask

One of the key elements of robbery with a mask is the use of a disguise. A defense strategy may focus on challenging the evidence that the defendant was wearing a mask or disguise. The defense can raise questions about whether the mask was actually used during the robbery or whether it was even worn at all.

- **Lack of Mask Evidence**: If the mask cannot be physically linked to the defendant, or if there is no evidence that the defendant wore the mask during the robbery, the charges may be reduced or dismissed.
- **Eyewitness Testimony**: Eyewitnesses who claim to have seen the defendant wearing a mask can be cross-examined to assess the credibility and reliability of their testimony. Inconsistent descriptions or uncertainties can undermine the prosecution's case.

B. File Pre-Trial Motions to Suppress Evidence

If the defendant's arrest or the seizure of evidence, such as the mask or other items related to the robbery, was conducted unlawfully (without probable cause or a warrant), the defense can file a motion to suppress the evidence. This could result in the exclusion of critical evidence, weakening the prosecution's case.

For example:

- **Illegal Search or Seizure**: If the police violated the defendant's constitutional rights during the arrest or investigation, any evidence obtained through an illegal search may be excluded from the trial.
- **Failure to Read Rights**: If the defendant's rights were not read to them during the arrest, or if there was a failure to provide Miranda warnings, statements made by the defendant may not be admissible.

C. Negotiate a Plea Deal

In cases where the evidence against the defendant is strong but there are mitigating factors (e.g., no prior criminal record, minor role in the crime, or cooperation with authorities), negotiating a plea deal with the prosecution may be an effective strategy. A plea deal can result in reduced charges or a lighter sentence in exchange for a guilty plea.

---

4. Conclusion

Robbery with a mask is a serious charge in Florida, but it is not a charge that is necessarily impossible to beat. There are numerous defenses available, including challenges to the evidence of the mask, lack of intent, lack of identification, duress, and insufficient evidence. An experienced criminal defense attorney will evaluate the facts of the case, craft the appropriate defense strategy, and fight for the best possible outcome for the defendant. Whether through challenging the evidence, filing pre-trial motions, or negotiating a plea deal, there are legal avenues available to contest a robbery with a mask charge and protect one's future.

CHAPTER SIXTY SIX.

BEATING SOLICITING PROSTITUTION CHARGES IN FLORIDA

INTRODUCTION

Soliciting prostitution is a serious offense in Florida, as it involves the offer or request for sexual services in exchange for money or other goods. The state takes a firm stance against prostitution and related crimes, and those charged with soliciting prostitution can face significant legal consequences. This chapter will explore the charge of soliciting prostitution under Florida law, the penalties associated with it, potential defenses, and strategies to challenge or mitigate these charges.

---

1. Understanding the Law on Soliciting Prostitution in Florida

In Florida, soliciting prostitution is defined under **Florida Statutes Section 796.07**. This statute makes it illegal to solicit, entice, or procure another person to engage in sexual activity in exchange for money, goods, or services.

Key Elements of Soliciting Prostitution

To convict someone of soliciting prostitution in Florida, the prosecution must prove the following elements beyond a reasonable doubt:

1. **The Defendant's Request**: The defendant must have made a request, offer, or agreement with another person to engage in sexual activity in exchange for money or other consideration (such as goods or services).

2. **Intent to Engage in Prostitution**: The defendant must have had the intent to engage in prostitution, meaning that the solicitation was for sexual activity with an exchange of money or something of value.
3. **Communication of the Solicitation**: The solicitation must have been communicated to another person. This could involve verbal communication, gestures, or other forms of communication indicating the offer or request for sexual services.

It's important to note that the crime does not require that the prostitution transaction actually occurs—simply making the solicitation is enough to be charged under this law.

Penalties for Soliciting Prostitution

Soliciting prostitution in Florida is typically classified as a **misdemeanor of the first degree** for a first offense, but it can escalate in certain situations.

- **First Offense**: A first offense of soliciting prostitution carries penalties of:
    - Up to **1 year in jail**
    - Fines of up to **$1,000**
    - **Probation** or community service
    - Completion of a **prostitution-related education program** (often required by the court)
- **Subsequent Offenses**: If the defendant has been convicted of soliciting prostitution before, the charge can be elevated to a **felony of the third degree**, carrying harsher penalties, including:
    - Up to **5 years in prison**
    - Fines up to **$5,000**
    - Longer probation or mandatory counseling programs

In addition to criminal penalties, being convicted of soliciting prostitution can carry significant collateral consequences, such as a permanent criminal record, which could impact employment, housing, and reputation.

---

2. Common Defenses to Soliciting Prostitution Charges

Although soliciting prostitution is a serious charge, there are several defenses that may be raised to challenge or reduce the charges. In some cases, the evidence may be insufficient, or the defendant may have a legitimate reason for their actions that does not involve solicitation. A skilled defense attorney will evaluate the details of the case and may employ one or more of the following defenses.

A. Lack of Intent

One of the most effective defenses to a solicitation charge is the argument that the defendant did not intend to solicit prostitution. Intent is a key element of the crime, and if the prosecution cannot prove that the defendant had the specific intent to engage in prostitution, the case may be dismissed or reduced.

Possible scenarios for this defense include:

- **Misunderstanding or Miscommunication**: The defendant may have been involved in a conversation or interaction that was misunderstood by law enforcement or a third party as soliciting prostitution. If the defendant did not express a clear intention to engage in illegal activity, this could be a defense.
- **Innocent Discussion**: The defendant may have been discussing matters related to prostitution or similar activities, but without any intention to participate in them. If there is no direct evidence of the defendant

asking for or offering sexual services, the defense could argue that there was no solicitation.

B. Entrapment

Entrapment occurs when law enforcement induces or pressures a person to commit a crime they would not otherwise have committed. If a defendant can demonstrate that they were coerced or encouraged to solicit prostitution by undercover officers or informants, they may have a valid defense based on entrapment.

To successfully argue entrapment, the defendant must show:

- **Law Enforcement Overreach**: The defendant was not predisposed to engage in prostitution, but law enforcement officials induced or pressured them to do so. For example, if an undercover officer actively engaged the defendant in a conversation, making repeated offers or promises to engage in sexual activity, the defense could argue that the defendant would not have acted without this inducement.
- **Lack of Criminal Intent**: The defendant was not already planning to engage in prostitution and was persuaded or manipulated by law enforcement into committing the crime.

If the defense can show that the defendant was entrapped into committing the offense, the charges could be dropped or reduced.

C. False Allegations or Mistaken Identity

Sometimes, defendants are wrongly accused of soliciting prostitution due to mistaken identity or false allegations. The defendant might argue that they were misidentified by the complainant, or that the situation was misinterpreted by law enforcement.

Possible examples include:

- **False Accusations**: The defendant could argue that they were wrongly identified as the person attempting to solicit prostitution. For example, a person may be in the wrong place at the wrong time, and law enforcement may mistakenly believe they were involved in a solicitation.
- **Lack of Evidence**: The defense can challenge the sufficiency of the evidence against the defendant. If there is no clear communication or evidence that the defendant made an offer for prostitution, the case may be dismissed or reduced.

D. No Offer of Money or Goods

In order to convict someone of soliciting prostitution, there must be evidence that the defendant made an offer of money or other goods in exchange for sexual services. If the defendant did not actually offer any compensation or exchange, the defense can argue that no crime occurred.

The defendant could claim:

- **No Agreement Was Made**: While there may have been an exchange of words or gestures, there was no agreement to engage in sexual acts for money. If the defendant never offered money or other goods, the defense could argue that the solicitation charge does not apply.
- **Lack of Transaction**: If the police cannot demonstrate that the defendant engaged in a transaction or had a serious intent to exchange something for sexual services, the defense can argue that the elements of the crime are not met.

E. Improper or Unlawful Police Procedure

In some cases, the way the police conducted their investigation may be flawed. If the police used improper tactics or violated the defendant's rights during the arrest or investigation, this may form the basis for a defense. For example:

- **Violation of Miranda Rights**: If the defendant was not informed of their rights during the arrest or interrogation, statements made by the defendant may be inadmissible in court.
- **Illegal Search or Seizure**: If the police obtained evidence against the defendant through an unlawful search or seizure, the defense could argue that the evidence should be excluded from trial.

F. Lack of Jurisdiction or Legal Issues with the Arrest

If the arrest was made in an area or under circumstances where the law does not apply, the charges could be contested. For instance, if the defendant was not in the appropriate jurisdiction, or if the undercover operation did not adhere to legal requirements, this may form the basis of a defense.

---

3. Key Legal Strategies for Beating Soliciting Prostitution Charges

A. Challenge the Evidence of Solicitation

One of the most common and effective legal strategies is challenging the evidence that the defendant made an actual solicitation. This includes:

- **Cross-examining Witnesses**: If the charge is based on witness testimony (e.g., law enforcement officers), cross-examining the witnesses to uncover inconsistencies or biases can be effective.
- **Lack of Recorded Evidence**: Many modern law enforcement operations use undercover officers and often record communications. If there is no recorded evidence of the defendant soliciting prostitution, the defense can argue that the prosecution's case is weak.

B. File Pre-Trial Motions

A skilled defense attorney may file pre-trial motions to dismiss the charges or suppress evidence. Some potential motions could include:

- **Motion to Dismiss**: If the prosecution's evidence is insufficient to support the charge of solicitation, the defense may file a motion to dismiss the case.
- **Motion to Suppress Evidence**: If the evidence against the defendant was obtained through unlawful means, such as an illegal search or failure to advise the defendant of their rights, the defense can file a motion to suppress the evidence.

C. Negotiate a Plea Agreement

In cases where the evidence is strong but the defendant has no prior criminal history or mitigating factors, negotiating a plea agreement may be the best option. In exchange for a guilty plea to a lesser charge or for a reduced sentence, the defendant may avoid a lengthy trial and secure a more favorable outcome.

---

4. Conclusion

Soliciting prostitution charges in Florida can carry serious legal consequences, but there are various defenses available to challenge these charges. Whether through disputing the intent to commit the offense, proving entrapment, questioning the sufficiency of the evidence, or arguing procedural errors, there are multiple strategies that can be employed to defend against solicitation charges. A skilled criminal defense attorney will be essential in navigating the complexities of the case, challenging the evidence, and securing the best possible outcome for the defendant. By understanding the law and legal defenses, individuals accused of soliciting prostitution can take the necessary steps to protect their rights and minimize the impact of the charges on their future.

CHAPTER SIXTY SEVEN.

BEATING SHOPLIFTING CHARGES IN FLORIDA

INTRODUCTION

Shoplifting is a common crime in Florida that can lead to serious legal consequences. Whether it's taking merchandise from a store, attempting to conceal items, or using deceptive means to avoid paying for goods, Florida law treats shoplifting offenses seriously. However, shoplifting charges are not always straightforward, and there are several defenses that can be used to challenge such accusations. This chapter will provide an in-depth look at the laws surrounding shoplifting in Florida, the potential penalties, and the most effective strategies to fight a shoplifting charge.

---

1. Understanding Shoplifting in Florida

In Florida, shoplifting is a form of **theft**, and it is defined as the act of willfully and intentionally taking merchandise from a retail store or other commercial establishment without paying for it or without the store's consent.

Under **Florida Statutes Section 812.015**, shoplifting includes actions such as:

- **Taking or concealing merchandise** with the intent to steal it.
- **Altering or removing price tags** or labels on items to reduce their price.
- **Under-ringing** items at checkout or causing the cashier to ring them up incorrectly.
- **Leaving the store with the merchandise** without paying for it.

Key Elements of Shoplifting

To secure a conviction for shoplifting, the prosecution must prove the following elements:

1. **The Defendant Took Property**: The defendant must have taken property from a retail establishment, whether it was concealed or carried away.
2. **Intent to Steal**: The defendant must have had the intent to permanently deprive the store of the property. This intent is often inferred from actions like concealing items or bypassing the checkout process.
3. **No Consent or Payment**: The store did not consent to the removal of merchandise, and the defendant did not pay for the goods.

Even if the defendant did not leave the store with the merchandise, actions like attempting to conceal an item or bypass the checkout process can still result in a charge of shoplifting if the intent to steal is evident.

Penalties for Shoplifting in Florida

The penalties for shoplifting in Florida depend on the value of the merchandise stolen and whether it is classified as a misdemeanor or a felony. The severity of the crime is typically determined by the **value of the stolen property**.

1. **Petty Theft (Misdemeanor)**: If the value of the merchandise is less than $750, it is generally considered a **second-degree misdemeanor** (petty theft). Penalties include:
    - **Up to 60 days in jail**
    - **Fines up to $500**
    - **Probation**
    - **Community service**
    - **Restitution to the store** for the value of the stolen items

2. **Grand Theft (Felony)**: If the value of the stolen property exceeds $750, the charge is typically upgraded to **grand theft** (a felony). There are different degrees of grand theft depending on the value of the items:

   - **Third-degree felony**: Stolen items worth between $750 and $20,000 (up to 5 years in prison and fines up to $5,000).
   - **Second-degree felony**: Stolen items worth between $20,000 and $100,000 (up to 15 years in prison and fines up to $10,000).
   - **First-degree felony**: Stolen items worth over $100,000 (up to 30 years in prison and fines up to $10,000).

In addition to criminal penalties, individuals convicted of shoplifting may also face civil penalties. Florida law allows retailers to sue shoplifters for the value of the merchandise, plus additional civil damages.

---

2. Common Defenses to Shoplifting Charges in Florida

Shoplifting charges are not always easy to prove, and a skilled criminal defense attorney can raise a number of defenses to challenge the prosecution's case. Some of the most common defenses include:

A. Lack of Intent to Steal

One of the most common defenses to a shoplifting charge is the claim that the defendant did not have the intent to steal. Shoplifting requires specific intent—meaning that the defendant must have consciously and purposefully intended to deprive the store of its property.

Possible arguments include:

- **Mistaken Intent**: The defendant may have accidentally taken or concealed an item without realizing it, or may have intended to pay for the item but got distracted.

- **No Theft Intent**: The defendant may have intended to purchase the item but forgot to check out, or they may have been planning to return the item after a trial of it.

If the defense can show that there was no intent to steal or that the defendant was not acting with criminal intent, the charge could be reduced or dismissed.

B. Mistaken Identity

Mistaken identity is a defense in shoplifting cases when the defendant is wrongly accused of committing the crime. For example, the defendant may be misidentified by a store employee, a security camera, or a witness.

Possible ways to challenge mistaken identity include:

- **Inconsistent Descriptions**: If the store employee or security cameras give inconsistent descriptions of the suspect, the defense could argue that the defendant was not the person who committed the crime.
- **Alibi**: The defendant may have an alibi proving they were not in the store at the time of the alleged shoplifting, such as surveillance footage, witness testimony, or records showing they were elsewhere.

If there is doubt about the defendant's identity or evidence that they were not the person involved, the defense can argue for a dismissal of the charges.

C. No Evidence of Theft

The prosecution must prove the elements of the crime beyond a reasonable doubt, and if they fail to provide sufficient evidence, the defendant may have a valid defense. For example:

- **No Concealment**: If there is no evidence that the defendant concealed items or attempted to leave the store without paying, the charge may be unsupported.

- **No Video or Witness Testimony**: If there is no video footage or credible witness testimony to show that the defendant took or intended to take property, the defense can argue that the prosecution has no evidence to prove guilt.

If there is insufficient or unreliable evidence linking the defendant to the alleged shoplifting, the charges may be dropped or reduced.

D. Entrapment

Entrapment is a defense that can be raised if law enforcement or a store employee coerced or encouraged the defendant to commit the crime. In cases of **sting operations** or when undercover officers are involved, the defendant may argue that they were pushed into committing the offense.

To use the entrapment defense, the defendant must show:

- **Law Enforcement Action**: The defendant was induced by law enforcement or another official to commit the theft.
- **No Predisposition**: The defendant was not predisposed to shoplift and would not have committed the crime if not for law enforcement's actions.

If the defense can show that the defendant was coerced into committing the shoplifting crime, the charges may be dismissed.

E. Unlawful Search or Seizure

In some cases, police may unlawfully search the defendant or their belongings, or seize evidence without a warrant or probable cause. If the defendant's constitutional rights were violated during the arrest or investigation, the evidence obtained may be inadmissible.

Possible violations include:

- **Illegal Search**: If police searched the defendant's bags or person without a warrant or probable cause, any evidence found may be excluded.
- **Improper Detention**: If the defendant was detained without reasonable suspicion or probable cause, statements or evidence obtained during that detention may not be allowed in court.

If the defense can prove that the search or seizure was unlawful, the court may suppress the evidence, making it difficult for the prosecution to prove the case.

---

3. Key Legal Strategies for Beating Shoplifting Charges

A. Challenge the Evidence

The strongest defense in a shoplifting case is often challenging the evidence the prosecution presents. If the prosecution cannot prove beyond a reasonable doubt that the defendant took the property with the intent to steal, the case will likely be dismissed. The defense may:

- **Challenge Surveillance Video**: If the prosecution relies on video evidence, the defense can argue that the footage is unclear, tampered with, or does not show the defendant committing the crime.
- **Cross-Examine Witnesses**: The defense can cross-examine store employees, security personnel, or other witnesses to question their reliability and consistency.

B. Negotiate a Plea Deal

If the evidence against the defendant is strong and a conviction seems likely, negotiating a plea deal may be a good option. A plea deal may result in:

- **Reduced Charges**: The defendant may be able to plead guilty to a lesser offense, such as a misdemeanor, which carries less severe penalties.
- **Alternative Sentencing**: The defense may negotiate for alternative sentencing options, such as community service, probation, or diversion programs, instead of jail time.

C. Pre-Trial Motions

Pre-trial motions are requests made to the court before the trial begins to dismiss the case or suppress certain evidence. Common pre-trial motions include:

- **Motion to Dismiss**: If there is insufficient evidence or a procedural error, the defense may file a motion to dismiss the charges.
- **Motion to Suppress Evidence**: If the evidence against the defendant was obtained illegally, the defense may file a motion to suppress that evidence, weakening the prosecution's case.

---

4. Conclusion

Shoplifting charges in Florida can carry serious consequences, but there are numerous legal defenses available to challenge these charges. From disputing the intent to steal to challenging the sufficiency of the evidence or raising constitutional violations, there are many strategies that can be used to defend against shoplifting allegations. By working with an experienced criminal defense attorney, individuals accused of shoplifting can explore their options, safeguard their rights, and work toward the best possible outcome. Whether through contesting the charges in court or negotiating a favorable plea deal, there are effective ways to beat a shoplifting charge in Florida.

CHAPTER SIXTY EIGHT.

BEATING A CONCEALED WEAPONS CHARGE IN FLORIDA

David's heart pounded as he sat in the holding cell, staring at the cold concrete walls. One mistake, one moment of forgetfulness, and now he was facing a felony weapons charge.

He had always carried a firearm for protection. It was legally purchased, registered, and locked in his glove compartment—where he thought it was supposed to be. But during a routine traffic stop, the officer asked if he had any weapons in the car. David answered honestly.

Moments later, he was in handcuffs.

Understanding Florida's Concealed Carry Laws

Florida has strict laws regarding carrying firearms. Under Florida Statute 790.01, it is illegal to carry a concealed weapon without a valid Concealed Weapon License (CWL). A person found with a concealed firearm can face:

- Third-Degree Felony (for a concealed firearm) – Punishable by up to 5 years in prison and a $5,000 fine.
- First-Degree Misdemeanor (for a concealed weapon other than a firearm, like a knife or taser) – Punishable by up to 1 year in jail and a $1,000 fine.

The key legal issue? What counts as "concealed"?

In Florida, a weapon is considered concealed if it is on or about a person and not visible to ordinary sight. That means even if the gun was in a car, purse, or under a jacket, it could still lead to charges if the person did not have a CWL.

David was in trouble—but he wasn't out of options.

Building the Defense

His attorney, Sarah Mitchell, was a criminal defense lawyer who had successfully defended dozens of weapons cases.

"This isn't an open-and-shut case," she said, flipping through the arrest report. "We can fight this."

David listened as she laid out a multi-pronged defense strategy.

1. The Firearm Was Not "Readily Accessible"

Florida law allows people to transport firearms in their vehicle, even without a CWL, as long as the gun is securely encased and not easily accessible.

David had his gun in his locked glove compartment, which fit the legal requirement.

"We'll argue that the firearm wasn't readily accessible," Sarah said. "If the jury agrees, the charge should be dropped."

2. No Criminal Intent

To convict, the prosecution needed to prove that David knowingly and willfully concealed the firearm.

"If you didn't know the law or had no intent to break it, that creates reasonable doubt," Sarah explained.

David had never been arrested before. He had no criminal history. If the jury saw him as a responsible gun owner who simply made a mistake, they would be more likely to side with him.

3. The Police Conducted an Illegal Search

"How did they find the gun?" Sarah asked.

David hesitated. "They asked if I had any weapons. I said yes. Then they searched my car."

Sarah's eyes narrowed. "Did they ask for permission to search?"

David shook his head. "No."

That was a potential Fourth Amendment violation. Unless David had given clear consent or the officer had probable cause, the search could have been illegal.

"If the search was unconstitutional, we can file a motion to suppress the evidence," Sarah said. "If we win, they can't use the gun as evidence."

Without the gun, there was no case.

Pretrial Strategy: Getting the Charges Dropped

Sarah immediately filed two motions:

1. A Motion to Dismiss – Arguing that David's gun was securely encased, meaning no crime was committed.
2. A Motion to Suppress – Challenging the legality of the search.

Meanwhile, she negotiated with the prosecutor.

David had a clean record. He wasn't a felon. He wasn't carrying the gun with criminal intent.

The prosecutor offered a plea deal—plead guilty to a misdemeanor, avoid jail time, and pay a fine.

David refused. "I didn't break the law," he said. "I want to fight this."

Winning in Court

In court, Sarah attacked the state's case.

- First, she proved the gun was not readily accessible.
    - She showed that Florida law allows guns in locked compartments without a CWL.
    - The judge agreed.
- Next, she challenged the illegal search.
    - The officer admitted he never asked for consent.
    - Without probable cause, the search was unconstitutional.

With the search ruled unlawful, the gun was suppressed as evidence.

Without evidence, the prosecutor had no choice: Case dismissed.

Aftermath

David left the courthouse a free man.

"I won't make that mistake again," he said. "I'm applying for a concealed carry license tomorrow."

Sarah smiled. "Good. But the real lesson? Know your rights."

CHAPTER SIXTY NINE.

BEATING DRUG PARAPHERNALIA CHARGES IN FLORIDA

INTRODUCTION

Drug paraphernalia charges in Florida can result in significant legal consequences, including fines, imprisonment, and a criminal record that may impact one's future. Drug paraphernalia refers to items used in the consumption, manufacture, or concealment of illegal drugs. These items can include pipes, bongs, syringes, scales, baggies, and other objects that are associated with drug use or trafficking. While being charged with drug paraphernalia does not mean an individual is automatically involved in drug distribution or abuse, these charges can still be serious. However, there are several defenses and strategies that can be used to fight or reduce these charges. This chapter will discuss the law surrounding drug paraphernalia in Florida, potential defenses, and strategies to challenge such charges.

---

1. Understanding the Law on Drug Paraphernalia in Florida

In Florida, the possession, sale, or manufacture of drug paraphernalia is prohibited under **Florida Statutes Section 893.147**. This law makes it illegal for any person to possess, use, or sell items intended for use in the consumption or distribution of controlled substances.

Definition of Drug Paraphernalia

The law defines drug paraphernalia as any equipment, product, or material that is:

1. **Primarily intended for use** in the planting, cultivating, harvesting, manufacturing, compounding, converting, producing, processing,

preparing, testing, packaging, storing, or introducing a controlled substance into the human body.
2. **Used in connection with a controlled substance**, including marijuana, cocaine, heroin, methamphetamine, and other illegal drugs.

Examples of drug paraphernalia include:

- Pipes, bongs, and smoking devices.
- Syringes, needles, and spoons.
- Scales, baggies, and small containers.
- Roach clips, blenders, or grinders used for drug preparation.
- Straws or tubes used for inhaling or snorting drugs.

Penalties for Drug Paraphernalia Charges

The penalties for drug paraphernalia charges in Florida depend on the type of offense and whether the individual has prior convictions. The severity of the charges may also depend on whether the paraphernalia was intended for personal use or for distribution.

1. **Possession of Drug Paraphernalia**: Possessing drug paraphernalia is a **first-degree misdemeanor** under Florida law. Penalties can include:
    - Up to **1 year in jail**.
    - Fines up to **$1,000**.
    - Probation or community service.
    - Mandatory drug counseling or rehabilitation programs.
2. **Sale or Distribution of Drug Paraphernalia**: Selling, offering to sell, or distributing drug paraphernalia is considered a **third-degree felony** under Florida law. Penalties can include:
    - Up to **5 years in prison**.
    - Fines up to **$5,000**.

- Probation or community service.
- Civil liability for damages caused by the sale of the paraphernalia.

3. **Manufacturing Drug Paraphernalia**: Manufacturing, creating, or designing drug paraphernalia with the intent to distribute is also a felony offense under Florida law, carrying similar penalties to selling or distributing paraphernalia.

---

2. Common Defenses to Drug Paraphernalia Charges

Although drug paraphernalia charges can be serious, there are several defenses that can be used to challenge the prosecution's case. A knowledgeable criminal defense attorney will evaluate the specific circumstances of the case and may employ one or more of the following strategies.

A. Lack of Knowledge or Intent

For a conviction of possessing drug paraphernalia, the prosecution must prove that the defendant had knowledge of the paraphernalia and intended to use it in connection with illegal drugs. If the defendant did not know the object was drug paraphernalia or did not intend to use it for illegal purposes, the charge may be difficult to prove.

Possible defenses include:

- **Unaware of the Paraphernalia**: The defendant may argue that they were unaware the item was considered drug paraphernalia. For example, if a pipe or other item was found in the defendant's vehicle or home but was not used for drugs, they could argue that they did not know it was intended for drug use.

- **Innocent Possession**: The defendant may have possessed the paraphernalia but had no intention of using it for drugs. For example, an item could have been owned for a legitimate non-drug-related purpose (e.g., a decorative pipe) but was mistakenly associated with drug use.
- **No Intent to Use for Illegal Drugs**: Even if the defendant knew the object was paraphernalia, they may argue that they did not intend to use it for illegal drug consumption. For example, the defendant could argue that they had the item for a lawful purpose, such as collecting or display.

B. Mistaken Identity or False Allegations

Another common defense in drug paraphernalia cases is mistaken identity or false allegations. If the prosecution's case relies on witness testimony, store surveillance footage, or other evidence that misidentifies the defendant, the charge may be reduced or dismissed. Possible scenarios include:

- **Wrongful Arrest**: The defendant may have been wrongfully identified as the individual who possessed or used the paraphernalia. In this case, the defense could argue that the defendant was at the wrong place at the wrong time or that they were misidentified by law enforcement.
- **Lack of Evidence**: If there is no physical evidence linking the defendant to the paraphernalia, the defense could argue that the charges are based on insufficient or circumstantial evidence. For example, if the paraphernalia was found in a shared space and it's unclear who it belonged to, the defense can argue there's no proof the defendant owned or used it.

C. Unlawful Search and Seizure

Under the **Fourth Amendment** of the U.S. Constitution, individuals are protected against unreasonable searches and seizures. If the police searched the defendant's property, vehicle, or person without a valid warrant or probable cause, the evidence obtained may be inadmissible in court. If the defendant's rights were violated during the arrest or investigation, the charges could be dropped or reduced.

Common examples of unlawful search and seizure include:

- **No Warrant**: If police officers conducted a search of the defendant's home, car, or personal belongings without a warrant or without consent, any evidence seized could be excluded.
- **Probable Cause**: If law enforcement lacked probable cause to stop or search the defendant, the defense can argue that the search was illegal and that the evidence of drug paraphernalia should be suppressed.

D. The Paraphernalia Was Not Intended for Drug Use

In some cases, drug paraphernalia may appear to be intended for drug use but is actually intended for a legal or legitimate purpose. The defense can argue that the item in question was not meant to be used in connection with drugs. Common examples include:

- **Decorative Items**: The defendant may have items that resemble drug paraphernalia but are actually intended for decoration, such as ornamental pipes or glassware.
- **Dual-Use Items**: An item may have a legitimate non-drug use. For example, a pipe or scale may have been used for a lawful purpose, such as for smoking tobacco or weighing non-illegal items. In such cases, the defense can argue that the item was not primarily intended for drug use.

E. Lack of Possession or Control

To be convicted of possessing drug paraphernalia, the prosecution must prove that the defendant had possession and control of the item. If the paraphernalia was found in a location where the defendant had no control or ownership, the charge could be dismissed. Common situations where this defense applies include:

- **Shared Ownership**: If the paraphernalia was found in a shared space, such as a roommate's home or a family car, the defendant may argue that the item did not belong to them.
- **Lack of Knowledge**: Even if the item was found with the defendant, they may argue that they were unaware of its existence or purpose. This defense could apply if the paraphernalia was found in someone else's bag or in an area the defendant does not regularly access.

---

3. Key Legal Strategies for Beating Drug Paraphernalia Charges

A. Challenge the Prosecution's Evidence

The most effective strategy in defending against drug paraphernalia charges is often challenging the evidence. A skilled defense attorney will look for holes in the prosecution's case, such as:

- **Lack of Clear Evidence**: If the prosecution cannot prove that the item was actually drug paraphernalia or that it was used for illegal purposes, the defense may argue for a dismissal of charges.
- **Unreliable Testimony**: The defense may cross-examine witnesses or challenge the reliability of the evidence presented by law enforcement.

B. File Pre-Trial Motions

A defense attorney may file pre-trial motions to have the charges reduced or dismissed based on insufficient evidence or constitutional violations. These motions may include:

- **Motion to Dismiss**: If there is insufficient evidence to support the paraphernalia charge, the defense may file a motion to dismiss the case.
- **Motion to Suppress Evidence**: If evidence was obtained through an unlawful search or seizure, the defense may file a motion to suppress that evidence.

C. Negotiate a Plea Deal

In some cases, negotiating a plea deal may be the best option. The defendant may agree to plead guilty to a lesser charge or accept a reduced sentence in exchange for avoiding trial. A plea deal may include:

- **Reduced Charges**: The defendant may plead guilty to a lesser offense, such as a misdemeanor with less severe penalties.
- **Alternative Sentencing**: The defendant may be able to avoid jail time and instead receive probation, community service, or enrollment in a drug diversion program.

---

4. Conclusion

Drug paraphernalia charges in Florida can carry serious penalties, but there are many legal defenses available to fight these charges. From challenging the evidence of possession or intent to raising issues of unlawful search and seizure, there are numerous strategies a defense attorney can use to protect the defendant's rights and minimize the consequences of the charges. By understanding the law and the available defenses, individuals facing drug paraphernalia charges can take steps to defend themselves and achieve the best possible outcome in their case. Whether through contesting the charges in court or negotiating a favorable plea deal, it is essential to work with an experienced attorney to navigate the complexities of Florida's drug laws.

CHAPTER SEVENTY

FIGHTING BURGLARY CHARGES IN FLORIDA

James never thought he'd need a criminal defense attorney. He was a construction worker, not a criminal. But here he was, sitting in a jail cell, charged with burglary of an occupied dwelling—a felony that could put him away for life.

The police said he broke into a house. He said he was there for work. Now, his future depended on proving his innocence.

Understanding Florida's Burglary Laws

In Florida, burglary is defined under Florida Statute 810.02 as:

Entering a dwelling, structure, or conveyance with the intent to commit a crime inside.

The key factor? Intent. If James didn't intend to commit a crime, he wasn't guilty of burglary.

Florida categorizes burglary based on the type of property entered:

- Burglary of an Occupied Dwelling (First-Degree Felony)
    - A home or residence where people are present.
    - Punishable by life in prison if armed or if assault occurs.
    - Otherwise, up to 30 years in prison.
- Burglary of an Unoccupied Dwelling (Second-Degree Felony)
    - A home where no one is present.
    - Punishable by up to 15 years in prison.
- Burglary of a Structure (Third-Degree Felony)

 - A non-residential building (e.g., a store or warehouse).
 - Punishable by up to 5 years in prison.

James was facing first-degree felony burglary—the worst kind.

Building the Defense

His attorney, Melissa Carter, had one job: prove James never intended to commit a crime.

"This whole case hinges on intent," she told him. "If we can show you were there legally or had no criminal intent, we win."

James took a deep breath. "I was there to do a job. I wasn't breaking in."

That was the foundation of his defense.

1. Lack of Intent to Commit a Crime

Florida law requires that a burglary suspect enters a property with the intent to commit a crime inside. If there was no intent, there was no burglary.

Melissa planned to argue that:

- James was hired for a job and had no intention to steal or commit any crime.
- He had tools for work, not burglary.
- The entire incident was a misunderstanding.

2. Consent & Authorization

James had been at the house before. The homeowner had hired his company for renovations.

"Do you have a contract or work order?" Melissa asked.

James nodded. "Yeah, in my truck."

That was a key piece of evidence. If James had permission to be there, he couldn't be guilty of burglary.

3. Mistaken Identity

The police report claimed that a neighbor had seen James entering the house and called 911. But the witness had only seen a man in a hoodie—not James specifically.

Melissa hired a private investigator to:

- Interview the witness.
- Check surveillance cameras nearby.

KIf they could prove the witness misidentified James, the case would fall apart.

4. Illegal Search & Seizure

"How did the police arrest you?" Melissa asked.

James frowned. "They showed up, handcuffed me, and searched my truck."

"Did they have a warrant?"

"No."

That was a Fourth Amendment violation. Without a warrant or probable cause, the search was illegal. Melissa filed a motion to suppress any evidence found in James's truck.

Pretrial Strategy: Pushing for Dismissal

Before trial, Melissa attacked the prosecution's case from every angle:

1. Filed a motion to dismiss – arguing James had legal permission to be there.

2. Filed a motion to suppress evidence – since the police conducted an illegal search.
3. Challenged witness testimony – proving the neighbor couldn't clearly identify James.

Meanwhile, the prosecution offered a plea deal: 5 years in prison for a guilty plea.

James refused. "I'm not pleading guilty to something I didn't do."

Winning in Court

In court, Melissa tore apart the state's case:

- The homeowner testified that James was hired for work—he had no reason to break in.
- The contract proved James had a legitimate reason to be there.
- The neighbor admitted they didn't see the suspect's face—just a "man in a hoodie."
- The judge ruled that the search of James's truck was unconstitutional, throwing out key evidence.

With no criminal intent, no reliable witness, and no admissible evidence, the prosecutor had no choice: Case dismissed.

Aftermath

James walked out of court a free man.

"I can't believe they almost sent me to prison for this," he said.

Melissa nodded. "It happens more than you think. But the law is clear—without intent, it's not burglary."

CHAPTER SEVENTY ONE.

THE WRONG PLACE AT THE WRONG TIME

James never thought of himself as a criminal. He was a 22-year-old college student, working part-time as a delivery driver. But one night, a simple decision turned into a nightmare—one that almost cost him his freedom.

The Arrest

It was late, and James had just finished his last delivery for the night. Driving home, he noticed his gas tank was running low. He pulled into a dimly lit neighborhood, hoping to find a gas station. His GPS directed him down a road he had never been on before. As he passed a row of houses, he spotted a small, abandoned home with an overgrown yard and boarded-up windows.

James parked his car nearby and stepped out to stretch his legs. Curious, he walked up to the house and peeked inside through a broken window. He had always been interested in real estate and often watched YouTube videos about flipping abandoned homes. Maybe this was a foreclosure, he thought. Maybe he could buy it cheap one day.

What James didn't know was that someone was inside.

A homeless man, using the abandoned house for shelter, saw James outside and panicked. Thinking he was about to be attacked or thrown out, he called 911. He told the dispatcher that a man was "trying to break in." Minutes later, flashing blue lights surrounded James.

James tried to explain to the police that he hadn't broken into the house, that he was just looking inside, but they weren't listening. Officers searched him, found nothing illegal, and arrested him anyway—charging him with burglary of an occupied dwelling, a first-degree felony in Florida, carrying a penalty of up to 30 years in prison.

The Legal Challenge

James' parents hired a defense attorney, Maria Lopez, who had handled dozens of burglary cases. She knew immediately that this was a case of misinterpretation and overcharging.

"Burglary requires intent," she told James during their first meeting. "The prosecution has to prove you entered that property with the purpose of committing a crime inside. Just looking inside isn't enough."

Maria built her defense around three key arguments:

1. No Intent to Commit a Crime

Under Florida Statute 810.02, burglary isn't just about entering a building—it's about entering with the intent to commit a crime. James never entered the home, and he had no tools or weapons that could suggest he planned to commit theft or vandalism.

Maria gathered James' phone records, which showed his GPS activity. He had been following his navigation system when he stopped. She also collected text messages he sent to his friend minutes before, saying he was looking for gas.

2. Mistaken Witness Testimony

The homeless man's 911 call described a "suspicious man trying to break in," but Maria subpoenaed the full recording. In the audio, the man admitted he only saw James outside the house, looking in. He never saw him enter or attempt to enter.

When Maria cross-examined the witness in court, she asked, "Did you actually see my client break into the house?"

"Well, no," the witness admitted. "But I thought he was going to."

3. No Forced Entry or Damage

The prosecution claimed James was trying to commit burglary, but there was no evidence of a break-in. No broken locks, no pried doors, no damage to the property. Maria highlighted this lack of evidence to weaken the state's case.

The Verdict

The jury deliberated for less than an hour. With no proof of criminal intent, no actual break-in, and an unreliable witness, they returned with a not guilty verdict.

James was free.

Outside the courthouse, he took a deep breath. "I can't believe I almost lost my future over something so stupid."

Maria nodded. "It happens all the time. But the law is clear—intent matters. Just because something looks suspicious doesn't mean it's a crime."

James walked away with a lesson he'd never forget: Sometimes, being in the wrong place at the wrong time can change everything—but knowing your rights can change it back.

Got it! Here's a fresh take for the final chapter—something informative yet engaging.

CHAPTER SEVENTY TWO.

UNDERSTANDING FLORIDA BURGLARY LAWS—WHAT YOU NEED TO KNOW

Burglary charges in Florida can be life-changing, and many people misunderstand what legally qualifies as burglary. It's not just about breaking into a home—many cases involve misunderstandings, mistaken identity, or even being in the wrong place at the wrong time.

This chapter breaks down what you need to know about burglary laws, penalties, and possible defenses in Florida.

What Legally Counts as Burglary?

According to Florida Statute 810.02, burglary is when a person:

1. Enters a dwelling, structure, or vehicle
2. Without permission (or stays after permission is revoked)
3. With the intent to commit a crime inside

Key Takeaways:

- You don't need to steal anything—intent to commit any crime inside is enough.
- Even lawful entry can turn into burglary if you refuse to leave.
- A locked or enclosed area is a critical factor—an open porch is not the same as entering a house.

Penalties for Burglary in Florida

The punishment for burglary depends on where it happens and whether people are inside:

- Burglary of an Occupied Dwelling – First-degree felony (Up to life in prison)
- Burglary of an Unoccupied Dwelling – Second-degree felony (Up to 15 years in prison)
- Burglary of a Structure or Vehicle – Third-degree felony (Up to 5 years in prison)

If a weapon is used or an assault occurs, the penalties increase dramatically.

Common Defenses to Burglary Charges

Many people accused of burglary aren't criminals—they were either misunderstood or wrongfully arrested. Some common defenses include:

1. Lack of Criminal Intent – If you entered a place but had no intention of committing a crime, it's not burglary.
2. Permission to Enter – If you had permission to be there, burglary charges don't apply.
3. Mistaken Identity – Surveillance footage or witness testimony is often unreliable.
4. Illegal Search & Seizure – If evidence was obtained without a warrant or probable cause, it may be thrown **out.**

How to Protect Yourself from a Wrongful Burglary Charge

- Know your rights – Never admit to anything without a lawyer present.
- Don't enter abandoned or private property – Even if it seems empty, someone may claim you trespassed.
- Keep records of permission – If you have a reason to be on a property (contract work, rental, etc.), keep written proof.

Final Thought

Burglary charges can be devastating, but a strong defense can make the difference between freedom and years in prison. Understanding the law and your rights is the best way to protect yourself.

CHAPTER SEVENTY THREE.

BEATING MANUFACTURING AND CULTIVATING MARIJUANA CHARGES IN FLORIDA

INTRODUCTION

In Florida, marijuana laws have become increasingly complex, especially with the rise of medical marijuana use and ongoing discussions about marijuana legalization. However, despite these changes, the illegal cultivation or manufacture of marijuana remains a serious offense under Florida law. Individuals charged with manufacturing or cultivating marijuana face substantial penalties, including imprisonment, hefty fines, and a criminal record that could impact their future. Fortunately, there are multiple defenses and legal strategies available to challenge such charges. This chapter will provide an overview of Florida's laws regarding the manufacturing and cultivating of marijuana, discuss the penalties associated with these crimes, and outline key defense strategies to help individuals fight these charges.

---

1. Understanding the Law on Manufacturing and Cultivating Marijuana in Florida

Florida law takes marijuana cultivation and manufacturing offenses seriously, and the penalties reflect the state's tough stance on drug-related crimes. **Florida Statutes Section 893.13** outlines the criminal penalties for cultivating or manufacturing marijuana, and these penalties vary depending on the amount of marijuana involved and the circumstances surrounding the offense.

Definition of Manufacturing and Cultivating Marijuana

Under Florida law:

- **Cultivating marijuana** involves planting, growing, harvesting, or nurturing marijuana plants with the intent to distribute or possess for distribution.
- **Manufacturing marijuana** involves producing or creating marijuana for sale, including processing marijuana into concentrated forms (such as oils or edibles), as well as cultivating marijuana for the purpose of creating a larger-scale operation.

While medical marijuana is legal in Florida under certain conditions, the law still prohibits the unlicensed cultivation or manufacturing of marijuana. Cultivating marijuana outside the bounds of the state's medical marijuana program is illegal, and individuals found growing marijuana without the necessary licensing can be charged with a crime.

Penalties for Manufacturing and Cultivating Marijuana

The severity of the penalties for cultivating or manufacturing marijuana in Florida depends on the quantity of marijuana involved, the individual's prior criminal record, and other factors. Below are the general penalties associated with marijuana cultivation and manufacturing:

1. **Possessing Fewer than 25 Plants**:
    - If a person is found cultivating fewer than 25 marijuana plants, they can be charged with a **third-degree felony**.
    - Penalties for a third-degree felony include up to **5 years in prison**, **fines of up to $5,000**, and potential probation.
2. **Possessing 25 to 2,000 Plants**:
    - Cultivating between 25 and 2,000 marijuana plants is considered a **second-degree felony**.

    - Penalties can include **up to 15 years in prison**, **fines of up to $10,000**, and potential probation.
3. **Possessing More Than 2,000 Plants**:
    - Cultivating more than 2,000 marijuana plants is classified as a **first-degree felony** under Florida law.
    - Penalties can include **up to 30 years in prison**, **fines of up to $10,000**, and potential probation.
4. **Manufacturing Marijuana**:
    - Manufacturing marijuana, including processing marijuana into concentrates or edibles, is typically classified as a **first-degree felony**.
    - Penalties include **up to 30 years in prison** and **fines of up to $10,000**.

The penalties associated with these offenses can be severe, and those convicted may also face civil consequences, such as asset forfeiture (seizing of property or money connected to illegal activities).

---

2. Common Defenses to Manufacturing and Cultivating Marijuana Charges

While the penalties for manufacturing and cultivating marijuana in Florida are steep, there are several defense strategies that can be employed to challenge these charges. A skilled criminal defense attorney will evaluate the specific details of the case and may use one or more of the following defenses:

A. Lack of Knowledge or Intent

In order to be convicted of manufacturing or cultivating marijuana, the prosecution must prove that the defendant had knowledge of and intent to cultivate or manufacture the drug. If the defendant did not know about the marijuana plants or did not intend to cultivate marijuana for illegal purposes, the charge may be difficult to prove.

Possible defenses include:

- **Unaware of the Plants**: The defendant may argue that they did not know marijuana plants were being cultivated on their property. This defense can be used if marijuana plants were found on a property they were renting or in a location they did not have control over (e.g., a shared garden or property).
- **Lack of Intent**: The defendant could argue that they were not intending to grow marijuana for distribution or sale. For example, if the marijuana was for personal use or was mistakenly planted without intent to sell or manufacture, the defense could challenge the prosecution's claims of illegal intent.

B. No Control or Ownership of the Marijuana

If the marijuana plants were found on property the defendant did not own or control, they may not be liable for cultivating or manufacturing the marijuana. In order to be convicted, the prosecution must prove that the defendant had control or ownership of the marijuana plants or manufacturing equipment.

Possible arguments include:

- **Shared Property**: If the marijuana was found on property the defendant did not own, such as a shared residence or rental property, the defense may argue that the defendant had no control over the marijuana cultivation or manufacturing process.
- **Lack of Possession**: The defense could argue that the defendant did not have possession of the marijuana plants, particularly if the

defendant was merely present at the scene or lived in the residence where the marijuana was found.

C. Improper Search and Seizure

Under the **Fourth Amendment** of the U.S. Constitution, individuals are protected against unreasonable searches and seizures. If law enforcement conducted an illegal search—whether in the defendant's home, car, or property—the evidence obtained may be inadmissible in court.

Possible Fourth Amendment violations include:

- **Lack of Warrant**: If the police searched the defendant's home, vehicle, or property without a warrant or without consent, the search may be unlawful. If the evidence was obtained during an illegal search, it could be excluded from the case.
- **No Probable Cause**: Law enforcement must have probable cause to believe that a crime is being committed in order to search a property. If the search was conducted without probable cause, the evidence obtained could be suppressed.

D. Entrapment

Entrapment occurs when law enforcement officers induce a person to commit a crime that they would not have otherwise committed. This defense can be used if the defendant was encouraged or coerced by law enforcement to engage in marijuana cultivation or manufacturing.

To establish an entrapment defense, the defendant must prove:

- **Inducement by Law Enforcement**: Law enforcement officers or agents may have pressured or encouraged the defendant to cultivate or manufacture marijuana.

- **No Predisposition**: The defendant must show that they were not predisposed to commit the crime and would not have done so without law enforcement's involvement.

If the defense can show that the defendant was entrapped, the charges may be dismissed.

E. Improper or Insufficient Evidence

The prosecution must prove the defendant's involvement in marijuana cultivation or manufacturing beyond a reasonable doubt. If the prosecution fails to present sufficient evidence to establish the defendant's guilt, the charges may be dropped or reduced.

Possible challenges to evidence include:

- **Unclear or Insufficient Evidence**: If the marijuana plants or manufacturing equipment were found in an area that does not clearly link the defendant to the crime, the defense can argue that the evidence is insufficient.
- **Mistaken Identification**: The defendant may argue that they were wrongly identified as the individual responsible for the marijuana cultivation or manufacturing.

---

3. Key Legal Strategies for Beating Manufacturing and Cultivating Marijuana Charges

A. Challenge the Evidence

A critical strategy in defending against marijuana cultivation and manufacturing charges is challenging the evidence that the prosecution presents. An experienced criminal defense lawyer will examine the evidence and may challenge the reliability or legality of the search that led to the marijuana discovery. The attorney may also question the authenticity or chain of custody of evidence, such as marijuana plants or manufacturing materials.

B. File Pre-Trial Motions

In cases where the evidence is weak or the search was conducted improperly, the defense may file pre-trial motions to suppress evidence or dismiss charges. These motions include:

- **Motion to Suppress Evidence**: If the marijuana was discovered in violation of the defendant's constitutional rights (such as through an unlawful search), the defense can file a motion to suppress that evidence.
- **Motion to Dismiss**: If there is insufficient evidence to support the cultivation or manufacturing charges, the defense can file a motion to dismiss the case.

C. Negotiate a Plea Deal

In cases where the evidence against the defendant is strong, the defense may negotiate a plea deal to reduce the charges or penalties. This could involve pleading guilty to a lesser offense, such as a reduced felony or misdemeanor, or seeking alternative sentencing options such as probation, community service, or participation in a drug diversion program.

---

4. Conclusion

The charges for manufacturing and cultivating marijuana in Florida are serious and can lead to severe penalties, including lengthy prison sentences. However, there are numerous defenses available to challenge these charges, ranging from questioning the sufficiency of the evidence to raising issues of constitutional violations such as unlawful searches or entrapment. By working with an experienced criminal defense attorney, individuals facing marijuana cultivation and manufacturing charges can explore their options, protect their rights, and seek the best possible outcome in their case. Whether through challenging the evidence in court or negotiating a plea deal, there are ways to fight back against these serious charges.

CHAPTER SEVENTY FOUR

BEATING DEALING IN STOLEN PROPERTY CHARGES IN FLORIDA

INTRODUCTION

Being charged with dealing in stolen property in Florida is a serious offense that can have significant consequences. Under Florida law, dealing in stolen property is classified as a felony, and those convicted face severe penalties, including imprisonment, fines, and a criminal record. However, there are several legal defenses and strategies available that can help individuals fight these charges. This chapter will discuss the laws surrounding dealing in stolen property in Florida, the penalties for such charges, common defenses, and strategies that could potentially help reduce or dismiss the charges.

---

1. Understanding the Law on Dealing in Stolen Property in Florida

Under **Florida Statutes Section 812.019**, dealing in stolen property refers to the act of knowingly selling, buying, or trafficking stolen goods. This statute applies not only to people who are directly involved in the theft of property but also to individuals who receive or distribute stolen property with the knowledge that it was stolen. This offense can encompass a wide variety of actions, from reselling stolen electronics to trafficking in stolen vehicles or other high-value goods.

Elements of the Crime

For a person to be convicted of dealing in stolen property, the prosecution must prove the following elements:

1. **Knowledge of the Property's Stolen Nature**: The individual must know or have reason to believe that the property they are dealing with was stolen.
2. **Dealing with the Stolen Property**: The individual must engage in one of the following actions:
   - **Receiving** stolen property.
   - **Selling** stolen property.
   - **Buying** stolen property.
   - **Possessing** stolen property with the intent to sell or distribute it.
3. **Intent**: The defendant must have the intent to benefit from the stolen property. This could be through resale, trade, or any action that benefits the defendant or another party by transferring the stolen goods.

If the defendant did not have knowledge that the property was stolen or was not involved in the transaction of stolen property, they may be able to mount a successful defense.

---

2. Penalties for Dealing in Stolen Property in Florida

The penalties for dealing in stolen property in Florida depend on the value of the stolen property involved in the crime. The crime is classified as a **second-degree felony** in most cases, but the penalties can vary based on the specific circumstances.

1. **Second-Degree Felony**:
   - If the property involved is worth less than **$20,000**, the offense is classified as a second-degree felony.
   - Penalties include up to **15 years in prison, fines of up to $10,000**, and potential probation.
2. **First-Degree Felony**:

- If the property involved is worth **$20,000 or more**, the offense is classified as a first-degree felony.
- Penalties can include up to **30 years in prison, fines of up to $10,000**, and probation.

In addition to these criminal penalties, individuals convicted of dealing in stolen property may also face civil consequences, such as asset forfeiture (seizing assets or property connected to the offense), and the destruction of their reputation, which could affect future employment and other opportunities.

---

3. Common Defenses to Dealing in Stolen Property Charges

Although dealing in stolen property charges in Florida can be serious, several defense strategies can be employed to challenge these charges. The right defense strategy depends on the facts of the case and the circumstances surrounding the alleged crime. Here are some common defenses that could potentially be used in these cases:

A. Lack of Knowledge That the Property Was Stolen

One of the most common defenses in dealing with stolen property charges is that the defendant did not know the property was stolen. Florida law requires that the defendant have actual knowledge or reasonable belief that the property was stolen. If the defendant did not know the goods were stolen, they cannot be convicted of this crime.

Possible scenarios for this defense include:

- **Purchasing from an Untrustworthy Source**: The defendant may argue that they bought the property from someone who misrepresented it as being legitimate, and they did not have any reason to believe it was stolen.

- **Innocent Possession**: If the defendant received or possessed the property without realizing it was stolen, they can argue that they did not have the requisite knowledge to be guilty of dealing in stolen property.

B. Lack of Intent to Sell or Distribute the Property

In some cases, a person may possess stolen property without the intent to sell or distribute it. Florida law requires that the defendant have the intent to deal in the stolen property (i.e., to sell or distribute it). If the property was intended for personal use or if the defendant was not trying to benefit from it, the defense could argue that there was no intent to commit the crime.

For example:

- **Personal Use Defense**: The defendant could argue that they received the property for personal use, not for resale, and had no intention of distributing or selling it.

C. Entrapment

Entrapment occurs when law enforcement officers or agents induce an individual to commit a crime that they would not have otherwise committed. If the defendant was coerced or encouraged by law enforcement to buy, sell, or deal in stolen property, they could argue that they were entrapped.

To establish an entrapment defense, the defendant must show:

- **Law Enforcement Induced the Crime**: The defendant may argue that law enforcement officers created the opportunity for the crime and encouraged them to act in a way they would not have otherwise.

- **Lack of Predisposition**: The defendant must demonstrate that they were not predisposed to commit the crime without law enforcement's influence.

D. Mistaken Identity or False Allegations

Sometimes, individuals are wrongfully identified or falsely accused of dealing in stolen property. If the defendant was wrongly connected to the stolen goods or was misidentified as the person involved in the illegal transaction, the defense could argue mistaken identity or false allegations.

Possible scenarios for this defense include:

- **Wrongful Arrest**: The defendant may argue that they were at the wrong place at the wrong time or were falsely identified by a witness or law enforcement.
- **No Evidence Linking the Defendant to the Stolen Property**: If the defendant was not physically involved with the stolen property and the evidence does not clearly connect them to the crime, they may argue that the charges should be dropped.

E. Improper Search and Seizure

If law enforcement conducted an illegal search and seizure that resulted in the discovery of stolen property, the evidence obtained may be inadmissible in court. Under the **Fourth Amendment** of the U.S. Constitution, individuals are protected against unreasonable searches and seizures. If the search violated the defendant's rights, the evidence may be suppressed.

Common Fourth Amendment violations include:

- **No Search Warrant**: If the search was conducted without a valid warrant or consent, the evidence may be inadmissible.

- **Lack of Probable Cause**: Law enforcement must have probable cause to believe a crime has been committed in order to justify a search. If the search was conducted without probable cause, the evidence can be excluded from the case.

---

4. Key Legal Strategies for Beating Dealing in Stolen Property Charges

A. Challenge the Prosecution's Evidence

One of the most effective strategies in defending against dealing in stolen property charges is to challenge the prosecution's evidence. A skilled criminal defense attorney will scrutinize the evidence to find weaknesses in the prosecution's case. Possible areas to challenge include:

- **Lack of Clear Evidence**: If the prosecution cannot prove that the defendant knowingly dealt in stolen property, the charges may be reduced or dismissed.
- **Unreliable Witnesses**: If the case relies on witness testimony, the defense may cross-examine witnesses to show that their testimony is unreliable.

B. File Pre-Trial Motions

In cases where there is insufficient evidence or constitutional violations, the defense attorney may file pre-trial motions to have the charges dropped or evidence suppressed. These motions include:

- **Motion to Suppress Evidence**: If the stolen property was discovered during an unlawful search or seizure, the defense may file a motion to suppress that evidence.

- **Motion to Dismiss**: If the evidence is insufficient to support the charges, the defense may file a motion to dismiss the case.

C. Negotiate a Plea Deal

If the evidence against the defendant is strong, the defense may negotiate a plea deal with the prosecution. A plea deal may involve the defendant agreeing to plead guilty to a lesser offense or accepting a reduced sentence in exchange for avoiding a lengthy trial. A plea deal may include:

- **Reduced Charges**: The defendant may plead guilty to a lesser felony or misdemeanor charge, reducing the potential penalties.
- **Alternative Sentencing**: The defendant may be able to avoid lengthy prison time and instead receive probation, community service, or drug or theft diversion programs.

---

5. Conclusion

Dealing in stolen property is a serious offense in Florida, with significant legal consequences, including long prison sentences and hefty fines. However, there are multiple defenses available that can help individuals fight these charges. By challenging the prosecution's evidence, proving lack of knowledge, or showing that the defendant had no intent to sell or distribute the property, it may be possible to reduce or even dismiss the charges. A skilled criminal defense attorney will be able to evaluate the specific facts of the case and employ the most appropriate defense strategies to protect the defendant's rights and achieve the best possible outcome. Whether through challenging the evidence in court or negotiating a favorable plea deal, there are effective ways to fight against dealing in stolen property charges in Florida.

CHAPTER SEVENTY FIVE.

BEATING THE TWO-WAY COMMUNICATIONS DEVICE CHARGES IN FLORIDA

INTRODUCTION

Florida law takes the illegal use of two-way communications devices seriously, especially in cases involving criminal activity. Under Florida Statutes Section 934.215, it is a criminal offense to use a two-way communications device (such as a cell phone or radio) to facilitate certain crimes, including drug trafficking, fraud, and organized criminal activity. Charges related to the use of two-way communications devices are often added to other criminal charges and can significantly increase penalties, making them a critical issue in a criminal defense.

This chapter will provide an overview of the law surrounding two-way communications devices in Florida, the penalties for using such devices in connection with criminal activities, common defenses to these charges, and strategies for beating these charges.

---

1. Understanding the Law on Two-Way Communications Devices in Florida

Florida Statutes Section 934.215 criminalizes the use of a two-way communications device to facilitate the commission of certain illegal activities. These devices, including cell phones, radios, and other forms of communication that allow for verbal exchange between two parties, are considered critical tools for law enforcement in investigating and preventing crimes. However, when these devices are used to facilitate criminal conduct, such as drug trafficking, organized crime, or fraud, they become an illegal instrumentality under the law.

Elements of the Crime

To be convicted of using a two-way communications device to commit a crime, the prosecution must prove the following elements beyond a reasonable doubt:

1. **Use of a Two-Way Communications Device**: The defendant must have used a device capable of two-way communication (e.g., a cell phone, radio, or walkie-talkie).
2. **Criminal Activity**: The device must have been used in furtherance of criminal activity. This includes crimes such as:
   - Drug trafficking or distribution.
   - Engaging in organized crime.
   - Committing fraud, theft, or other felonies.
3. **Intent to Facilitate the Crime**: The defendant must have used the device with the intent to assist in the commission of the criminal activity. This means the device was used to plan, execute, or promote the crime.

A person does not have to directly commit the crime using the device, but rather, they must have used it to enable, further, or promote the illegal activity. For instance, if someone is coordinating drug sales through text messages or phone calls, they could be charged under this statute.

---

2. Penalties for Using a Two-Way Communications Device in Florida

The penalties for using a two-way communications device in furtherance of criminal activity are serious and can vary depending on the nature of the underlying crime and the defendant's criminal history.

1. **Second-Degree Felony**: In most cases, using a two-way communications device to facilitate a crime is considered a **second-degree felony** in Florida. This charge is typically applied when the underlying offense involves crimes like drug trafficking or organized crime, but the value or severity of the crime does not warrant a higher charge.
    - **Penalties**: A second-degree felony in Florida carries a potential sentence of up to **15 years in prison**, **fines of up to $10,000**, and probation.
2. **First-Degree Felony**: If the two-way communications device is used to facilitate more severe crimes, such as the trafficking of large amounts of drugs, the penalties can escalate. The charge may be classified as a **first-degree felony**.
    - **Penalties**: A first-degree felony can result in **up to 30 years in prison**, **fines of up to $10,000**, and probation.

Given these severe penalties, it is essential to mount an effective defense to fight these charges. A conviction on charges involving two-way communications devices can significantly impact one's future, so understanding potential defenses is key to avoiding conviction.

---

3. Common Defenses to Two-Way Communications Device Charges

There are several legal defenses available that can be used to contest charges of using a two-way communications device to facilitate a crime in Florida. Depending on the facts of the case, some of these defenses may result in charges being reduced, dismissed, or significantly mitigated.

A. Lack of Knowledge or Intent

One of the most common defenses in cases involving two-way communications devices is that the defendant did not know or intend to use the device to further a crime. Under Florida law, simply using a two-way communications device is not enough to support a conviction; the prosecution must prove that the defendant used the device intentionally to facilitate criminal activity.

Key points to challenge may include:

- **Lack of Knowledge**: The defendant may not have been aware that their communication was being used for criminal activity. For example, if someone used their phone to arrange a meeting with a person who later used the opportunity for illegal purposes, the defense could argue that the defendant had no knowledge that the meeting was for a criminal purpose.
- **No Intent to Facilitate the Crime**: The defendant might argue that the communication was innocent or unrelated to the criminal conduct. For example, if phone calls were made for personal reasons rather than to further a crime, this defense can undermine the prosecution's argument.

B. No Criminal Activity or Unrelated Crime

For a conviction under Section 934.215 to occur, the defendant must have used the device to facilitate criminal activity. If the communication did not involve a criminal activity, this could form a solid defense.

Potential arguments include:

- **Unrelated Communications**: The defendant might claim that the communication was unrelated to any illegal conduct. For example, if a phone call or text message was made to schedule a social meeting rather than facilitating a drug transaction, there may be insufficient evidence to link the communication to a crime.

- **No Evidence of Criminal Intent**: If the prosecution fails to present clear evidence that the communications were part of a broader criminal enterprise or conspiracy, this can be an effective defense.

C. Unlawful Search and Seizure

In some cases, the evidence of illegal use of a two-way communications device may have been obtained through an unlawful search and seizure. The **Fourth Amendment** protects individuals from unreasonable searches and seizures, and if law enforcement violated this protection, any evidence obtained could be inadmissible in court.

Some possible violations to consider include:

- **No Warrant for Phone Search**: If law enforcement searched the defendant's phone, computer, or other communications devices without a valid search warrant, the evidence obtained from that search could be challenged and excluded.
- **Lack of Probable Cause**: If the search of the defendant's communication device occurred without probable cause or a warrant, the evidence may be deemed inadmissible. This can lead to a dismissal of the charges.

D. Mistaken Identity

Sometimes, individuals are wrongfully accused of crimes they did not commit. In the context of two-way communications devices, a defendant could argue that they were mistakenly identified as being involved in a criminal transaction or conspiracy.

Possible strategies include:

- **Alibi**: If the defendant can prove they were not involved in the communications at the time the crime was occurring, this can be a powerful defense.
- **Misidentification**: The defense could argue that the defendant was misidentified by law enforcement or witnesses as the person involved in the communications leading to the crime.

E. Entrapment

Entrapment occurs when law enforcement officers or agents induce someone to commit a crime that they would not have otherwise committed. This defense may apply in cases where law enforcement officers actively encouraged or coerced the defendant to use a two-way communications device to facilitate illegal activity.

To prove entrapment, the defendant must show:

- **Coercion or Encouragement by Law Enforcement**: Law enforcement agents may have set up a situation in which the defendant was encouraged to use the device to facilitate criminal activity.
- **Lack of Predisposition**: The defendant must show that they were not predisposed to commit the crime and would not have committed the offense without law enforcement's involvement.

---

4. Key Legal Strategies for Beating Two-Way Communications Device Charges

A. Challenge the Evidence

A critical defense strategy involves challenging the evidence that the prosecution has presented. The defense attorney may question the reliability of the evidence, including phone records, call logs, or text messages. This may include showing that the communications were misinterpreted or that the defendant's actions were unrelated to any criminal activity.

B. File Pre-Trial Motions

If there are grounds to suppress evidence, the defense attorney may file pre-trial motions to exclude evidence obtained through an unlawful search or seizure, or if there is insufficient evidence to connect the defendant to the crime. Key motions include:

- **Motion to Suppress Evidence**: If the defendant's phone or communication records were obtained unlawfully, the defense can file a motion to suppress that evidence.
- **Motion to Dismiss**: If there is no clear evidence of criminal activity facilitated by the device, the defense may file a motion to dismiss the charges.

C. Negotiate a Plea Deal

If the evidence against the defendant is strong, a defense attorney may negotiate a plea deal with the prosecution. This could involve pleading to lesser charges or negotiating for reduced penalties in exchange for cooperation. This may result in a more favorable outcome, such as reduced prison time or probation instead of incarceration.

---

5. Conclusion

Charges involving the use of a two-way communications device in Florida can lead to serious legal consequences, including lengthy prison sentences and significant fines. However, there are several defenses that can be employed to challenge these charges. Whether it's proving lack of knowledge, demonstrating that the communications were unrelated to criminal activity, or challenging the evidence on constitutional grounds, there are multiple ways to fight back against these charges. By working with an experienced criminal defense attorney, individuals facing two-way communications device charges can explore all available defenses and pursue the best possible outcome for their case.

CHAPTER SEVENTY SIX.

Filing and challenging claims of ineffective assistance of counsel (IAC) In a case, especially if you're concerned about its impact on your case via social media platforms like Facebook, is a complex process. However, I'll guide you through how to file such a claim and provide general advice on how to approach this issue in Florida, or any state, even if Facebook or social media plays a role in your defense or claim.

What is Ineffective Assistance of Counsel?

Ineffective assistance of counsel is a legal claim asserting that your defense attorney failed to provide effective representation, violating your constitutional right to a fair trial under the Sixth Amendment. To succeed in such a claim, the burden is on the defendant to prove that their attorney's performance was below the standard expected, and that this failure directly impacted the outcome of the case.

Two-Part Test to Prove Ineffective Assistance

The U.S. Supreme Court's decision in **Strickland v. Washington** (1984) set forth the standard for proving ineffective assistance of counsel. Under **Strickland**, to succeed on an ineffective assistance of counsel claim, the defendant must show:

1. **Deficient Performance**: The attorney's performance was **below an objective standard of reasonableness**. This means that the attorney's actions (or lack of actions) were outside the scope of what is considered competent in the legal profession.

2. **Prejudice**: The defendant must show that the deficient performance **prejudiced the defense**. Specifically, the defendant must demonstrate that there is a **reasonable probability** that, but for the attorney's errors,

the outcome of the case would have been different (e.g., a not-guilty verdict, reduced sentence, etc.).

How to File an Ineffective Assistance of Counsel Claim

If you believe that your attorney's performance was ineffective and that it negatively affected your case, here's how you can go about filing such a claim.

1. Post-Conviction Relief

If you were convicted, and you believe your attorney was ineffective, you will need to file a **post-conviction motion** to raise the claim. In Florida, this would typically be done through a **Florida Rule of Criminal Procedure 3.850 Motion for Post-Conviction Relief**.

Here's how the process works:

1. **File a Rule 3.850 Motion**: This is the formal motion for post-conviction relief in Florida. You can file this in the court where you were convicted. In your motion, you need to specify the errors your attorney made (deficient performance) and how those errors affected the outcome of your case (prejudice).
2. **Grounds for IAC**: In your motion, outline the specific ways in which your attorney's actions were deficient. For example, if your attorney failed to object to improper evidence, failed to investigate certain aspects of your case, or failed to raise a certain defense, this could be grounds for IAC.
3. **Provide Evidence**: Provide any evidence to support your claims. This can include statements, affidavits, or anything else showing that your attorney's actions were ineffective and harmful.
4. **Filing with the Court**: Once you've completed the motion, file it with the court. After filing, the court will review your claims. If your

motion is accepted, the case may be re-opened for further proceedings, or it may lead to a new trial or resentencing.

2. Appeal if Necessary

If you believe the court's denial of your post-conviction motion is wrong, you can **appeal** that decision. The appellate court will review whether your attorney's performance was truly ineffective and whether it had a prejudicial impact on your case.

How Facebook or Social Media Can Affect Ineffective Assistance Claims

If **Facebook** or social media played a role in your case—either by your attorney failing to investigate social media evidence, not using certain social media evidence in your defense, or making comments on Facebook related to your case—this could be part of your IAC claim.

For example:

- **Failure to Investigate Social Media**: If your attorney didn't look into important social media evidence (e.g., messages, posts, or photos) that could have helped your case, that could be grounds for a claim of ineffective assistance.
- **Inappropriate Social Media Use by Your Lawyer**: If your attorney posted about your case on Facebook or shared details publicly, this could be a violation of legal ethics and could support a claim that your attorney was ineffective.
- **Failure to Object to Social Media Evidence**: If the prosecution used evidence from Facebook (like posts or private messages) that should have been excluded, and your attorney failed to object, this could be seen as ineffective assistance.

To pursue such a claim, you will need to:

- **Document the Issue**: If your attorney failed to investigate or misused social media evidence, document this as part of your claim. For example, you can provide screenshots, affidavits, or testimony showing that social media evidence was crucial and overlooked.
- **Consult an Expert**: If social media evidence was central to your case, it might be worth consulting a digital forensics expert who can explain how this evidence could have been used in your favor.
- **Raise the Issue in Your Motion**: If you believe that your lawyer's handling of Facebook or social media evidence (or their failure to do so) amounted to ineffective assistance, you must raise this in your **3.850 Motion**.

What to Do if You Want to File an Ineffective Assistance Claim Involving Facebook

1. **Document Everything**: Collect all social media evidence, including posts, messages, and screenshots, which support your claim that social media was involved in your case or was mishandled by your attorney. If your lawyer made inappropriate comments on Facebook or failed to use social media evidence that could help your case, gather this documentation.

2. **Consult with a New Attorney**: If you're serious about pursuing an IAC claim, it is crucial to consult a new attorney. A second opinion can help you understand whether the actions of your previous lawyer truly amounted to ineffective assistance, especially concerning Facebook or social media.

3. **File a Rule 3.850 Motion (in Florida)**: Include a detailed explanation of how your attorney's actions regarding social media or Facebook were ineffective. This could involve failing to investigate social media evidence, not presenting crucial evidence from social media, or mishandling online communications in the case.
4. **Explain How the Failure Prejudiced Your Case**: In your motion, show how your attorney's failure to properly handle social media evidence impacted your case. For example, you could explain that certain posts or messages on Facebook could have contradicted the prosecution's case or supported your defense.
5. **Prepare for Appeal**: If your motion is denied, you may consider appealing the decision to a higher court. You'll need to argue that your attorney's deficiencies were not only unreasonable but also prejudicial to your case.

Conclusion

If you believe that your defense attorney was ineffective in handling your case, especially in relation to Facebook or other social media issues, you can file a post-conviction motion to challenge the conviction based on **ineffective assistance of counsel**. By proving that your attorney's performance fell below a reasonable standard and prejudiced your case, you can have your conviction potentially overturned or reduced. Social media plays an increasingly important role in criminal cases, so a failure to properly handle it may be a strong argument for an IAC claim. Working with a skilled post-conviction attorney is essential to navigating this complex legal process.

CHAPTER SEVENTY SEVEN.

GETTING BACK INTO COURT FROM FLORIDA PRISON

INTRODUCTION

If you are incarcerated in a Florida prison and believe that your conviction was unjust or that you were wrongfully sentenced, you have the right to pursue legal avenues to challenge your conviction or sentence and potentially get back into court. Whether you are seeking to have your conviction overturned, request a reduced sentence, or address legal errors made during your trial, Florida law provides several mechanisms for inmates to petition the courts for relief. This chapter will guide you through the various processes involved in getting back into court from Florida prison, the options available to you, and how to maximize your chances of success.

---

1. Post-Conviction Relief: Rule 3.850 Motion

The most common method for getting back into court after a conviction in Florida is through a **post-conviction motion**. One of the primary vehicles for this is a **Florida Rule of Criminal Procedure 3.850 Motion for Post-Conviction Relief**.

What is Rule 3.850?

A **3.850 Motion** is a legal request to the court to review and overturn your conviction or sentence based on errors made during the trial or the legal process. This motion can address various issues, including:

- **Ineffective assistance of counsel** (e.g., if your lawyer failed to properly represent you or made mistakes that harmed your case).

- **Newly discovered evidence** that could have changed the outcome of your case.
- **Violation of constitutional rights** during the trial (e.g., illegal search and seizure, improper jury instructions, or prosecutorial misconduct).
- **Sentencing errors** (e.g., an incorrect calculation of your sentence, or if you received a harsher sentence than required by law).

How to File a Rule 3.850 Motion

1. **Grounds for the Motion**: You must clearly state the reasons why you believe your conviction or sentence should be overturned or modified. Common grounds include ineffective counsel, newly discovered evidence, or violations of constitutional rights. Ensure that your claims are supported by facts and evidence.

2. **Filing the Motion**: To file a Rule 3.850 motion, you need to submit the motion to the court where you were convicted. The motion must be filed within **two years** from the date your conviction became final (the time when the judgment is no longer subject to appeal).

3. **Supporting Documents**: Along with your motion, you may need to submit any supporting documents, such as affidavits, evidence of new facts, or expert opinions that support your claims.

4. **Court Review**: After filing, the court will review your motion and the claims you've made. If the court finds merit in your claims, it may schedule a hearing to reconsider your case. If your motion is denied, you have the right to appeal the decision.

---

2. Rule 3.800 Motion: Correcting Sentencing Errors

If you believe there was an error in the calculation or imposition of your sentence, you can file a **Rule 3.800 Motion** to challenge the sentence itself. This is a faster procedure than Rule 3.850 motions and is focused on sentencing errors rather than broader issues related to your conviction.

When to Use Rule 3.800

- **Illegal sentences**: If your sentence is unlawful (for example, if you were sentenced beyond the maximum allowable sentence or the court imposed a sentence not supported by the law).
- **Sentencing mistakes**: If the judge made a mistake in sentencing, such as failing to consider certain factors or imposing an incorrect sentence based on prior convictions.

How to File Rule 3.800

1. **Identify the Error**: Carefully review your sentencing documents and identify the specific errors.
2. **File the Motion**: You can file a Rule 3.800 motion directly with the court that imposed your sentence. This motion must be filed as soon as possible after identifying the error.
3. **Court Decision**: The court may correct the error without a hearing if the facts are clear. If the court denies the motion, you can appeal the decision to a higher court.

---

3. Appealing a Conviction or Sentence: Direct Appeal

If your case is still within the time limits for an appeal, you can pursue a **direct appeal** to challenge your conviction or sentence.

What is a Direct Appeal?

A direct appeal is a formal request to a higher court (the **Florida District Court of Appeal**) to review your case and the legal issues raised during the trial. You typically file an appeal after a conviction or sentencing, but it must be done within **30 days** from the date of sentencing.

Grounds for Appeal

You can appeal on several legal grounds, including:

- **Errors in trial procedure**: For example, improper jury instructions or wrongful admission of evidence.
- **Constitutional violations**: For example, violations of due process, the right to a fair trial, or protection against self-incrimination.
- **Legal errors**: If the judge made an error in applying the law.

How to File an Appeal

1. **Notice of Appeal**: You must file a **Notice of Appeal** with the trial court to inform them that you are appealing your conviction.
2. **Appellate Brief**: Your attorney (or a new attorney) will write an **appellate brief** outlining the legal errors that occurred during your trial.
3. **Oral Argument**: After reviewing your case, the appellate court may schedule an oral argument where your attorney will present the case for overturning your conviction.

What Happens After the Appeal?

- **Appellate Review**: The appellate court will review the trial transcript and legal arguments presented in your brief. They will decide if there were any legal errors that affected your conviction or sentence.
- **Outcome**: The appellate court may:
    - Affirm the conviction (uphold the decision).

- Reverse the conviction or sentence, resulting in a new trial, a reduced sentence, or dismissal of the charges.

---

4. Filing for Post-Conviction Relief Based on Newly Discovered Evidence

In cases where new evidence comes to light after a conviction, you can file for post-conviction relief based on **newly discovered evidence**. This evidence must be significant enough to likely alter the outcome of your case.

What is Newly Discovered Evidence?

Newly discovered evidence refers to information or materials that were not available during your trial and could prove your innocence or show that you were wrongly convicted. Examples include:

- DNA evidence.
- Testimony from new witnesses.
- Physical evidence that was overlooked.

How to File Based on Newly Discovered Evidence

1. **Prepare Your Evidence**: Gather the newly discovered evidence that could help your case. It must be credible, material, and likely to change the outcome of the trial.
2. **File a Motion**: File a motion in the court that convicted you, arguing that the new evidence warrants a new trial or a reexamination of your case.
3. **Hearing**: If the court accepts the motion, a hearing will be scheduled to determine whether the new evidence warrants relief.

---

5. Florida's Clemency Process

If you are serving a lengthy prison sentence, you may be eligible to apply for **clemency** in Florida. Clemency involves a pardon or a reduction in your sentence by the **Florida Board of Executive Clemency**. Clemency is not automatic and is only granted in certain cases.

Types of Clemency

- **Pardon**: A pardon erases the conviction and restores your civil rights, including the right to vote.
- **Sentence Commutation**: A commutation reduces the length of your sentence.
- **Reprieve**: A temporary delay in your sentence, often for health reasons.

How to Apply for Clemency

1. **Eligibility**: You must meet certain eligibility requirements, such as serving a specific portion of your sentence and having a clean disciplinary record.
2. **Clemency Petition**: Submit a petition for clemency to the Florida Office of Clemency. This petition includes personal information, a statement of your case, and reasons for seeking clemency.
3. **Review Process**: The Florida Board of Executive Clemency will review your case, and they may schedule a hearing or make a decision based on your petition.

---

6. Conclusion

Getting back into court from a Florida prison is a complex process, but it is possible through various avenues such as post-conviction motions, direct appeals, and clemency petitions. Whether you are seeking to correct an unjust conviction, reduce your sentence, or prove your innocence with newly discovered evidence, understanding the procedures and having the right legal support can make a significant difference. By working with experienced legal counsel and following the appropriate procedures, you can maximize your chances of success in getting back into court and improving your situation.

CHAPTER SEVENTY EIGHT

BEATING IMMIGRATION DEPORTATION IN FLORIDA

Immigration law in the United States is intricate, and Florida, with its significant immigrant population, stands as one of the states where deportation cases are commonly fought. Whether you are facing deportation due to overstaying a visa, a criminal conviction, or other grounds, understanding the deportation process and the legal options available to you is critical to fighting the case.

In this chapter, we will explore how immigrants facing deportation in Florida can protect themselves and possibly avoid removal from the country.

Understanding the Deportation Process in Florida

Deportation, also known as removal, is the formal process by which the U.S. government forces an immigrant to leave the country. The process can begin for various reasons such as overstaying a visa, entering the country unlawfully, committing a crime, or violating immigration terms.

For individuals residing in Florida, the process typically involves the following steps:

1. **Notice to Appear (NTA):** The first step in the deportation process is when the Department of Homeland Security (DHS) issues a Notice to Appear, which is a formal notice that the individual is being placed into removal proceedings. It typically happens after an immigration violation is discovered.

2. **Immigration Court Hearing:** After receiving the NTA, the immigrant will have to appear before an immigration judge in one of Florida's

immigration courts. The judge will determine whether the immigrant has a valid defense against deportation.

3. **Fighting Deportation:** This is the stage where an immigrant can present defenses. Common defenses against deportation include cancellation of removal, adjustment of status, asylum, or demonstrating that the immigrant has U.S. citizen or lawful permanent resident family members who will suffer hardship if the immigrant is removed.

4. **Appeals Process:** If the immigration judge rules against the immigrant, the decision can be appealed to the Board of Immigration Appeals (BIA), and in some cases, further appeals may be made to federal courts.

Common Grounds for Deportation

Several grounds could lead to deportation proceedings in Florida. Some of the most common include:

- **Overstaying a Visa:** One of the most common reasons immigrants face deportation is overstaying their visa. If you entered the U.S. on a tourist, student, or work visa and remained after your visa expired, you are at risk of being deported.

- **Criminal Convictions:** Certain criminal convictions, particularly drug offenses, violent crimes, or crimes of moral turpitude, can lead to deportation. Even lawful permanent residents are not immune if they are convicted of specific crimes.

- **Unlawful Entry:** Individuals who entered the U.S. without inspection, meaning they crossed the border without permission, may face deportation if caught.

- **Violation of Immigration Terms:** If you violate the terms of your visa or status, like working without authorization or engaging in other prohibited activities, it can lead to deportation.

Possible Defenses Against Deportation

If you are facing deportation in Florida, there are various defenses available depending on your situation:

1. **Cancellation of Removal:** This defense applies to certain individuals who have lived in the U.S. for an extended period, have good moral character, and can show that their deportation would cause exceptional hardship to their U.S. citizen or lawful permanent resident family members.

2. **Asylum or Refugee Status:** If you are in fear of persecution in your home country, you may apply for asylum, which, if granted, allows you to stay in the U.S. even if you were previously facing deportation.

3. **Adjustment of Status:** If you are married to a U.S. citizen or a lawful permanent resident, you may be able to apply for a green card, thereby adjusting your immigration status and avoiding deportation.

4. **Prosecutorial Discretion:** In some cases, the U.S. government may choose to exercise prosecutorial discretion and not pursue deportation. This is often seen in cases involving young individuals, individuals who have been long-time residents, or those with strong ties to the U.S.

5. **Waivers for Certain Crimes:** In certain cases, immigrants who have committed specific crimes may apply for a waiver. A waiver, if granted, may allow the immigrant to remain in the U.S. despite their criminal record.

The Role of Legal Counsel

Deportation proceedings can be complex, and it's essential to have experienced legal counsel to navigate the process effectively. In Florida, there are numerous immigration attorneys specializing in deportation defense. Here's how a lawyer can help:

- **Legal Advice:** An immigration attorney can help you understand the specifics of your case, advise you on your options, and help you develop the best defense strategy.
- **Representation:** Attorneys represent clients in immigration courts, ensuring that your case is presented effectively and that all legal defenses are raised.
- **Appeals:** If your case does not go in your favor, an attorney can assist with the appeal process, representing you before the Board of Immigration Appeals or even in federal court.

Taking Action Early

If you are facing deportation in Florida, it's essential to take action as soon as possible. Waiting too long can result in missed deadlines, missed opportunities to apply for relief, and unnecessary delays. Here's what you can do:

1. **Consult an Immigration Attorney:** The sooner you have legal representation, the better your chances are of avoiding deportation or at least delaying proceedings.
2. **Gather Evidence:** Collect any documentation that may support your defense, such as proof of employment, family ties, or any other evidence of hardship if you were deported.
3. **Understand the Impact of Deportation:** Deportation can have severe consequences on your ability to return to the U.S. in the future.

Understanding the long-term consequences is key to making informed decisions.

Conclusion

Fighting deportation in Florida is a challenging process, but it is not impossible. By understanding the legal procedures, knowing your rights, and working with an experienced immigration attorney, you can maximize your chances of avoiding removal. Whether through an appeal, a defense like asylum, or proving hardship for your family members, the right strategy can help you remain in the U.S. and continue building your life.

CHAPTER SEVENTY NINE.

NAVIGATING SPECIFIC DEFENSES AGAINST DEPORTATION IN FLORIDA

Deportation proceedings can be a daunting and complex process, but it's important to remember that not all is lost. Many immigrants facing deportation in Florida can present defenses that may allow them to remain in the United States. This chapter will delve deeper into some of the most common and effective defenses used to fight deportation, including **Asylum**, **Cancellation of Removal**, and the role of **Family-Based Relief**.

1. Asylum: Protection for Refugees

Asylum is one of the most common forms of relief for immigrants facing deportation, particularly for those who fear persecution in their home countries. If you have a well-founded fear of persecution based on race, religion, nationality, political opinion, or membership in a particular social group, you may be eligible to apply for asylum.

The Asylum Process

To apply for asylum, you must file a **Form I-589**, Application for Asylum and for Withholding of Removal. You must submit this application within one year of arriving in the U.S. (unless you can show that extraordinary circumstances prevented you from applying within that time frame). Here's how the process generally works:

1. **Application Submission:** File Form I-589 with the U.S. Citizenship and Immigration Services (USCIS) or, if already in deportation proceedings, with the Immigration Court.
2. **Interview or Hearing:** If applying affirmatively (i.e., not in removal proceedings), you will attend an interview with an asylum officer. If

you're in removal proceedings, you will have a hearing before an immigration judge.

3. **Adjudication:** The asylum officer or judge will determine if you meet the criteria for asylum. If granted, you will be able to stay in the U.S. and may later apply for a green card. If denied, you can appeal the decision.

Common Challenges to Asylum Applications

- **Credibility Issues:** Asylum applicants must prove their case with credible testimony and supporting evidence. This can be difficult, especially if there are inconsistencies in your story or if you lack documentation to support your claims.

- **One-Year Filing Deadline:** You must file your asylum application within one year of arriving in the U.S. Unless you qualify for an exception, failing to meet this deadline can result in ineligibility for asylum.

- **Past Persecution:** You must show that you've either been persecuted in the past or that you have a well-founded fear of future persecution. This often requires providing country-specific information, affidavits, or expert testimony.

Asylum as a Defense to Deportation

If you are in deportation proceedings and can establish eligibility for asylum, you may be able to avoid removal to your home country by demonstrating a fear of persecution. However, the burden of proof is on you, and you must present convincing evidence of your situation.

2. Cancellation of Removal: A Second Chance

Cancellation of removal is a form of relief available to certain immigrants who have been in the U.S. for many years and have strong ties to the country. This relief allows a judge to cancel the removal order, allowing the immigrant to remain in the U.S. and apply for lawful permanent resident status (a green card).

Eligibility Requirements

To be eligible for cancellation of removal in Florida, you must meet the following criteria:

- **Continuous Physical Presence:** You must have been continuously present in the U.S. for at least 10 years immediately before your removal hearing.
- **Good Moral Character:** You must show that you have been of good moral character for the entire 10-year period.
- **Hardship to U.S. Citizen or Lawful Permanent Resident Family:** You must prove that your deportation would cause extreme hardship to your U.S. citizen or lawful permanent resident spouse, children, or parents. The hardship must go beyond the typical challenges associated with deportation.

The Process

1. **Filing for Cancellation:** If you meet the above criteria, you can apply for cancellation of removal by filing a motion with the immigration court. This is typically done during your deportation hearing.
2. **Proving Hardship:** You must present evidence showing how your removal would cause extreme hardship to your family members. This might include medical records, financial documents, or testimony from family members about the hardship they would face without you.

3. **Court Decision:** The immigration judge will decide whether to grant cancellation of removal. If granted, you may be able to remain in the U.S. and eventually apply for a green card.

Challenges to Cancellation of Removal

- **Meeting the Hardship Requirement:** Demonstrating "extreme hardship" can be difficult. It's important to provide specific evidence that supports how your family would suffer if you were deported.
- **Criminal History:** If you have a criminal history, it could negatively impact your application for cancellation of removal. However, depending on the crime and how long ago it occurred, you may still be eligible.

3. Family-Based Relief: The Power of Family Ties

Family ties are one of the most significant factors in many deportation cases. If you are a close relative of a U.S. citizen or a lawful permanent resident, you may be eligible for relief from deportation through **family-based immigration**. There are several routes this can take.

Adjustment of Status

If you are married to a U.S. citizen, or if you are the immediate relative of a U.S. citizen or lawful permanent resident, you may be eligible to adjust your status to that of a lawful permanent resident (green card holder), even if you are in deportation proceedings.

To adjust your status:

1. **File for Adjustment of Status (Form I-485):** This process can occur concurrently with your deportation proceedings, allowing you to stay in the U.S. while your application is being reviewed.

2. **Eligibility for Immediate Relatives:** Spouses, parents, and children of U.S. citizens typically have the easiest path to adjustment of status.
3. **Overcoming Prior Violations:** In some cases, you can still adjust your status even if you violated immigration laws (e.g., overstayed a visa), provided you meet other criteria and have strong family ties.

Waivers for Certain Grounds of Inadmissibility

If you are facing deportation due to certain immigration violations (such as unlawful presence or a criminal conviction), a **waiver** may allow you to remain in the U.S. if your U.S. citizen or lawful permanent resident spouse or parent would suffer extreme hardship if you were deported.

1. **I-601 Waiver:** This waiver applies to certain grounds of inadmissibility, including unlawful presence or prior criminal convictions. You must prove that your U.S. citizen or lawful permanent resident family member would face extreme hardship if you were deported.
2. **I-601A Waiver:** If you are in the U.S. unlawfully but have a qualifying family member, this waiver allows you to apply for a provisional waiver before leaving the U.S. to attend a consular interview abroad.

4. Prosecutorial Discretion and Deferred Action

In some cases, the government may choose not to pursue deportation against certain individuals through **prosecutorial discretion** or **deferred action**. While this is not a legal defense in itself, it can prevent deportation.

- **Prosecutorial Discretion:** This is when the government decides not to pursue deportation for certain individuals due to factors such as long-term residence, family ties, or community involvement. While prosecutorial discretion is not a permanent solution, it can delay deportation and provide time for other legal options.

- **Deferred Action:** This is a form of relief that grants temporary protection from deportation. It is often given to individuals who came to the U.S. as children (e.g., **DACA** recipients) or those with strong humanitarian cases.

Conclusion

While deportation is a serious and often frightening process, there are multiple defenses and relief options available to those facing removal from Florida. From asylum and cancellation of removal to family-based relief and waivers, there are many pathways that could allow an immigrant to stay in the U.S. It's crucial to understand these options, consult with an experienced immigration attorney, and act quickly to protect your rights.

CHAPTER EIGHTY.

PREPARING YOUR CASE: EVIDENCE AND STRATEGY FOR IMMIGRATION COURT

Fighting deportation in Florida requires more than just understanding your legal options—it demands careful preparation, strategic thinking, and effective presentation of evidence. Immigration courts are incredibly strict and fact-driven, so the success of your defense largely depends on how well you present your case. In this chapter, we will explore how to gather the necessary evidence, build a strong defense strategy, and effectively prepare for your immigration court hearing.

1. Understanding the Role of Evidence in Your Case

Evidence is the backbone of any legal case, and deportation proceedings are no different. The immigration judge will rely heavily on the evidence you provide to determine whether you are eligible for relief or should be deported. As such, the evidence you present must be thorough, organized, and compelling.

There are two main categories of evidence you will need to consider:

- **Documentary Evidence:** These are physical records that support your case. They can include everything from immigration forms, birth and marriage certificates, and financial records to medical records and country conditions reports.
- **Testimonial Evidence:** This type of evidence consists of statements made by you and others who can support your case. This can include affidavits from family members, friends, colleagues, or experts who can testify on your behalf.

2. Gathering Documentary Evidence

Documentary evidence is crucial for establishing the facts of your case and supporting your claims. Below are some types of documents that could be important for your defense:

a. Immigration Documents

- **Form I-589 (Asylum Application):** If you're seeking asylum, this form and any supplementary documents you've filed should be included.
- **Form I-485 (Adjustment of Status):** If you're applying for adjustment of status, make sure to gather all documentation associated with your application.
- **Any Notices or Orders:** Keep copies of all notices from the Department of Homeland Security (DHS), the immigration court, or other government agencies related to your case.

b. Identity and Relationship Documents

- **Birth Certificates and Marriage Certificates:** These are vital for proving your identity and relationships to U.S. citizens or lawful permanent residents, particularly in family-based defense claims.
- **Passport or Travel Documents:** These will show when and how you entered the U.S. and whether you overstayed your visa or entered without inspection.

c. Proof of Residence and Employment

- **Tax Returns and Pay Stubs:** These documents can help establish that you have been living and working in the U.S. for a long period and have strong ties to the community.
- **Utility Bills or Lease Agreements:** Documents like electricity, water, or phone bills, along with rental agreements, can serve as proof of your continuous physical presence in the U.S.

d. Medical Records and Hardship Evidence

If you're seeking a defense based on hardship (for example, family-based relief or cancellation of removal), medical records, psychological evaluations, or documents showing the impact your deportation would have on family members can be essential.

- **Medical Evidence:** If a family member has a serious medical condition that would be worsened by your deportation, you will need medical records to prove this.
- **Psychological Reports:** Mental health assessments showing the emotional and psychological toll your removal would have on family members or yourself can also be important.

e. Country Conditions Reports

For asylum claims, you will need evidence showing that your home country is unsafe for you. This often includes reports from human rights organizations, U.S. government reports, or expert testimony about conditions in your country of origin, such as political unrest, violence, or discrimination.

3. Testimonial Evidence: Affidavits and Witness Testimonies

Testimonial evidence can help bring your case to life by adding personal stories that provide context to the documentary evidence. Immigrants often use affidavits or witness testimony to strengthen their claims. Here's how to effectively utilize this type of evidence:

a. Affidavits

An affidavit is a sworn written statement from you or others that supports your case. They can be used to provide details of your experiences, personal background, or the hardship your family will face if you are deported. Some key points to keep in mind when preparing affidavits:

- **Be Clear and Specific:** The affidavit should be clear, specific, and provide detailed explanations of the facts that support your case. For example, if you are claiming asylum, describe any specific incidents of persecution you have faced and how you have been affected.
- **Include Relevant Details:** The affidavit should include dates, locations, and specific instances that are pertinent to your claim. The more specific you can be, the better.
- **Sworn Statement:** The affidavit must be signed and notarized to be considered valid in court.

b. Witness Testimonies

Witnesses can be family members, friends, coworkers, or experts who can provide testimony that supports your case. For instance, if you are applying for cancellation of removal, family members can testify about the hardship your deportation would cause them.

- **Character Witnesses:** If you are arguing that you have demonstrated good moral character, character witnesses can speak to your behavior, your contributions to the community, and your reputation in the U.S.
- **Expert Witnesses:** Expert witnesses, such as country conditions experts or psychologists, can testify about conditions in your home country or the emotional impact of your deportation.

4. Organizing and Presenting Your Case in Court

Once you have gathered your evidence, it's time to organize it and prepare to present it in court. Immigration court is a formal environment, and presenting your case in a clear, professional manner is crucial. Here's how to prepare:

a. Create a Timeline

It is helpful to create a timeline of events that are central to your case. This can help the judge understand the sequence of events and how the evidence supports your defense. For example, if you're applying for asylum, you can create a timeline detailing key incidents of persecution.

b. Prepare an Evidence Binder

Organize your documentary evidence into a binder that is easy to navigate. Label each section clearly and make sure that everything is in order. You'll want to be able to access documents quickly during the hearing.

c. Practice Your Testimony

You'll likely be asked to testify in immigration court, so it's important to practice speaking clearly and confidently. Your testimony is a critical part of your case, and you'll want to explain your situation and answer questions without sounding defensive or evasive.

- **Stay Calm and Honest:** The immigration judge will be evaluating your credibility, so it's important to remain calm, straightforward, and honest. Don't exaggerate or fabricate your story.
- **Rehearse with Your Attorney:** Before your court date, rehearse your testimony with your attorney. They will help you understand the questions you might be asked and ensure your testimony is focused and coherent.

d. Address Potential Weaknesses

No case is perfect. If there are weaknesses in your case—such as gaps in your documentation or inconsistencies in your testimony—be prepared to address them. Your attorney can help you develop strategies to minimize the impact of these weaknesses.

5. The Role of Legal Counsel in Preparing Your Case

An experienced immigration attorney is an invaluable asset in preparing for immigration court. They will help you:

- **Assess Your Evidence:** Your attorney can review all of your evidence to ensure that it is strong and relevant. They will advise you on what additional evidence may be necessary and help you gather it.
- **Strategize Your Defense:** Your attorney will create a legal strategy that aligns with the specific facts of your case and the available defenses. They will also help you anticipate potential arguments from the government.
- **Present Your Case in Court:** During your hearing, your attorney will represent you in court, presenting your evidence, cross-examining witnesses, and arguing on your behalf.

Conclusion

Successfully fighting deportation in Florida hinges on the strength of your case preparation. Gathering thorough, compelling evidence, preparing strong witness testimony, and working with an experienced immigration attorney will significantly improve your chances of success. Be diligent and proactive in assembling your case, and ensure that you present it clearly and confidently in court.

In the next chapter, we will discuss the appeals process—how to handle a negative ruling, what options are available for appealing a deportation order, and how to approach federal court if necessary.

CHAPTER EIGHTY ONE

NAVIGATING THE APPEALS PROCESS: CHALLENGING A DEPORTATION ORDER IN FLORIDA

After months of preparation, hearings, and the emotional toll of fighting deportation, you may find yourself facing a negative ruling from the immigration judge. While this outcome is disappointing, it's important to know that all is not lost. The deportation process includes options for appealing the decision and, in some cases, taking the matter to federal court. In this final chapter, we will explore how to handle a negative ruling, the appeals process, and what steps you can take to continue your fight to remain in the U.S.

1. Understanding the Appeals Process

If the immigration judge rules against you, the first step is to file an appeal with the **Board of Immigration Appeals (BIA)**. The BIA is the highest administrative body that reviews decisions made by immigration judges.

a. Filing the Appeal

If you disagree with the immigration judge's decision, you can file a notice of appeal to the BIA. The notice must typically be filed within **30 days** of the judge's decision, so it's critical to act quickly. Here are the key steps in filing an appeal:

1. **File a Notice of Appeal (Form EOIR-26):** This form must be submitted to the BIA to initiate the appeals process.
2. **Pay the Filing Fee:** There is a filing fee associated with the appeal, although some individuals may request a fee waiver if they are unable to afford it.

3. **Provide Written Briefs:** You may be required to submit a brief, which is a written argument explaining why the immigration judge's decision should be overturned. Your attorney will typically handle this step, ensuring the brief thoroughly addresses the legal errors or factual inaccuracies in the judge's ruling.
4. **Submit Evidence:** If new evidence has become available after your hearing, you may submit it to the BIA to support your appeal.

b. What Happens After the Appeal is Filed?

Once the appeal is submitted, the BIA will review the case. The process typically takes several months, and you will be notified of the decision. There are a few possible outcomes:

1. **Affirming the Judge's Decision:** If the BIA agrees with the immigration judge's ruling, your deportation order will stand.
2. **Overturning the Decision:** If the BIA finds that the judge made an error in the law or facts, they may overturn the decision and allow you to stay in the U.S. or grant other relief.
3. **Remanding the Case:** In some cases, the BIA may send the case back to the immigration court for further proceedings, possibly with instructions to the judge to reconsider the case under different legal standards or guidelines.

2. Taking the Case to Federal Court

If the BIA upholds the immigration judge's decision and denies your appeal, you have the option to take the case further by appealing to the federal courts. This is a more complex and time-consuming process, but it may be the final opportunity to fight deportation.

a. Filing a Petition for Review

To appeal a BIA decision, you must file a **petition for review** with the appropriate federal appeals court. The court of appeals for Florida is the **11th Circuit Court of Appeals**, and you must file your petition within **30 days** of the BIA's decision. The process involves:

1. **Petitioning the Federal Court:** You will need to submit a petition to the court, outlining why you believe the BIA's decision was wrong. This petition must be filed with the appropriate court of appeals, and there is no further action required from the BIA at this stage.
2. **Submitting Briefs:** The federal court will review written briefs from both parties, including any legal arguments made by your attorney. This is your chance to present a compelling legal argument, identifying any errors in the BIA's analysis.
3. **Oral Arguments:** In some cases, the court may schedule oral arguments. If this happens, your attorney will have the chance to argue your case in person before a panel of judges.

b. What Happens After the Petition is Filed?

The federal court will review the BIA's decision and may take one of the following actions:

1. **Affirm the BIA's Decision:** If the court agrees with the BIA's ruling, the deportation order will be upheld, and you will be required to leave the U.S.
2. **Reverse or Remand the Case:** If the court finds that the BIA made a legal or procedural error, it may reverse or remand the case for further review. If the case is remanded, it will go back to the BIA or immigration court for additional proceedings.
3. **Grant Relief:** In rare cases, the court may grant relief from deportation directly, allowing you to stay in the U.S.

The federal court process is complex and often takes several months, but it is a vital part of ensuring that all legal avenues have been exhausted.

3. Other Options After the Appeal Process

In addition to filing an appeal, there are other options that may allow you to avoid deportation after the BIA or federal court decision:

a. Motion to Reopen or Reconsider

If new evidence becomes available or if you believe there was a legal error in your case that was not addressed in the appeal, you can file a **motion to reopen** or **motion to reconsider** with the BIA. These motions request that the BIA review the case again based on new facts or legal arguments.

- **Motion to Reopen:** This motion is typically filed if new evidence has surfaced that could significantly affect the outcome of your case. For example, if you've obtained a new witness statement or medical records showing the impact of deportation on your family, this could justify reopening your case.
- **Motion to Reconsider:** This motion asks the BIA to reconsider its decision due to errors in the law or facts.

These motions do not guarantee success but are an important tool to challenge deportation if new information arises.

b. Request for Prosecutorial Discretion

In some cases, individuals who have been denied relief may still be able to avoid deportation through **prosecutorial discretion**. This is a decision made by the U.S. government to forgo pursuing deportation in certain cases based on humanitarian or other considerations.

While this is not a formal legal defense, individuals who have strong family ties, long-term residence in the U.S., or other compelling factors can request that the government exercise prosecutorial discretion in their case. This could lead to a temporary stay of deportation, giving you time to pursue other avenues of relief.

4. Deportation and Voluntary Departure

If your appeals fail, and deportation becomes imminent, you may still have the option of **voluntary departure**. Voluntary departure allows you to leave the U.S. on your own terms, avoiding the formal removal process. While it's not ideal, voluntary departure may have less severe consequences than a deportation order, particularly when it comes to re-entering the U.S. in the future.

- **Eligibility for Voluntary Departure:** You must be able to prove that you have the financial means to depart the U.S. and that you are not a threat to public safety. Additionally, you must apply before your removal order is executed.

Choosing voluntary departure may help you avoid a formal deportation on your record, but it comes with its own risks and limitations, including the potential to be barred from re-entering the U.S. for several years.

5. Conclusion: The Final Steps in Your Fight

The fight against deportation is challenging, but it is far from over after an adverse ruling. Through the appeals process, motions to reopen, and even federal court intervention, there are still paths to preventing your deportation.

No matter how your case progresses, having an experienced immigration attorney by your side is essential. They can guide you through the complex appeals process, assist with filing motions, and represent you in federal court if necessary. Each step of the process involves careful legal strategy and preparation, and a knowledgeable attorney can be the difference between success and deportation.

The most important thing is to stay proactive, keep all your options open, and continue to explore every possible avenue for relief. While the road may be long and uncertain, your legal options remain, and with the right strategy, you can still achieve the outcome you deserve.

In this final chapter, we've covered how to challenge a deportation order through appeals, the potential role of federal courts, and how to take the next steps even after the appeals process. Deportation is a serious matter, but it is not the end of the road. Your fight to stay in the U.S. can continue, and with careful planning and legal expertise, it is possible to overcome the challenges ahead.

CHAPTER EIGHTY TWO.

BEATING A DUI CHARGE IN FLORIDA: LEGAL STRATEGIES AND DEFENSES

Facing a DUI (Driving Under the Influence) charge in Florida is a serious matter. DUI convictions can lead to severe consequences, including fines, license suspension, mandatory alcohol education programs, and even jail time. However, a DUI charge is not the same as a DUI conviction, and there are various legal strategies and defenses that can help you fight the charge. In this chapter, we will explore the most effective ways to challenge a DUI charge in Florida, outlining potential legal defenses, steps you can take during the arrest, and how to approach your case with the help of an experienced DUI attorney.

1. Understanding Florida's DUI Laws

Florida law defines DUI as operating a motor vehicle with a blood alcohol concentration (BAC) of **0.08% or higher**, or under the influence of drugs or alcohol to the extent that your normal faculties are impaired. DUI charges can be classified as either:

- **First-Degree Misdemeanor DUI:** Typically occurs when your BAC is 0.08% or higher, or if you were impaired by alcohol or drugs, but no aggravating circumstances exist.
- **Felony DUI:** If you have multiple prior DUI convictions, or if you cause serious injury or death while driving under the influence, your charge could be upgraded to a felony.

In Florida, you can also be arrested for DUI if an officer believes you are impaired, even if your BAC is below 0.08%. This could be due to drugs (prescription, recreational, or illegal) or a combination of substances.

2. Key Factors in a DUI Case: Challenging the Evidence

There are several ways to challenge a DUI charge in Florida, focusing primarily on the evidence presented by the prosecution. Below are some of the key factors and how you can challenge them:

a. The Traffic Stop

For a DUI charge to be valid, the police officer must have had a valid reason to pull you over in the first place. If the officer did not have reasonable suspicion of a violation or criminal activity, any evidence obtained during the stop may be inadmissible in court.

- **Unlawful Stop Defense:** If the officer cannot prove they had reasonable suspicion (e.g., erratic driving, speeding, or running a red light), you can argue that the stop was unlawful, and therefore, the evidence gathered should be suppressed.

b. Field Sobriety Tests (FSTs)

During a DUI stop, an officer may ask you to perform field sobriety tests, which typically include the one-leg stand, walk-and-turn, and horizontal gaze nystagmus (HGN) tests. While these tests are often used as evidence of impairment, they are not foolproof.

- **Challenging FST Results:** Field sobriety tests are subjective and can be affected by various factors, such as:
    - **Weather conditions** or **road surface issues** (e.g., uneven roads).
    - **Medical conditions** or **physical disabilities** that could affect your performance.
    - **Nervousness** or **fatigue**, which can also impact your ability to perform well on these tests.

  - **Improper administration**: If the officer did not follow proper procedures when conducting the test, you can challenge the results.

c. Breathalyzer and Blood Tests

One of the most important pieces of evidence in a DUI case is the breathalyzer or blood test that measures your BAC. However, there are several ways to challenge the reliability of these tests:

- **Breathalyzer Calibration and Maintenance:** Breathalyzer machines must be calibrated and maintained according to state regulations. If the machine was not calibrated properly or was malfunctioning, you can challenge the results.

- **Officer Certification:** Officers must be properly trained to administer breath tests. If the officer was not properly trained, the results may be inadmissible.

- **Rising BAC Defense:** Your BAC may be over the legal limit when tested, but you may have been under the limit when you were initially pulled over. This can occur if alcohol has not yet fully absorbed into your system at the time of the stop. An experienced DUI lawyer can present this defense by showing the timing of the stop and the test.

- **Blood Test Issues:** Blood tests are usually more accurate than breath tests but can still be challenged. Possible issues include:
  - **Chain of custody problems:** If there was any break in the chain of custody, the results might be unreliable.
  - **Improper handling or contamination** of the blood sample can lead to inaccurate results.

- **Delay in testing:** Blood alcohol content can decrease over time, and if there was a delay between the arrest and the test, your BAC at the time of driving might have been lower than the test result indicates.

d. Impairment by Drugs (DUI Drugs)

If you are accused of driving under the influence of drugs, whether prescription, over-the-counter, or illegal substances, your defense will focus on challenging the evidence of impairment.

- **Drug Recognition Expert (DRE):** In many DUI drug cases, a police officer may rely on a Drug Recognition Expert to determine if you are impaired by drugs. However, these experts are not always accurate, and there may be flaws in their evaluation. Your attorney can challenge their qualifications or the methods they used to assess your impairment.
- **Prescription Medications:** If you were impaired by prescription medication, it's important to show that the medication was taken as prescribed and that you were not exceeding the recommended dose. Additionally, many prescription medications do not impair driving ability in the same way that alcohol does.

e. Breath Test Refusal

If you refused to take a breath test, Florida law provides an automatic **license suspension** for up to 12 months for a first refusal and 18 months for subsequent refusals. However, refusing a breath test can still be challenged in court.

- **Refusal Defense:** You can argue that the officer did not properly inform you of the consequences of refusal or that your refusal was based on a legitimate concern (e.g., being physically unable to provide a sample).

3. Defensive Strategies to Fight a DUI Charge in Florida

Several legal strategies can be employed to fight a DUI charge in Florida. The key to winning a DUI case is to expose weaknesses in the prosecution's evidence, create reasonable doubt, and protect your rights throughout the process.

a. Lack of Impairment

One common defense in DUI cases is to argue that you were not actually impaired at the time of the arrest. Even if your BAC was above the legal limit, you may not have been impaired in a way that affected your ability to drive safely. The prosecutor must prove that your impairment was severe enough to impact your ability to operate the vehicle.

- **Video Evidence:** Many police departments now have dashcam or bodycam footage of DUI stops. This footage can show how you interacted with the officer, your physical condition, and your behavior. If you appear calm, coherent, and capable of driving safely, this evidence can be used to challenge the claim of impairment.

b. Medical or Physical Conditions

Certain medical conditions can mimic signs of impairment, such as slurred speech, unsteady movements, or difficulty concentrating. Some conditions that may lead to false DUI accusations include:

- **Neurological disorders** such as stroke or multiple sclerosis.
- **Physical injuries** that affect your ability to perform field sobriety tests, such as back pain or leg injuries.

- **Nervousness or anxiety**, which can cause shaking, sweating, or difficulty speaking clearly.

If you have a medical condition that could have affected your behavior during the DUI stop, presenting medical records or expert testimony from a physician can be an effective defense.

c. Improper Police Conduct

The actions of law enforcement during your DUI arrest are critical. If the police officer violated your constitutional rights during the arrest, such as performing an unlawful search and seizure or failing to inform you of your rights, it could lead to the suppression of evidence. A skilled DUI attorney will thoroughly review the details of your arrest to ensure that proper procedures were followed.

4. The Importance of Legal Representation

Successfully fighting a DUI charge in Florida requires knowledge of the law, familiarity with local courts, and the ability to challenge the evidence presented against you. DUI cases are complex, and having an experienced attorney by your side is crucial to mounting a strong defense.

A skilled DUI lawyer will:

- Review the circumstances of your arrest and ensure your rights were upheld.
- Investigate the accuracy of the breathalyzer or blood test results.
- Challenge the field sobriety tests and any other evidence presented by the prosecution.
- Negotiate plea deals when appropriate to reduce penalties or avoid a conviction.
- Represent you in court, fighting for the best possible outcome.

5. Conclusion

Facing a DUI charge in Florida can be overwhelming, but it's important to remember that you have rights and legal options to fight the charge. By challenging the traffic stop, field sobriety tests, breathalyzer or blood test results, and any other evidence, you can increase your chances of winning the case or achieving a favorable outcome. With the right legal strategy and expert representation, it is possible to avoid a DUI conviction and minimize the impact on your life.

In the following chapter, we will explore the potential penalties for DUI convictions in Florida and discuss how to minimize those penalties through plea agreements, diversion programs, or alternative sentencing options.

CHAPTER EIGHTY THREE

PENALTIES FOR DUI CONVICTIONS IN FLORIDA AND HOW TO MINIMIZE THEM

If you have been charged with a DUI in Florida, understanding the potential penalties for a conviction is essential. The consequences can range from fines and license suspension to mandatory alcohol education classes and even imprisonment. However, not all DUI convictions result in the maximum penalties. This chapter will explore the range of penalties associated with a DUI conviction in Florida, and discuss strategies for minimizing the severity of those penalties.

1. Penalties for DUI in Florida: An Overview

Florida law outlines a variety of penalties for DUI convictions, with different levels of punishment depending on factors like your blood alcohol concentration (BAC), whether you have prior DUI convictions, and whether your actions caused harm to others.

a. First-Time DUI Offender

For individuals facing a **first DUI offense**, the penalties can include:

1. **Fines:** A fine ranging from **$500 to $1,000**.
2. **License Suspension:** A **180-day** license suspension. However, you may be eligible for a **restricted license** that allows you to drive to work, school, or for other essential purposes after a 30-day period.
3. **Jail Time:** Up to **six months in jail**, though jail time is often not imposed for a first offense, especially if there are no aggravating factors.
4. **Probation:** A judge may impose probation, which typically lasts for **six months**. During probation, you will be required to comply with

specific conditions set by the court, including regular check-ins with a probation officer.

5. **Alcohol Education Classes:** You will be required to complete a **DUI education program** (often 12 hours long) that covers the dangers of impaired driving and substance abuse.
6. **Community Service:** A court may impose up to **50 hours** of community service.

b. DUI with a BAC of 0.15% or Higher

If your BAC is found to be **0.15% or higher**, you will face enhanced penalties, even if it is your first DUI offense:

1. **Fines:** The fines increase to **$1,000 to $2,000**.
2. **Jail Time:** A **mandatory minimum of 2 days** in jail is required, with up to **9 months** of jail time possible.
3. **License Suspension:** The license suspension is extended to **180 days to 1 year**.
4. **DUI Education:** You will be required to attend a more intensive **DUI education program**.
5. **Ignition Interlock Device:** The court may require you to install an **ignition interlock device** on your vehicle, which prevents the car from starting if alcohol is detected on your breath.

c. Second DUI Offense

If you are convicted of a **second DUI offense** within **5 years** of your first offense, the penalties become more severe:

1. **Fines:** The fines increase to **$1,000 to $2,000**.
2. **License Suspension:** A **5-year license suspension** is imposed, with eligibility for a restricted license after **1 year**.

3. **Jail Time:** You may face a minimum of **10 days in jail**, with up to **9 months** in jail possible.
4. **Probation:** You may be sentenced to **12 months** of probation.
5. **DUI Education Classes:** You must complete a **DUI program**, with a longer duration of classes.
6. **Ignition Interlock Device:** For second-time offenders, an **ignition interlock device** may be required, and this can be extended to **5 years**.

d. Third DUI Offense

A **third DUI conviction** within **10 years** is classified as a **third-degree felony**. The penalties for a third offense are severe and can include:

1. **Fines:** The fines range from **$2,000 to $5,000**.
2. **License Suspension:** Your license will be permanently revoked. However, you may be able to apply for a **restricted license** after **5 years**.
3. **Jail Time:** The sentence can range from **30 days to 5 years** in prison, depending on the circumstances of the case.
4. **Probation and DUI Education:** A third conviction usually includes probation and mandatory alcohol and substance abuse education programs.
5. **Ignition Interlock Device:** You will be required to install an **ignition interlock device** for an extended period.

e. Aggravating Factors

Certain aggravating factors can increase the penalties for a DUI conviction. These factors include:

- **Driving with a minor passenger**: If you have a child under 18 in the vehicle at the time of the DUI, you may face additional penalties.

- **DUI causing injury or death**: If you cause an accident resulting in injury or death, you can face much more severe penalties, including **felony charges**, longer prison sentences, and larger fines.
- **Refusal to submit to a breath test**: Refusing to take a breath test can lead to automatic suspension of your license and can be used against you in court.

2. Minimizing the DUI Penalties: Legal Strategies

While the penalties for a DUI conviction can be severe, there are various strategies that a skilled attorney can use to minimize the consequences. Below are some of the most effective legal strategies for reducing the severity of your sentence:

a. Negotiating a Plea Bargain

In many DUI cases, the prosecution and defense may agree to a **plea bargain**, where you agree to plead guilty to a lesser charge or accept a reduced penalty in exchange for avoiding a trial. Common outcomes of a plea bargain might include:

- A **reduced charge**: In some cases, your attorney may be able to negotiate a reduction in the charge (e.g., from DUI to reckless driving).
- **Reduced penalties**: This may include lowering fines, reducing the length of license suspension, or eliminating mandatory jail time.

Plea bargaining is often a favorable option if the evidence against you is strong, as it can help avoid the uncertainties of a trial.

b. Diversion Programs and Alternative Sentencing

Florida offers **diversion programs** and **alternative sentencing** for eligible offenders. These programs allow you to avoid jail time and may offer a chance to have your record expunged or your sentence reduced if you meet certain conditions.

For example, Florida has a **First-Time Offender Program** that may allow individuals with no prior criminal record to participate in alcohol education classes, community service, and probation, with the possibility of having the DUI charge dismissed upon successful completion of the program.

c. Challenging the Evidence

If your attorney is able to challenge the evidence against you, the prosecution may be forced to reduce or drop the charges. Some common ways to challenge DUI evidence include:

- **Challenging the traffic stop**: If the police officer did not have probable cause to pull you over, the evidence obtained during the stop may be inadmissible.
- **Challenging the field sobriety tests**: If the officer administered the tests improperly or if your performance was affected by a medical condition, your attorney can argue that the results are not valid.
- **Challenging the breathalyzer or blood test**: If the breathalyzer machine was improperly calibrated or maintained, or if the blood test was mishandled, this could create reasonable doubt in the prosecution's case.

d. Showing Mitigating Circumstances

Mitigating circumstances are factors that may reduce the severity of your punishment. These may include:

- **First-time offense**: If this is your first DUI offense and you have no prior criminal record, the court may be more lenient in sentencing.

- **Good character references**: Letters from employers, family members, or community leaders can show that you are a responsible person who made a mistake.
- **Participation in counseling**: Voluntarily seeking counseling for alcohol or substance abuse may demonstrate your commitment to addressing the root cause of your behavior and could result in a lighter sentence.

e. Requesting Hardship License

If your license is suspended as a result of a DUI conviction, you may be able to apply for a **hardship license**. A hardship license allows you to continue driving for specific purposes, such as commuting to work or attending school, during your suspension period. This request is typically made during a hearing, and the judge will consider factors like your need for transportation and whether you have completed alcohol education classes.

3. Conclusion

A DUI conviction in Florida can have serious and lasting consequences, including fines, license suspension, mandatory classes, and even jail time. However, there are ways to minimize these penalties through effective legal strategies, such as negotiating a plea bargain, participating in diversion programs, challenging the evidence, and presenting mitigating circumstances. An experienced DUI attorney will work closely with you to explore all your options and help you achieve the best possible outcome.

CHAPTER EIGHTY FOUR.

DEFENDING A DUI CASE IN COURT: WHAT TO EXPECT

When you are facing a DUI charge in Florida, and after exploring options to resolve the case through plea bargaining or diversion programs, the next possible step is going to trial. Defending a DUI case in court is complex and requires both strategic planning and a deep understanding of the legal process. This chapter will guide you through the typical steps in a DUI trial, what you can expect during the trial, how the prosecution will build its case, and how your defense attorney can effectively challenge the evidence against you.

1. What to Expect Before the Trial

Before the trial begins, your attorney will work on several aspects of your case. This includes gathering evidence, reviewing police reports, speaking with witnesses, and consulting with expert witnesses, such as toxicologists or accident reconstructionists. Below are key stages leading up to the trial:

a. Pre-Trial Motions

Before the actual trial, your defense attorney may file pre-trial motions. These motions aim to challenge certain aspects of the case, such as:

- **Motion to Suppress Evidence:** If there were any constitutional violations during the arrest or traffic stop (e.g., unlawful search or seizure), your attorney may file a motion to suppress evidence gathered after the violation.
- **Motion to Dismiss the Case:** If there is insufficient evidence to support the DUI charge, your attorney may ask the court to dismiss the case entirely.

If the judge grants these motions, it could lead to the dismissal of the charges or the exclusion of certain evidence, which can significantly weaken the prosecution's case.

b. Discovery

Discovery is the process where both parties exchange evidence. Your defense attorney will review all the evidence that the prosecution has gathered against you, including police reports, field sobriety test results, breathalyzer test results, and witness statements. Your lawyer will also interview any witnesses, including the arresting officers, and examine any video footage from dashcams or bodycams that might exist.

c. Consulting Expert Witnesses

In many DUI cases, expert witnesses are brought in to challenge the scientific evidence, such as breathalyzer or blood test results. Expert witnesses in DUI cases might include:

- **Toxicologists** to discuss the accuracy of the breathalyzer test or blood test.
- **Accident Reconstructionists** to examine whether there was an accident or impairment involved.
- **Medical Experts** to discuss any medical conditions or medications that may have caused impairment.

These experts can testify on your behalf, making the case stronger that you were not impaired, or that the tests were inaccurate.

2. What Happens During the Trial?

If your case goes to trial, it will generally follow a structured process. Below is a breakdown of what you can expect at each stage of the trial:

a. Jury Selection

Most DUI cases in Florida will be decided by a jury. During the jury selection process, both the prosecution and the defense will question potential jurors to ensure they can be fair and impartial. This is a critical part of the trial because the jury will ultimately decide your fate.

Your defense attorney will attempt to ensure that jurors are unbiased and open to considering the facts of the case without prejudice. The prosecution will similarly look for jurors who are more likely to convict.

b. Opening Statements

After jury selection, both the prosecution and the defense will give their opening statements. The **prosecution** will outline the case against you, explaining the evidence they plan to present, including your BAC, field sobriety test results, and witness testimonies. The **defense attorney** will explain why the evidence does not prove guilt beyond a reasonable doubt and how they plan to challenge the prosecution's case.

Opening statements are not the time for arguing guilt or innocence. Instead, they set the stage for what each side plans to prove.

c. The Prosecution's Case

After the opening statements, the prosecution will present its case first. This includes calling witnesses and presenting evidence to support the DUI charge. The most common evidence presented by the prosecution includes:

- **Testimony from the arresting officer(s):** The officer will testify about the circumstances surrounding your traffic stop, the reason they suspected you of DUI, how you performed on field sobriety tests, and whether you submitted to a breathalyzer or blood test.

- **Breathalyzer or Blood Test Results:** If a breathalyzer or blood test was conducted, the prosecution will present the results, showing that your BAC was above the legal limit.
- **Field Sobriety Test Results:** The prosecution will present the officer's observations of your performance on field sobriety tests, if applicable.

Your defense attorney will have the opportunity to cross-examine the prosecution's witnesses. Cross-examination is an essential part of the trial because it allows your attorney to challenge the credibility and reliability of the evidence presented.

d. The Defense's Case

Once the prosecution has finished presenting its case, the defense will have the opportunity to present its side. The defense may call witnesses to testify, such as:

- **You, the defendant:** Your attorney may decide to have you testify in your defense, although this decision should be carefully considered. Testifying can provide the jury with your perspective on the events, but it also opens you up to cross-examination by the prosecution.
- **Expert witnesses:** If the defense has expert witnesses, they may be called to testify about the accuracy of the breathalyzer or blood test, potential medical issues, or other factors that could have influenced your impairment.
- **Character witnesses:** In some cases, the defense may call character witnesses who can speak to your general behavior and whether it is consistent with someone who would normally engage in reckless driving or substance abuse.

e. Closing Arguments Once both the prosecution and the defense have presented their cases, each side will give closing arguments. The prosecution will summarize the evidence they believe proves your guilt, while the defense will summarize how the evidence fails to prove guilt beyond a reasonable doubt.

Closing arguments are your defense's last opportunity to appeal to the jury and emphasize the weaknesses in the prosecution's case. Your attorney will argue that the prosecution has failed to meet its burden of proof.

f. Jury Deliberation and Verdict

After closing arguments, the jury will deliberate in private. They will discuss the case and try to reach a unanimous decision. If the jury finds you **not guilty**, the case is over, and you will be acquitted. If the jury finds you **guilty**, you will be convicted of DUI.

In some cases, if the jury cannot reach a unanimous verdict, the judge may declare a **hung jury**, leading to a mistrial. If this happens, the prosecution can choose to retry the case or offer a plea deal.

3. Possible Outcomes of a DUI Trial

At the end of the trial, there are several possible outcomes:

a. Not Guilty Verdict

If the jury finds you not guilty, the charges are dismissed, and you are free to go. This is the ideal outcome, especially if the evidence against you was weak or your defense effectively created reasonable doubt.

b. Guilty Verdict

If you are found guilty, the court will proceed to sentencing. The judge will consider the evidence, any mitigating factors, and the penalties associated with your conviction before imposing a sentence. This could include fines, license suspension, community service, DUI education programs, or even jail time.

c. Hung Jury / Mistrial

In the case of a hung jury, a mistrial is declared. The prosecution will then decide whether to retry the case or offer a plea deal. If the prosecution decides to retry the case, the process will begin again with a new trial.

4. How Your Attorney Defends You in Court

Your defense attorney plays a critical role in defending you during trial. Some of the ways they will work to protect your interests include:

- **Challenging the evidence:** Your attorney will scrutinize the prosecution's evidence, including the arrest process, field sobriety tests, breathalyzer or blood test results, and the actions of the arresting officer.
- **Presenting alternative explanations:** Your attorney may present reasonable alternative explanations for your behavior, such as medical conditions that may have caused impaired driving or errors made by the police during the arrest process.
- **Raising reasonable doubt:** The core strategy of any criminal defense is to create doubt in the minds of the jurors about the prosecution's case. If your attorney can show that there is reasonable doubt regarding your guilt, you can be acquitted.

5. Conclusion

Defending a DUI case in court can be a daunting process, but with the right legal strategy and an experienced DUI defense attorney, you can fight the charges and seek the best possible outcome. It's important to understand the trial process, the role of your defense attorney, and the various defenses that can be raised to challenge the prosecution's case. By working closely with your attorney and taking a strategic approach, you increase your chances of securing a favorable verdict in your DUI case.

CHAPTER EIGHTY FIVE.

POST-CONVICTION RELIEF: HOW TO CHALLENGE A DUI CONVICTION

Even if you have been convicted of a DUI in Florida, there may still be opportunities to reduce or eliminate the consequences of your conviction. This chapter will explore the options for **post-conviction relief**, including the **appeals process**, the possibility of **expungement**, and other legal remedies to challenge your DUI conviction after the trial is over.

1. What is Post-Conviction Relief?

Post-conviction relief refers to legal remedies that are available to a defendant after a conviction has been handed down. These remedies aim to address errors that may have occurred during the trial, such as legal mistakes, ineffective representation, or new evidence that was not available at the time of the trial. Post-conviction relief can help reduce or even eliminate the consequences of a DUI conviction, such as jail time, fines, and a permanent criminal record.

Post-conviction relief options can vary depending on the circumstances of your case, but they generally involve **appealing the conviction** or seeking **modifications** to your sentence.

2. The Appeals Process: Challenging a DUI Conviction

If you have been convicted of DUI, one of the most common methods of post-conviction relief is filing an **appeal**. An appeal is a legal process in which you ask a higher court to review the decision made in your trial to see if there were errors in how the law was applied. It's important to understand that an appeal is not a new trial; it focuses only on whether any legal errors were made during the trial process that could have affected the verdict or sentence.

a. Grounds for Appeal

In Florida, there are several grounds on which you can base an appeal in a DUI case:

- **Errors in the Trial Process**: This can include procedural mistakes that may have affected the fairness of your trial, such as improper jury instructions, wrongfully admitted evidence, or an inappropriate ruling by the judge.
- **Legal Errors**: If the judge made a legal mistake, such as incorrectly applying the law, the appeal court may find that this error affected the outcome of your case.
- **Ineffective Assistance of Counsel**: If your defense attorney made significant mistakes or failed to provide effective representation, you may have grounds for an appeal. Examples include failing to challenge critical evidence or not properly investigating the case.
- **Insufficient Evidence**: If the prosecution did not present enough evidence to prove your guilt beyond a reasonable doubt, your attorney may argue that your conviction should be overturned because of insufficient evidence.
- **Misapplication of the Law**: If the trial court misinterpreted or misapplied the DUI laws, this may be a valid ground for appeal.

b. The Appeal Process

Here is an overview of the steps in the appeal process:

1. **Notice of Appeal**: The first step is to file a **Notice of Appeal** with the court that convicted you. This must be done within **30 days** of your conviction.

2. **Appellate Brief**: Your attorney will file an **appellate brief**, which outlines the legal arguments and the errors that occurred during the trial. This document will explain why the conviction should be overturned.
3. **Prosecution's Response**: The prosecution will file a response to your appeal, arguing why the conviction should stand.
4. **Oral Arguments**: In some cases, the appellate court may schedule oral arguments, where both sides have the opportunity to present their case in person. However, many DUI appeals are decided based solely on the written briefs.
5. **Appellate Court Decision**: After reviewing the case, the appellate court will issue a decision. Possible outcomes include:
    - **Affirming the Conviction**: The court may uphold your conviction if they find no legal errors.
    - **Reversing the Conviction**: If the court finds that legal errors occurred, they may overturn the conviction, which could result in a new trial or dismissal of charges.
    - **Remanding the Case**: The court may send the case back to the trial court with instructions for a new trial or a modification of the sentence.

An appeal can be a lengthy and complicated process, and there is no guarantee that a conviction will be overturned. However, if your case involves significant legal errors or ineffective representation, an appeal may offer you a second chance.

3. Expungement of a DUI Conviction

Another option for post-conviction relief is **expungement**. Expungement is the legal process of having your criminal record sealed or erased. If a DUI conviction is expunged, it means that, for most legal purposes, it will be as if the conviction never occurred. This can help you avoid the long-term consequences of a DUI conviction, such as difficulties finding employment, securing housing, or maintaining professional licenses.

a. Eligibility for Expungement

In Florida, expungement is not available for all DUI convictions. To be eligible for expungement, the following criteria generally apply:

- **First-Time Offender**: Expungement is more likely if this was your first DUI offense, and there were no aggravating factors (such as causing injury or death) involved in your case.
- **No Conviction**: You can only seek expungement if you were acquitted of the DUI charge or the charge was dismissed. If you pleaded guilty or were found guilty, you are not eligible for expungement.
- **Completion of Sentence**: If you were convicted but completed your sentence, including probation, community service, or DUI education classes, you may be eligible for expungement if you meet other criteria.

b. The Expungement Process

The process of expunging a DUI conviction in Florida involves several steps:

1. **Obtain a Certificate of Eligibility**: Before applying for expungement, you must obtain a **Certificate of Eligibility** from the Florida Department of Law Enforcement (FDLE). This certificate confirms that you are eligible for expungement under Florida law.
2. **File a Petition for Expungement**: Once you have the Certificate of Eligibility, your attorney will file a **Petition for Expungement** with the court. The petition must include all relevant details of the case,

including your criminal history, the DUI conviction, and the reasons why you are requesting expungement.

3. **Court Hearing**: A judge will review your petition and may schedule a hearing. The judge will consider factors such as your criminal history, whether you have been rehabilitated, and the specific circumstances of your DUI conviction.
4. **Judge's Decision**: If the judge grants the expungement, your DUI conviction will be sealed from public records, effectively erasing the record of the conviction. However, some records may still be accessible to law enforcement, and certain entities (such as government agencies or professional licensing boards) may still have access to your record.

Expungement is a powerful tool for clearing your record and moving forward after a DUI conviction. However, it is important to note that not all DUI convictions are eligible for expungement, and the process can be lengthy and complicated. Consulting with a qualified attorney is essential to determining whether you are eligible for expungement and ensuring that you follow the proper steps.

4. Other Forms of Post-Conviction Relief

In addition to appeals and expungement, there are other forms of post-conviction relief that may be available, depending on the specific facts of your case:

a. Motion for Post-Conviction Relief

If you believe your conviction was based on new evidence that wasn't available at the time of trial, you may file a **motion for post-conviction relief**. This is typically done when there is new evidence, such as witness testimony, that could have influenced the outcome of the trial. If the court accepts the motion, they may order a new trial.

b. Reduction of Sentence

In some cases, a defendant may seek a **sentence modification** after a DUI conviction. This is often done if you have served part of your sentence and demonstrated good behavior, or if there are changes in the law that would result in a less severe penalty. A motion for sentence reduction is filed with the court, and the judge will determine whether it is appropriate to reduce your sentence.

5. Conclusion

While a DUI conviction in Florida can have serious long-term consequences, post-conviction relief options provide a path for challenging your conviction or minimizing its effects. Whether through an **appeal**, **expungement**, or other forms of relief, there may still be ways to undo or reduce the impact of a DUI conviction.

If you are considering post-conviction relief, it's crucial to consult with an experienced DUI defense attorney who can guide you through the process and help you understand your options. With the right legal strategy, you may be able to move forward with a clean slate and minimize the lasting effects of a DUI conviction.

CHAPTER EIGHTY.SIX

THE CONSEQUENCES OF A DUI CONVICTION IN FLORIDA AND HOW TO MANAGE THEM

A DUI conviction in Florida can have far-reaching consequences, impacting various aspects of your life. Beyond the immediate legal penalties, such as fines, license suspension, or potential jail time, a DUI conviction can affect your employment, insurance rates, and professional licenses. Understanding these consequences and knowing how to manage them can help you move forward after a conviction. This chapter explores the long-term effects of a DUI and provides strategies to mitigate these challenges.

1. Impact on Employment

One of the most significant concerns for individuals facing a DUI conviction is the impact on their job and career. For some, a DUI can directly affect their ability to perform their job, while for others, it may have broader consequences, including losing their current job or facing difficulty finding new employment.

a. Employment and Criminal Records

In Florida, employers are allowed to conduct background checks as part of the hiring process, and a DUI conviction may appear on your record. While Florida law prevents employers from discriminating against you based solely on a criminal record, certain industries and positions may require a clean record, especially if your job involves driving or operating machinery. For example:

- **Commercial Drivers**: If you hold a Commercial Driver's License (CDL), a DUI conviction will have a severe impact on your career. A

DUI conviction can result in a suspension of your CDL, making it difficult or impossible to continue driving for a living.

- **Government Jobs**: Many government positions, including law enforcement, require a clean criminal record. A DUI conviction could disqualify you from applying for these types of jobs.
- **Professional Licenses**: For those in professions that require licensing (e.g., doctors, lawyers, accountants), a DUI conviction could lead to disciplinary action from the respective licensing boards, including suspension or revocation of your license.

b. Employment with a DUI Conviction

If you are already employed, the effects of a DUI conviction can vary:

- **Job Loss**: If your job requires driving (e.g., truck driving, delivery services), a DUI conviction may result in suspension or loss of employment. Additionally, some employers may have strict policies against criminal convictions, leading to termination.
- **Reputation Damage**: A DUI conviction can damage your professional reputation, especially if you work in a field where trust and accountability are paramount. This can affect relationships with clients, coworkers, and supervisors.

c. How to Manage Employment Challenges

- **Seek Legal Advice**: If you're concerned about the impact of a DUI conviction on your job, an attorney can help you understand your rights and how to address the situation with your employer. Some employers may be open to negotiating a solution, such as taking unpaid leave to resolve the legal issues.
- **Be Transparent**: If you're applying for a new job and the application asks about criminal history, be honest about your DUI conviction.

Some employers may appreciate your honesty and may offer opportunities for rehabilitation and employment.

- **Rehabilitation Programs**: If you're required to complete alcohol or drug treatment programs as part of your sentencing, consider showing your employer that you are taking steps to address the underlying issues. This can demonstrate your commitment to change and may soften the impact of your conviction.

2. Impact on Insurance Rates

A DUI conviction will typically result in higher car insurance premiums. Insurance companies view DUI offenders as higher-risk drivers, and as a result, they may increase your premiums substantially. In Florida, insurance premiums can rise anywhere from 30% to 100% after a DUI conviction, depending on various factors such as your previous driving history and the specifics of your DUI charge.

a. Florida's "SR-22" Requirement

In many cases, after a DUI conviction, Florida law requires drivers to carry **SR-22 insurance** for a period of three years. SR-22 is not a type of insurance, but a certificate that proves you have the required minimum coverage after a DUI conviction. This certificate is typically more expensive than standard insurance and can add to your financial burden.

SR-22 insurance is usually required if:

- Your driver's license was suspended.
- You are deemed a high-risk driver by the state.
- You are convicted of a DUI.

b. Managing Increased Insurance Costs

- **Shop Around**: After a DUI conviction, it's essential to compare insurance quotes from multiple providers. While your rates may go up, different insurance companies have varying policies on DUI offenders, and you might find a better rate elsewhere.
- **Complete a Defensive Driving Course**: Some insurance companies offer discounts if you complete a state-approved defensive driving course. This can help offset some of the increased insurance costs.
- **Maintain a Clean Driving Record**: The longer you go without any additional traffic violations or accidents, the more likely your insurance premiums will decrease. If you maintain a clean driving record after your DUI conviction, insurance companies may eventually reduce your rates.

3. Impact on Professional Licenses

For individuals with professional licenses, a DUI conviction can have serious consequences. Many Florida professional licensing boards require license holders to maintain a clean record, and a DUI conviction could trigger disciplinary actions, including suspension or revocation of your license.

a. Professions Affected by a DUI

- **Healthcare Professionals**: Doctors, nurses, and other healthcare providers can face disciplinary action from the **Florida Department of Health** after a DUI conviction. This could include suspension, probation, or even revocation of their professional license.
- **Attorneys and Other Legal Professionals**: A DUI conviction can impact your ability to practice law, as the **Florida Bar** can discipline lawyers convicted of criminal offenses, including suspension or disbarment.

- **Teachers and Educators**: If you hold a teaching certificate or other educational credential, a DUI conviction can lead to disciplinary action by the **Florida Department of Education**, including suspension or revocation of your license.

b. How to Manage Professional License Consequences

- **Report the Conviction Promptly**: Many licensing boards require professionals to report any criminal convictions. Failing to report a DUI conviction can result in additional disciplinary action. It's best to be proactive and report the conviction as required by the licensing body.
- **Seek Legal Representation**: If your professional license is at risk due to a DUI conviction, an attorney who specializes in professional license defense can help you navigate the disciplinary process. They can advocate for you and potentially reduce or eliminate the penalties.
- **Demonstrate Rehabilitation**: If you are facing disciplinary action, showing that you've taken steps to address the issues leading to your DUI conviction (such as completing a DUI education program, attending counseling, or seeking treatment) can help demonstrate that you are committed to changing your behavior.

4. Dealing with Social Stigma and Reputation Damage

A DUI conviction may also lead to social stigma and damage to your reputation. Friends, family members, and coworkers may perceive you differently, and you might experience feelings of shame or isolation.

a. Addressing the Social Impact

- **Acknowledge Your Mistake**: If you are facing judgment from others, acknowledging your mistake and taking responsibility can go a long way toward rebuilding trust. People are more likely to offer support if they see that you are sincere in your efforts to improve.

- **Focus on Rehabilitation**: Show others that you are taking steps to learn from the experience, such as attending therapy or enrolling in a DUI education program. This can demonstrate that you are actively working to make positive changes in your life.
- **Be Patient**: Reputation repair takes time. As you demonstrate your commitment to rehabilitation and self-improvement, others may gradually come to see you in a more positive light.

Conclusion: Moving Forward After a DUI Conviction

A DUI conviction in Florida can have significant consequences on many aspects of your life, including your employment, insurance rates, professional licenses, and reputation. However, it is important to remember that these challenges are not insurmountable. By understanding the potential consequences, taking proactive steps to mitigate them, and seeking professional help when needed, you can begin to rebuild your life after a DUI conviction.

While the road ahead may be difficult, demonstrating accountability and a commitment to change can help you regain control of your future. In the next chapter, we will explore resources for individuals convicted of DUI, including support groups, counseling options, and community programs that can assist in the recovery process.

CHAPTER EIGHTY SEVEN.

THE FLORIDA STATE PRISON SYSTEM

The Florida Department of Corrections (FDC) operates one of the largest prison systems in the United States. With over 80,000 inmates and approximately 140 facilities, including state prisons, private correctional institutions, work camps, and re-entry centers, the system is designed to manage offenders while focusing on rehabilitation, public safety, and reentry into society. This chapter explores the structure, policies, and challenges of Florida's prison system.

Structure of the Florida Prison System

The FDC oversees three primary types of facilities:

1. **State Prisons** – These are high-security institutions that house inmates serving long-term sentences. They include facilities designated for men, women, and specialized populations such as those requiring mental health treatment.
2. **Private Prisons** – Some correctional institutions in Florida are managed by private corporations under state contracts. These facilities operate under state oversight but may have different policies regarding staffing and rehabilitation programs.
3. **Work Camps and Re-Entry Centers** – These facilities focus on preparing inmates for release by providing vocational training, educational opportunities, and transitional housing.

Inmate Classification and Security Levels

Upon entering the system, inmates undergo an extensive classification process to determine their security level and housing assignment. The primary classifications include:

- **Minimum Security** – For non-violent offenders with short sentences, often housed in dormitory-style settings.
- **Medium Security** – For inmates with moderate criminal histories who may pose a higher escape risk or require increased supervision.
- **Maximum Security** – Reserved for violent or high-risk offenders, including those with disciplinary infractions while incarcerated.

Daily Life and Rehabilitation Programs

Life inside Florida's prisons is structured with strict schedules, including work assignments, education, and recreational time. The FDC emphasizes rehabilitation through several programs:

- **Education and Vocational Training** – Inmates have access to GED programs, technical training, and trade certifications in fields such as carpentry and plumbing.
- **Substance Abuse Treatment** – Many facilities offer addiction recovery programs to address underlying causes of criminal behavior.
- **Faith-Based and Reentry Programs** – Various religious organizations partner with the FDC to provide spiritual guidance and life skills training to prepare inmates for successful reintegration into society.

Challenges and Controversies

Despite efforts at rehabilitation, Florida's prison system faces several challenges:

- **Overcrowding** – The state's prisons frequently operate at or above capacity, leading to increased tensions and resource shortages.
- **Staffing Shortages** – High turnover rates among correctional officers have led to understaffing and security concerns.

- **Healthcare Concerns** – Access to medical and mental health care remains a significant issue, with lawsuits alleging inadequate treatment for inmates.
- **Recidivism** – A significant percentage of released inmates return to prison within a few years, highlighting the need for improved reentry support.

CHAPTER EIGHTY EIGHT

WHAT TO EXPECT IN FLORIDA WORK RELEASE

Facing time in prison is one of the most difficult challenges anyone can endure. However, in Florida, there is a chance to serve part of a sentence in a different way—through the Work Release Program. For those who qualify, work release offers the possibility of keeping a job while serving their sentence, helping to ease the transition back into society after incarceration. But what exactly does work release entail, and what should you expect?

What is Florida's Work Release Program?

The Florida Work Release Program allows eligible offenders to leave the facility during the day to work, earn a wage, and contribute to their families or the community. The program is run by the Florida Department of Corrections (FDC) and is designed to help inmates reintegrate into society while still fulfilling their sentence.

Eligibility for Work Release

Not everyone is eligible for work release, and eligibility depends on various factors:

- Type of Crime: Work release is generally available for non-violent offenders. Those convicted of violent crimes, such as murder, sexual assault, or armed robbery, are typically not eligible.
- Sentence Length: Inmates with shorter sentences or those who have served a substantial portion of their sentence may have a better chance of being accepted into the program. Typically, those with a sentence of less than five years are considered, but it depends on the nature of their offense.

- Behavior: Inmates must demonstrate good behavior while incarcerated. Poor conduct, disciplinary infractions, or being deemed a flight risk will disqualify someone from the program.
- No Serious Mental Health or Medical Issues: Inmates who require constant medical supervision or have severe mental health issues may not qualify for work release. However, they may be placed in programs suited to their medical needs.

How Does the Work Release Program Operate?

Once approved, inmates are allowed to leave the correctional facility during the day to work at a job outside. Here's how it works:

1. **Employment:**
   - Inmates must secure employment that is approved by the Florida Department of Corrections.
   - The job could be in any sector, but it must be legitimate and consistent with the individual's skills. This could include construction, manufacturing, office work, or various service industries.
   - The inmate must provide evidence that they are employed and show that their employer is willing to adhere to the terms of the work release program.
2. **Monitoring:**
   - While on work release, inmates are subject to strict monitoring.
   - They may be fitted with electronic monitoring devices, such as ankle bracelets, to ensure they stay on track and return to the facility at the designated times.

- Daily curfews are enforced—failure to return on time can result in severe consequences, including removal from the program and returning to regular incarceration.

3. **Transportation:**
   - Transportation is arranged by the correctional facility. Some inmates are provided with transportation to and from work, while others may need to arrange their own transportation under supervision.
   - Inmates typically are not allowed to use personal vehicles unless specifically authorized.
4. **Payment and Deductions:**
   - Inmates are paid for their work, and the majority of their wages are deducted for restitution, court fines, room and board, and other legal obligations.
   - However, inmates can keep a portion of their earnings to save up for the future or support their family. This money can help pay for things like personal hygiene, commissary items, or personal expenses during their time in the program.
5. **Curfews and Facility Rules:**
   - Inmates must adhere to strict curfews and report to the facility at the designated time.
   - The rules of the work release program are strict, and violations—such as failure to return on time or violating conditions of employment—can result in termination from the program and possible return to a regular prison sentence.

Benefits of Work Release

Work release offers several benefits to both the inmate and society:

1. **Preparing for Reentry:**

- Work release helps inmates develop job skills and get real-world experience, making it easier to find employment after their release. This improves their chances of successful reintegration into society and reduces the likelihood of reoffending.

2. **Family Support:**
   - For many inmates, the chance to earn money and contribute to their family's financial needs can be incredibly valuable. It helps reduce the strain on their loved ones and provides them with a sense of purpose during their sentence.
3. **Good Behavior Incentive:**
   - The work release program encourages positive behavior in prison. Inmates who qualify for work release are expected to follow the rules and show progress in their rehabilitation.
4. **Reduced Overcrowding:**
   - By allowing inmates to work outside the facility during the day, work release programs help ease overcrowding in Florida's correctional facilities.

Challenges and Restrictions

While work release offers many opportunities, there are also several challenges and restrictions:

1. **Strict Monitoring:**
   - The monitoring and rules surrounding work release can feel restrictive. Inmates must follow strict schedules, return to the facility on time, and comply with all rules or face termination from the program.
2. **Limited Employment Options:**
   - Not all inmates are able to find employment, and the types of jobs available may not always align with an inmate's skills. This

can make it difficult to secure stable work, which in turn impacts the effectiveness of the program.

3. **Severe Consequences for Violations:**
   - Violations of work release conditions—such as leaving the work site without permission or missing curfew—can lead to termination from the program and a return to regular prison time.

What Happens After Completing Work Release?

Once an inmate has completed their time in the work release program, they are often moved to a halfway house or released on probation. The transition from work release to freedom is an important step in reintegrating into society, and it's important to continue complying with the conditions set by the court or parole board.

In Conclusion: Preparing for Work Release

The Florida work release program provides a valuable opportunity for inmates to maintain a job, contribute to their community, and prepare for their return to society. However, it's important to understand the eligibility requirements, the rules and expectations, and the potential challenges that come with being part of the program.

If you or a loved one are considering work release, make sure to consult with a knowledgeable attorney who can help guide you through the process and ensure all conditions are met for a successful transition.

FINAL WORD

THE SYSTEM IS RIGGED.

This book was written to expose the flaws, corruption, and inherent biases within state institutions, particularly the legal and prison systems. Far too often, individuals are crushed by bureaucratic red tape, manipulated by the courts, and abandoned by lawyers who fail to fight for them. This book serves as a guide for those who refuse to be victims, offering practical strategies and critical insights to navigate and overcome the system's oppressive grip.

At its core, this book is about reclaiming power. The state thrives on ignorance and compliance, using complex laws and legal jargon to maintain control over individuals who don't understand how to defend themselves. By breaking down these barriers, this book gives readers the tools to challenge authority effectively, recognize legal traps, and counteract the tactics used against them.

A major theme throughout this book is the failure of legal representation. Many lawyers prioritize convenience, personal gain, or relationships within the system over their duty to defend their clients. This book equips readers with the knowledge to identify when they are being misled, push back against ineffective counsel, and take an active role in their own defense.

However, knowledge alone is not enough. Readers must be willing to apply what they learn, think critically, and act decisively. The information within these pages is meant to be a weapon—one that, when used correctly, can dismantle the state's ability to oppress and control. Whether dealing with criminal charges, civil disputes, or bureaucratic roadblocks, this book is a battle plan for those who refuse to surrender to a rigged system.

www.ingramcontent.com/pod-product-compliance
Lightning Source LLC
LaVergne TN
LVHW082023200926
848481LV00010B/2914
* 9 7 9 8 3 4 9 5 8 3 7 0 4 *